CREATING SPACE

CREATING SPACE

The Education of a Broadcaster

Andy O'Mahony

The Liffey Press

Published by
The Liffey Press
Raheny Shopping Centre, Second Floor
Raheny, Dublin 5, Ireland
www.theliffeypress.com

© 2016 Andy O'Mahony

A catalogue record of this book is
available from the British Library.

ISBN 978-1-908308-93-1

Printed in Spain by GraphyCems

CONTENTS

ACKNOWLEDGEMENTS

My thanks to Professor Finbarr McAuley, Monsignor Dermot Lane, Adrian Moynes, Michael Kealy, Dr. Bill Mathews S.J., Professor Tom Garvin, Michael Campion, Bernadette Comerford, Aoife Nic Cormaic, Paddy Glackin, Professor Vincent Comerford, Dr. Michael Casey, Fergal and Brid MacCabe, Nora and Gerry Rawson, Eddie and Bernie O'Mahony and Aidan Mathews.

I wish to thank Dr Bill McCormack for his perceptive editorial advice and my literary agent Jonathan Williams for his continuing encouragement and invaluable professional expertise. I would also like to register my gratitude to David Givens of The Liffey Press for his enthusiastic response to the manuscript.

Finally, I owe a special debt of thanks to the late Dennis O'Driscoll, who first urged me to write this book, and to Dr. Irene Goodman for ensuring that I completed it.

For Irene and Sarah

Chapter 1

THE GERMANS ARE COMING

I WAS ALREADY FORTY-EIGHT YEARS old when I began to keep a daily journal. You could call me a late developer in such matters. At the time, I regretted having left it so late. But when I began this autobiographical memoir a few years ago, I noticed that my memory of life *before* I kept a journal was surprisingly good. As a result, I began to wonder at first whether the fact that I hadn't been a journal-keeper all my life was all that great a loss. Nowadays I believe it was, because whenever I re-read my own journals of the past thirty-five years, I am made aware of how much I would have forgotten of that period alone, were it not for my written recollections.

Besides, journaling has a function other than that of being an aid to recollection: it can help us make better decisions. My late-in-the-day attraction to this daily practice occurred in late September 1982. I had just moved from Dublin to Cambridge, Massachusetts for a year's sabbatical from broadcasting. Were it not for that year off, it is doubtful if I would ever have taken up the practice of daily writing.

My original plan was to keep a journal for that year only, but the habit became mildly addictive. Those daily entries would become regular events in what had been an otherwise uneventful life. It is not merely that I had never flown the Atlantic solo or climbed Mont Blanc blindfolded, but I had tended to avoid

1

physical adventure of any kind. I am not particularly lazy but I *am* wary of anything that involves unnecessary bodily risk. It is the kind of attitude that can entail an uneventful life. That is, unless you're one of those people to whom interesting things happen. Even I have occasionally been heard to say, 'you'll never guess what happened to me', only to discover that losing a credit card or getting an airline upgrade to Malta on Christmas Eve doesn't cut much ice.

The exotic has not intruded on my life, be it anacondas in Florida or bandits in Peru. If mine was not a life of adventure, I did live in interesting times. I was born in Ireland in 1934 during the tail-end of the Great Depression. Roosevelt's New Deal was then getting under way in America; Hitler's Third Reich in Germany. At the end of that decade, the Second World War began. My native country declared itself neutral on that occasion, but it is now generally agreed that Ireland was neutral on the Allied side.

I was a television news anchor in Dublin in a decade that saw the assassinations of President John F. Kennedy and Martin Luther King Jr., landmark American Civil Rights legislation under Lyndon Johnson, the Vietnam war, worldwide student revolt and violence in Northern Ireland. The oil crisis of 1973 was a potent punctuation mark: a reminder that the previous decade, for all its turbulence, was still an era of plenty.

By the time Margaret Thatcher and Ronald Reagan had begun to change the face of social welfare capitalism in the 1980s, I was a broadcast journalist in my early fifties. The era of *financial* capitalism had arrived, and with it a period of unprecedented social inequality. Meanwhile the Soviet experiment had failed, Japan had stagnated, and China had re-emerged on the global stage after an interval of two hundred years. A major revolution in communications technology completed the picture.

Living a third of each year in the United States for the past thirty years has exposed me to a significantly larger slice of the modern world than would otherwise have been the case. What-ever the vantage-point, mine was never anything more than the life of an armchair observer. The closest I came to being directly involved in a life-threatening incident of any kind occurred in childhood in my home town of Clonmel, County Tipperary, during the Second World War.

Thankfully, the particular event the townspeople feared never came to pass, but the fear itself was real enough even to a child, maybe more so to a child. One day in what was prob-ably 1942, but possibly 1943, my home town lost all trace of its customary tranquil composure. The idea had taken root that German forces had landed that morning at Dungarvan, County Waterford, and were on their way inland. Dungarvan is about ten miles from Clonmel.

That day when it was thought that the Germans had invaded the south of Ireland was one in which all local attention was focused on the Convent Bridge in Clonmel. If German soldiers were to travel inland from Dungarvan, it is via that bridge they would reach the town. It was located quite close to the Presen-tation Convent, where I had gone to school. The bridge was lit-tered with tar barrels, the purpose of which stratagem escaped us youngsters. How could a string of tar barrels possibly halt the Hun?

There was talk of mines in and around the bridge. Oth-ers suspected that the barrels were just a ruse to deliberately slow down an impetuous, invading division, who would have to alight from their vehicles, smoke their foreign cigarettes and then search for potential booby traps while the nuns in the nearby convent looked on. There was a sturdy red-bricked house at the top of the Irishtown district which enjoyed a clear view of the Convent bridge. The house was a look-out post on that occasion. At a certain point, it seemed that our elders were beginning to wonder what was delaying the German forces on their way from Dungarvan.

Were these troops encountering stubborn resistance along the way? Surely not. Even if the Ballymacarbry Local Defence Force impressed all and sundry on its weekend manoeuvres, what chance did it have when confronted with the real thing? Perhaps the pubs in Dungarvan had supplied free drink to the invaders, who were now sampling the delights of crossroads country dancing, or playing pitch and toss with Nazi-sympathizing locals.

It is easy to make light of it now, but the general mood that day was one of deep uncertainty and confusion, which dissipated only with the eventual confirmation of a false alarm. That it wasn't all just childish imaginings was brought home to us in later years when we learned that the Germans had actually drawn up plans ('Operation Green') in 1940 for a planned invasion of Ireland. The plan proposed a German landing on the Waterford/Wexford coastline before establishing a beachhead between Gorey and Clonmel. This plan came into the hands of the Irish military authorities in 1942.

It is not certain whether the Germans had an actual attack on Ireland in mind at the time or were merely trying to wrong-foot the British with rumours of one, but the latter is now taken to be the more likely hypothesis. Shortly after the war, one of our teachers told us a story about a German bomber pilot who had returned to base from a supposed mission to bomb the city of Galway. He reported to the Luftwaffe high command that his journey had been in vain: the city looked as if it had been bombed already.

There is a certain irony in the manner in which I have thus far been highlighting the world of public events and adventurous action, as if to say it is these that should most command our attention. I confess to momentarily ministering to that particular prejudice in my opening paragraphs in order to make a point. However, an attitude that invariably assigns primacy to eventful action is not one I share. Take my working life. Once I quit as a television news anchor in 1972, I usually (though not always) regarded the world of ideas as offering more interesting broadcasting possibilities than either events or even issues.

Radio and television producers have five categories of material to work with: events, information, issues, people, and ideas. The programmes that generates most heat and audience involvement are those dealing with *issues*. It is hard to go wrong with gay marriage, immigration, abortion or taxation policy. There is nothing like an issue of a deeply polarizing kind to get us all going. I spent at least a decade of my own broadcasting life mining that particularly fertile vein. It is the kind of programme that gets attention and yet it may not be the most personally rewarding kind of programme to make or listen to. Probably the most popular kind of programme item is that which comes under the heading of 'people', especially when it features interviewees who have a really good story to relate.

The most neglected of the five categories mentioned is that of ideas. Programme items that aim to generate *understanding* of our world are few and far between. In fact, in the current affairs field, the discussion of ideas is gradually being squeezed out altogether, although BB2's *Newsnight,* Channel 4 *News,* Bloomberg's *Charlie Rose* and CNN's *The Global Public Square* with Fareed Zakaria are still defiantly flying the flag. These programmes do not confine themselves to events, issues or personalities; they also allow space to examine some of the fundamental ideas that govern our economic, social and political lives. Furthermore, they clearly believe that *cultural* matters should not be confined to arts programmes: they are as likely to make room for an Umberto Eco, a Judith Butler or a Richard Kearney as a political or financial titan.

My inclination to rate ideas above events and issues in a broadcasting context has also characterized my journal-keeping, not to the point of excluding something like hip surgery, but you know what I mean. Journal-keeping for me has been not so much a matter of chronicling events, but a recording of my attempts to make sense of the world whether eventful or not. What surprises me is that I did not begin the practice until I was forty-eight. It is a practice that paved the way for this autobiography.

Journal-keeping also provided research material for part of this book. A memoir is driven by memory and imagination, but research is no hindrance. We have good reason to believe that our efforts at recollection are predominantly governed by one of two broad impulses: a desire that our picture of the past be internally consistent; or that it conform to what actually happened. Research can minister to both impulses. It can obviously be enlisted to support an internally consistent picture of the past, but its more noble use, presumably, is in the service of truth or, if you prefer, in the service of 'getting things right'.

In any event, the extent to which autobiographical writing is primarily about truthful self-revelation is a moot point. It is not that a writer will necessarily set out deliberately to deceive but rather that the need to produce a piece of writing eventually takes precedence over everything else. The main objective will be to produce a *text* he or she is happy with, which usually means trying to generate a piece of work that the writer hopes will hold the reader's attention.

My own book sets out to be self-disclosing in a limited, clearly demarcated way, in that it is a profile of the intellectual life of the voyager: a chronicle of my efforts to understand the world. I should add that I am equally interested in conveying a flavour of the world I spent forever trying to understand, particularly how a given era appeared to someone of my background, education and interests.

In so far as books of this kind *are* about self-revelation, they tend to be governed by one major overriding tension; namely, that between our desire to disclose and our desire to conceal. And that is not an unfruitful tension. The psychoanalyst Donald

Winnicott was one who made much of it. As to how honest and forthright any of us can be is akin to asking how disinterested we can be. We are as prone to deception in rendering an account of our lives as we are liable to bias in assessing human affairs. But that does not rule out the possibility of *some* measure of honesty, *some* measure of disinterestedness.

In years to come, readers are certain to have access to the recollections of some of today's movers and shakers, our political, financial, technological and cultural titans. Perhaps readers will not have as much access to the musings and grumbles of those of us who did not shape events. The moral philosophy professor in Tom Stoppard's play *Jumpers* offers us a variant on that theme. He says to his loved one: 'You're the *wife* of an academic, dear; you're *twice* removed from the centre of events.'

Although some journalists are arguably closer to the centre of events than academics are, much of the broadcast journalism I practised was not. It is true that life in the RTÉ newsroom and at the helm of a current affairs show brought me closer at times to the centre, but for most of my working life I presided over programmes that favoured the discussion of ideas rather than issues or events.

On the other hand, it is easy to succumb to the temptation of false modesty: ideas do matter, even ones emanating from a radio or television studio or from casual conversations. This is a record that spans half of the twentieth century and part of the twenty-first. Given my natural predilections, it will include details of my reading, the reflections that it generated and, of course, the conversations. Above all I think, the conversations. But, whether it be reading, reflecting or conversing, I like the idea of preserving memories of these activities and then sharing them. This is what we do with a camera: we freeze the moment and then share the snapshots. Who knows how these written snapshots, if they survive at all, will appear to succeeding generations.

Who knows how altered our world will become: what new discoveries in physics, chemistry and biology are around the corner. Who can foretell the changes in geopolitics, technology and organized religions. I have read one forecast that predicts that Japan and Turkey will form an alliance against the United States in the middle of the twenty-first century. Maybe it was just their footballers the soothsayer had in mind. Whatever happens, snapshots, image-based or verbal, will retain their value. The fact that we had two major revolutions in physics in the early twentieth century, a world war after that, and a major revolution in biology in mid-century, has not altered the value we place on snapshot memorabilia of a century ago.

As a broadcast journalist, I have recorded many conversations for public transmission. RTÉ, the Irish public service network, has many hundreds of these in its archives, guarded day and night by a crack security team ready to sacrifice their lives in the interests of western civilization. These recordings with writers, thinkers, artists and scholars were gathered over a period of thirty-five years mostly in Dublin and London, but many in Oxford and Cambridge, and some in Paris and Rome.

Leaving traces of non-recorded conversations is a different matter. These casual colloquies are occasionally creative events of a kind that can shape our lives. We usually recognise these as they occur. The dynamic of such conversations is often difficult to capture but we can usually register what we have learned from them. Luckily, my natural recall is good; and my journals helped from 1982 onwards.

Students of autobiographical writing point out that individuals who write about their lives tend to go out of their way to claim that they are not writing about themselves, but about others, about the period they lived through, or whatever. Such claims are obviously disingenuous, given that, by definition, such accounts are engaged in constructing a narrative with the self at its centre. On the other hand, even narratives of that kind should be capable of occasionally moving away from their egocentric moorings. Confessional preambles like this are eminently lampoonable. They call to mind an old BBC television sketch, in which that one-time darling of the Cambridge Footlights Eleanor Bron is on her knees praying: 'Dear Lord, I feel nothing but humility in your presence. And yet I know that you see right through my pretence at humility. Not merely that, I know that you see through my *acknowledgement* of such pretence....' And on it goes.

There seem to be two ways of writing a book. You either begin writing straightaway or defer doing so until you have completed the necessary research. The first approach has two clear advantages: when we write, we discover what we think; we also find out what further reading we need to do or who else we need to talk to. Deferral, on the other hand, makes for an easier life. It certainly does so in the short term. Deferral isn't always a bad choice. In some contexts, it is a really useful one. Take politics, for example. Here is an arena where to choose *not* to act is often the really smart thing to do. If we are to believe the German sociologist Ulrich Beck, Chancellor Angela Merkel's power in Europe is due mainly to her tendency to procrastinate. Nor should we forget the old Vatican precept that the world is ruled by delay: *Cunctando regitur mundus*. For most of us, though, deferral is not a deliberate strategy; it is just our default response to not feeling ready. It was St Francis de Sales who forever nailed the perils of that perennially tempting posture when he said : 'If I were to wait until I were ready, I would never begin.' He is right, isn't he? You can feel that in your bones.

When we discover the benefits attached to writing early on, we cease to be inhibited by inadequate preparation. We see that writing is not only a vehicle for expressing what we already know, but a tool for unlocking what we don't. The historian Hugh Thomas told me in 1980 that the main reason he wrote *An Unfinished History of the World* (1979) was to make himself do the reading such a book required. He knew that once he began to write he would become more aware of the gaps in his reading.

As we get on in years, friends sometimes urge us to write. In doing so, they may be just telling us we are talking too much. For that reason, any encouragement we get in earlier days is more likely to be genuine. Over the years, some of the guests on my radio programmes were born encouragers. Two such contributors spring to mind: Sister Wendy Beckett, an art historian familiar to BBC television audiences; and Theodore Zeldin, an Oxford historian with an enviable knowledge of modern France.

Sister Wendy and I bonded early on in our encounter, perhaps because we shared the same reservations about a piece Germaine Greer had recently written for *Modern Painters.* In that particular essay, Dr. Greer had taken Sister Wendy to task for finding religious meanings in paintings where, Greer insisted, the artist had intended none. The problem was that Greer was clearly of the view that the intention of the artist is the only possible source of meaning. In other words, if the painter didn't consciously intend there to be a religious meaning, the art work could not possibly have one. Not true.

There is at least one other possible source of meaning: it usually resides in those who are tasked with appraising a work. A well-informed appraiser is likely to possess the necessary resources of experience and knowledge to *confer* meaning on the work of art. This may result in the generation of a fresh layer of meaning not consciously intended by the artist, but implicit in the work. I hold no brief for the importation of religious meanings in particular into an art work. My point is simply that we should remain hospitably open to all kinds of meaning, including the religious.

Whereas Sister Wendy lived in a mobile home in Quidenham, Norfolk in the grounds of a Carmelite monastery, Theodore Zeldin lived in an art deco house with a flat roof outside Oxford. I recorded two half-hour programmes with him in the mid-1990s about his book *An Intimate History of Humanity* (1994). He spoke that morning of wanting to break down the barriers between academic disciplines; he was aware that historian colleagues had mocked him for casting his net so wide. Historians at different specialist libraries had asked him what he was doing in their particular neck of the woods.

Professor Zeldin is best known as a historian of modern France and the author of *A History of French Passions* (1973-77). His advice has always been much sought after by leading French politicians, including Nicholas Sarkozy and Jacques Delors. Zeldin remarked to me that François Mitterrand was one of the cleverest politicians of the age. As an example of that, he cited the fact that Mitterrand had created the *extreme* right (he encouraged Le Pen) in an attempt to destroy the right *tout court*.

When these two gracious interviewees pressed me as to why I myself hadn't published, I cited lack of adequate knowledge about particular topics as the cause. But neither of them thought it mattered much *what* I wrote about, so long as I wrote. For them, the first steps consisted mainly of exercising a particular muscle. It is the kind of advice we get from writers like André Maurois.

Nothing came of those particular promptings, not even from reading Maurois, but I did eventually act on one from the poet and critic the late Dennis O'Driscoll, who collaborated with Seamus Heaney to produce *Stepping Stones* (2008). On a balmy day in November 2005, Dennis and I recorded a radio discussion with the critic Anthony Roche about Richard Bradford's biography of Philip Larkin. We continued the conversation outside Donnybrook Church, which is quite close to my living quarters on Ailesbury Road. We were both still mulling over critic James Wood's dismissal of Larkin as 'a minor registrar of disappointment'. Out of the blue, Dennis urged me to write about my life, or if not, at least to compile an edited version of the journals I had been keeping.

One of the pleasures of broadcasting is the schmoozing afterwards. That morning was different in that I was effectively commissioned to write something. Dennis' parting words that day were: 'Do it while you still can.' The remark was freighted with what in retrospect was a sad irony, given his own unexpected death in 2012 at the age of fifty-eight.

When I eventually began to write in late 2009, the principal lens through which I viewed my own past was one that sought to capture the story of my lifelong attempts at *understanding* the world. Given the lack of action in my life, this was no surprise. In that respect, I take consolation from Pascal's idea that the reason there is so much trouble in the world is that not enough people know how to sit at home quietly.

When I looked back on my early life, I was particularly struck by how little *politics* featured in my efforts to understand the world. The arts, philosophy and religion took precedence. Not until my mid-thirties did I develop any significant political awareness, though thereafter my understanding of it became quite multi-layered. My early life was also marked by timidity of thought; there was an excessive deference to authority, especially that of a religious kind. The great importance I attached early on in life to learning has remained, and I have managed to devote as much time, if not more, to my own continuing education as I have assigned to career activities.

There is usually a pattern to our attempts at understanding the world. We begin by trying to find out how some thoughtful predecessors made sense of things. And, then, perhaps, what knowledgeable contemporaries have to say on the matter. In time, we begin to devise maps of our own, even if we never cease to make use occasionally of the maps of others. It was in the summer of 1952 that I first embarked on that long voyage of discovery. I was seventeen years of age.

For the following twenty years, that process of educating myself was conducted in an unsatisfactory, episodic, hit-and-miss fashion. The main problem was lack of time. Not until 1972 did I begin to enjoy the kind of leisure such a project required. That increased free time came about because of an inspired if risky career decision: I left my job as a television news anchor with the fledgling Irish national television service. I swopped the television studios for the university library to pursue graduate research.

If there were those close to me who thought such a career choice was crazy, they didn't let on. Besides, I didn't abandon broadcasting altogether: I was still earning enough from radio work other than newsreading to get by. The sense of freedom the new life conferred more than outweighed financial anxieties. I knew I had to make the break at that point; I wouldn't get a second chance. So, not until I was thirty-seven years of age did I finally come to the conclusion that a life of reading, research, reflection and leisurely conversations wouldn't be possible unless I cut down on my broadcasting workload. I didn't know it then but such a decision would also facilitate many years of journal-keeping and more time for travel and living out of the country. I even, as I have said, managed a year's sabbatical.

Also relevant to the decision to work less is the fact that I never had to shoulder the responsibilities of marriage. Luckily, I was privileged over the years to enjoy intimate relationships consecutively with three remarkable women: Maireóg, Michaela and Irene. I was with Maireóg from 1968 to 1973, with Michaela from 1975 to 1980 and with Irene from 1980 onwards.

Maireóg Golden, born in Dublin, was twenty-one when we first met. She was living with her parents, was not attending college and did not have a job. She had manifest sketching talent, was intellectually curious and decidedly free-spirited. Equally independent-minded were Michaela and Irene, both Americans. Michaela O'Brien, born in Florida, had studied at the University of Georgia. When we met, she was a twenty-four-year-old graduate student in Anglo-Irish literature at Trinity College Dublin. Irene Goodman, born in Los Angeles, had graduated in psychology at UCLA. We first met in Cambridge, Massachusetts, when she was a twenty-nine-year-old doctoral student at Harvard. I am especially indebted to Irene in the matter of this book: without her constant cajoling and support it would never have surfaced.

My chosen life path made for a reasonably satisfying journey; that is to say, as contented as any journey can be, given the nagging awareness of a limited lifespan. It wasn't until my late fifties that I first had a real apprehension of mortality. The fact that I made a will at that point is testament to that. It is hard to disagree with Montaigne that the main task of the philosopher, indeed for all of us, is learning how to die. I'm sure Montaigne had something nobler in mind than drafting a will or looking up mortality estimates based on our existing age, both of which activities I have engaged in.

Montaigne's fellow countryman, the philosopher Paul Ricoeur, maintained that the two most difficult things for us to accept are the fact that we're going to die, and that not everybody loves us. For Sir Alex Ferguson, the former manager of Manchester United, the two things we can't change are our walk and our team. Readers are welcome to make their own binary-inflected contributions.

Ricoeur is right about dying; I'm not too sure about his second proposition. Not that one is querying the claim that not everybody loves us. That claim sounds reasonable enough. No, what's at issue here is whether or not that reality is the second most difficult thing to accept in life. For some it will be, but not for everyone. One can think of other things that are difficult to accept, such as, say, the fact that we become less open and tolerant as we get older, or that we no longer think as highly of human nature as we once did. Furthermore, the reality of not being universally loved is hedged in with possible qualifying circumstances of various kinds. Someone unlucky enough to have to interact with very demanding colleagues, friends and relations may be more accepting of not being universally loved than those more fortunate in their relationships. Whether the fact of not being universally loved is among the hardest things in life to accept is open to debate in a way that the fact of mortality is not. For most of our lives we have at best a flimsy grasp of mortality. It tends to deepen with the years and at a certain point will shift to a recognizably different register. After that sobering key change, which is minor in mode but major in remit, life is never the same. The sense of loss entailed gives us a glimpse of what the term 'prelapsarian' must mean for Christian believers, a sense of having lost the innocent, carefree world that preceded the Fall.

Evelyn Waugh claimed that for P. G. Wodehouse's characters there never was a Fall: Wodehouse's characters never tasted the forbidden fruit, and so, presumably, have no sense of their own mortality. Those of us who have doubts about a past Eden or a future Paradise can always use a strategy attributed to Carl Jung. The crafty Swiss psychotherapist is alleged to have recommended that we should live every day with a dual mind-set: as if it were the last day of our lives; and as if we were going to go on for ever. What a sly old Zurich fox.

My own quest for knowledge and wisdom took off with considerable vigour in my post-school years. What my approach lacked by way of not being systematic, it made up for in ardour. It was an approach heavily weighted towards the arts and philosophy. For the first fifteen years or so, my intellectual energies were devoted to music, literature, theatre, philosophy and religion.

I was nothing if not hungry for knowledge, but notably absent at that stage was any sustained interest in politics, either of a parliamentary, realpolitik or ideological kind. More lamentable was the absence of independence of thought owing largely to the particular manner in which I had appropriated my Catholic formation and upbringing. Those were the two main weaknesses of my early intellectual life: an indifference to politics; and a failure to think for myself. On the credit side was a vibrant curiosity, and an evolving openness of mind.

My knowledge of local Irish parliamentary politics was scant; I had little grasp of international affairs, and no interest in ideological politics. I was something of a slow learner on all those fronts. Listening to election candidates in my home town of Clonmel spin webs of rhetoric from the rear end of a stationary lorry was the extent of my early political education. That is, apart from hearing about the Locke's Distillery scandal in 1947 during my first year at boarding school. In that year, a foreign consortium had attempted to buy Locke's family distillery in the Irish midlands without having the necessary funds. A good old-fashioned scam, it seems. So why all the fuss? What gave the story a political resonance was that a Fine Gael Dáil deputy, Oliver J. Flanagan, accused the ruling Fianna Fáil administration of being complicit in the scam. The accused were subsequently exonerated by a tribunal.

It has always seemed odd to me that on political science courses, corruption is treated as a footnote, if mentioned at all, when the truth is that corruption may well define an entire system. Nonetheless, though deeply regrettable, a corrupt political system is somehow less morally grievous than a socially unjust one. At school in the late 1940s, I was being alerted to just one of those failings, but not to the larger and ultimately more morally significant one. That would take a while.

International affairs were a closed book to me until the Suez Crisis of 1956, at which point I was working for the Bank of Ireland in a town which boasts a memorably large square, the County Kerry market town of Listowel. Suez was the lead story in Raidió Éireann news bulletins at the time. That was the first occasion I was conscious of monitoring events from abroad.

I was a child during the Second World War, but was no more than five when it began. All I remember is the day the Germans were supposed to have landed at Dungarvan. The war was glided over during my school years as if it hadn't occurred. After the war, the Soviet Union meant little more than the threat of atheistic communism. During those post-war years at secondary school, 1947-51, the Holocaust was never mentioned. Nor was it adverted to later when I attended university in the late 1950s and early 1960s.

My *political* education came relatively late and had a piece-meal character. Not until my mid-thirties did the conventional political categories of left and right really register with me. Up to that point, the only bearing morality seemed to have on politics was in the condemnation of corrupt behaviour; it had nothing to do with evaluating how socially just the Irish political system itself was. Morality for my generation had mostly to do with correctness of sexual behaviour and the avoidance of theft. The idea that morality extended to something as large as the prevailing political system in Ireland was not widespread. There was little question then, of thinking in terms of a *system* being fair or not.

My interest in realpolitik, as opposed to political ideology, came about in the 1960s when I worked in Dublin as a news anchor in the newly established Irish national television station, Telefís Éireann (later RTÉ). My mentors included experienced journalists like Eddie Liston, who was unusual among Irish journalists in those days in having a solid background in Middle Eastern languages. Eddie and other colleagues alerted me to the dynamics of organizational politics.

Jim McGuinness, appointed Head of News at RTÉ in 1966, was deemed by old news hands as one of the great exemplars of realpolitik: for one thing, he was a master of the elliptical, which seemed to be an indispensable tool of political effectiveness. A conversation with McGuinness, a former prominent figure in the IRA, always seemed to be about something other than what was being overtly talked about.

That was the era of Antony Jay's influential book *Machiavelli and Management* (1967), reputedly based on Jay's experience with the BBC. Jay argued that the best way to understand the modern business corporation was to think of it in political terms, as a state. So he set about coaxing managers away from their cash flow charts to remind them that their true predecessors were the prime ministers and generals who had for aeons confronted the same problems as themselves. Jay transposed Machiavelli directly to the corridors of the modern corporation. One of Machiavelli's injunctions was that if you're going to harm an opponent, it has to be done so completely that the target cannot strike back: only half-wounding someone is pointless. Another was to make sure when appointing a deputy to oneself that he or she represented no threat to your own position.

It took me a while to figure out that one could usefully divide people into four categories: moralisers, apologists, explorers and problem-solvers. When a crisis occurs, the moraliser will *censure* or *condemn* someone or other; the apologist will *defend* whomever he's hired to defend; the explorer will try to *understand* what's happening; while the problem-solver looks for a *solution*.

The moraliser's primary impulse is to censure or condemn an action or individual. It is a valuable impulse because it ensures that certain values are kept in play. Its excesses can be regrettable if it involves pointing fingers precipitately. In this general category we find campaigning journalists, academics and politicians. They are vital to a society. The apologist's role is to defend sundry positions; essentially he's a gun for hire. In this group we find lawyers, public relations executives, corporate spokesmen, and all those who in any conflict defend 'the party line'. The explorer devotes his energies to trying to understand what's happening. In this category we find our dispassionate, disinterested thinkers. The problem solver is essentially a man of action. He will look at any crisis primarily for solutions. He will talk about options, implications of various courses of action and final decisions.

In the context of realpolitik, a question that particularly interested me from the 1970s onwards was what defined 'political intelligence'. What separates the most successful politicians from the others. As far as I could make out at the time, inscrutability ranked highly. It was noticeable that in the case of successful political operators, we tended not to know what they were really thinking or what they wanted. If there is a prototype for the kind of politician who is difficult to read, it is Franklin Delano Roosevelt. It is fair to say that de Gaulle, Macmillan, de Valera and Pope Leo XIII were no slouches either. And at RTÉ, the Irish national public broadcasting network, which I joined in 1961, there were senior executives who could have given master classes to them all.

Charles Lysaght, a friend of long standing, believes that Charles Stewart Parnell, the great late nineteenth-century Irish leader, is a perfect exemplar of the kind of political skill I have been talking about, namely that of playing everything very close to the chest. Charles is a lawyer, and the biographer of Tory politician Brendan Bracken; he's a shrewd judge of people. A number of his friends from student days at Cambridge in the 1960s later scaled the higher reaches of British politics, among them Norman Lamont, whom I met with Charles not too long ago in the company of economist Finola Kennedy. In a conversation that evening about the nature of political acumen, Lamont, a former Chancellor of the Exchequer in John Major's government, dissented from the view that inscrutability is a key component of political intelligence. Apart from working with Major, he had also served with Margaret Thatcher; later in life, he became a member of the House of Lords. One presumes that his experience of the Iron Lady determined his view of the matter for good. Mrs Thatcher always made clear what she wanted and what her intentions were. Her Irish counterpart, Charles J. Haughey, was no different in that respect. Lamont did not rule out inscrutability entirely, but he didn't see it as a *sine qua non* of political effectiveness. Undoubtedly, he has a point: not all successful politicians are necessarily hard to read.

Richard Sennett's fine book *The Fall of Public Man* (1977) is a reminder that journalists like myself who attach great importance to inscrutability in the context of realpolitik reveal themselves as true heirs of the kind of bourgeois psychology that first surfaced in the middle of the nineteenth century. At that point, concealment was the automatic position for *everybody*, not just for wily politicians.

At dinner in Sandymount, Dublin, sometime in the late 1970s, I heard one of the most unusual accounts of political acumen I had then come across. It was at the home of Michael and Marianne O'Gorman. Marianne had been a broadcasting colleague of mine at RTÉ in the 1960s. One of the guests that evening, an accountant by profession, made a novel contribution to a discussion about the nature of political intelligence. He suggested that if a gunman walked into the room as we were talking, most would deny it was happening. What signals the presence of political acumen, he argued, is the capacity to acknowledge an altered reality more quickly than others.

I suspect he may be right, at least to the extent that such a capacity is a significant, if not the sole, component. A Netflix documentary about the Republican Mitt Romney, who lost to President Obama in 2012, offers a good illustration of the foregoing kind of political intelligence. As he watched television coverage on the night of the results, despite encouraging noises from his trusted aides, Romney suddenly said: 'I'm out of here'. He was way ahead of his aides in recognizing the real state of play.

So far, two ingredients of a viable definition are emerging: inscrutability and speedy recognition that an environment has altered. These strike me now as the kind of qualities that are necessary but not sufficient conditions of political effectiveness. And one could argue that inscrutability isn't even a necessary condition. It's a fairly powerful one, though. As I write in 2012, the indicator of political intelligence that most impresses me is the capacity to transcend personal animosities. A classic example was President Obama's decision to appoint Hillary Clinton as Secretary of State in the wake of one of the most bitter campaign contests for the Democratic nomination in recent history.

That capacity or skill can, of course, be seen under the rubric of personal morality, when such action is taken mainly because it's the morally right thing to do. But that skill can also be seen (as in the case of President Obama's treatment of Hillary Clinton) under the heading of realpolitik: the action is taken not necessarily because it's the right thing to do, but because it is the most effective thing to do in the pursuit of a given end.

If political awareness both of an ideological and realpolitik kind were late arrivals in my case, the first stirrings of independent thought came later still. There was one saving grace, a persistent inclination to openness of mind. Those two pillars of a vigorous intellectual life are obviously intertwined: the capacity to make up one's mind, and the willingness to change it.

Openness of mind is a tricky variable: it is not always easy to distinguish the real thing from facsimiles of various kinds. I am reminded of an amusing line by the journalist Hugo Young about a junior member of the Thatcher government, whom he described as having not so much a mind that was open as one permanently vulnerable to opposing certainties. I take the former *Guardian* and *Sunday Times* journalist to be saying that although the individual in question was capable of changing allegiances, his actual mind-set remained unaltered: he was equally dogmatic, whatever his particular orientation at a given time. We all know them: erstwhile dogmatic left-wingers who become dogmatic right-wingers or vice versa, though we probably know more instances of the former than the latter.

I tend to the view that the capacity to make up one's mind is almost as rare as the willingness to change it. Let me amend that slightly, since it is the kind of claim that would be very difficult to verify. I suspect that coming to a firm conclusion is as difficult as a willingness to budge from that position. At any rate, let us agree that whatever the empirical realities, the relationship between the two is highly complex. There is no guarantee that the possession of either one capacity guarantees the emergence of the other. That they don't necessarily go hand in hand is spectacularly borne out by a remark made by a former Lord Chancellor of Britain, Viscount Hailsham, about his clever, controversial Tory colleague Enoch Powell. He said of Powell that he had the finest mind in British politics until it was made up.

The matter of personal convictions and our willingness to tweak or indeed abandon them has always interested me. In the 1960s I came to the conclusion that quite a number of people embraced ideological positions as a hasty response to pressures from others to define themselves. It is as if it's easier to say you're a socialist or, alternatively, a disciple of Ayn Rand than live with the uncertainty of not having decided. Anyway, who knows how we arrive at political positions. What I have said about the power of pressure may well be true in some cases. Then there are cases of straightforward conversions owing to charismatic personal influence.

For the past thirty years, I have been convinced that even the most rational people are guided initially in their political choices by gut feelings. Only afterwards does critical reason come into play, if and when we submit our initial preferences to critical scrutiny. It is illusory to think that anyone arrives at a basic political position by first assessing the evidence and then deciding. The point is we *begin* with a basic, gut-induced political posture, for which we may or may not subsequently seek intellectual support. Of greater significance than the impulse to seek support for that position is the willingness to submit it eventually to critical scrutiny.

W. S. Gilbert wasn't far off the mark when in *Iolanthe* he has Private Willis say that everyone is born either a little Liberal or else a little Conservative. The most commonly cited intellectual ancestry for the view that desire is our primary driving force is to be found in the work of the great Scottish philosopher David Hume. It is not that critical reflection doesn't count for him, but it is secondary to desire. While Hume is not my actual source, the fact that I think as I do indicates how deeply his ideas have infiltrated the culture of the last few hundred years.

We are initially drawn in a particular direction on the basis of a gut feeling, temperamental disposition, instinct, call it what you will. That primordial pull may be liberal, conservative, socialist, revolutionary or reactionary in character. Who knows whether we are in the grip of biochemical imperatives or are subject to early environmental conditioning. The reality is that these are our starting points. If enough of us are capable of submitting those initial impulses to critical scrutiny, and of treating other viewpoints fairly, then we can form a coherent political community. Implicit in what I am saying is this: *that* you think is more important than *what* you think.

Chapter 2

Much Religion, Some Culture, Little Politics

IF MY POLITICAL EDUCATION BEGAN ON a remarkably sluggish note, it gradually accelerated to a point that I didn't foresee. I am not talking about increased active political participation but about the extent to which politics has become central to my way of understanding the world. Like others who long for a more equitable social order, I occasionally find myself deploying the rhetoric of socialism, but in truth I am essentially a proponent of what one might call *welfare state* capitalism, a system under growing threat. The system we have is far from perfect, but in my opinion it is the best arrangement to date. In fact, I find it very difficult to conceive of any alternative economic system that could survive without the energizing potential of some kind of market-based framework. Unfortunately, it is not enough simply to have an efficient engine: if all our current dispensation can deliver are the recent unprecedented levels of social inequality, serious questions arise about its long-term survival.

The great challenge today for the fair-minded is to hold on to a system that defined the post-war years and is now fighting for its life, particularly in the United States. Whether welfare state capitalism can survive the next half-century or so is not at all clear. It is possible that if it fails, the entire house of cards will eventually come tumbling down in a manner hinted at by the Immanuel Wallersteins and Eric Hobsbawms of the world. Meantime, like many of my generation, I regard this system, imperfect though it be, as the best of a bad lot.

Politically, I am a child of that compassionate, government-directed, safety net approach to society that began in America with FDR in the early 1930s. I picked up an interesting story recently about FDR from Jeremy Adelman's book, *Worldly Philosopher: The Odyssey of Albert O. Hirschman (2013)*. Adelman reminds us that in Carlo Levi's novel *Christ Stopped at Eboli* (1949), Levi has a passage about impoverished Italian peasants displaying two portraits in their houses, one of Christ and and one of Franklin Delano Roosevelt. Although FDR's New Deal was pre-dated by some European welfare state programmes, the American effort surpassed these earlier initiatives in its worldwide impact. It set the tone for an even more interventionist approach by a post-war Labour government in Britain under Clement Attlee. Irish governments eventually followed suit, if not to the same extent as the UK, or indeed France and Germany, in the matter of universal health coverage. The arrival of Thatcher and Reagan in the 1980s presaged a serious threat to interventionist thinking, though it should be added that the British National Health Service survived the Thatcher era.

If I were not to be characterized as a proponent of *welfare state* capitalism, I could, alternatively, be described as the kind of socialist who accepts that the best we can do with the existing market system is to regulate it. Common to both descriptions is the realization that ultimately the choice is between different kinds of capitalism. I only became aware that we had taken social welfare capitalism for granted when *financial* capitalism began to hold sway from the 1980s onwards. I had assumed that the kind of political order we had before that was here to stay. I should add that it wasn't until a few years into the twenty-first century that I saw what was happening. That's how it usually is: only in retrospect do we see a pattern. I was, of course,

25

aware that Thatcher and Reagan shook things up, particularly the changes introduced to the city of London with the so-called 'big bang' of 1986. And yet, I didn't realize the significance of what was happening at the time. Eventually, a map of the terrain began to emerge.

Three years before the financial crash of 2008, historians like Steve Fraser and Tony Judt had begun to alert us to the defining economic contours of the post-war world. With hindsight, we can also see a measure of prediction in their work. Steve Fraser in *Wall Street: A Cultural History* (2005) looked at Wall Street over two centuries; Tony Judt in *Postwar* (2005) looked at Europe since 1945. Each drew attention to the collapse of both Rooseveltian capitalism and the Keynesian consensus from the 1980s onwards.

The western political world in the decades after 1945 was one in which we took the welfare state for granted. In such a dispensation, the arts, education and broadcasting could count on generous government financial support. That era began to come to an end in the early 1980s. Since then it has been not just funding for education, the arts and broadcasting that is under increasing threat, but basic social welfare itself, the bedrock of the old system. The old compassionate order of social welfare capitalism is now being powerfully assailed. We are living in a different world: one reminiscent of a late nineteenth-century robber baron era. When the financial collapse occurred in 2008, it all looked eerily familiar to those aware of past events.

As I write, in the middle of the second decade of the twenty-first century, there is some surprise that the political left has not managed to capitalize on the 2008 financial collapse. One of the reasons being advanced for that outcome is that the right was catapulted into action by the scale of U.S. government intervention that was necessary to bail out the banks: it feared a socialist takeover. What is being overlooked here is that without public money, the financial disaster would have been compounded.

The failure of the left thus far to benefit from the crisis has been overshadowed by the rise of China as an economic super-power. There were significant signs of that development around 2000, but after 2008 China took the place of the U.S as the leading power in economic globalization. The post-war map had altered substantially. And in the context of a larger time frame, China, which had been on the global fringes for the previous two hundred years, was back.

I have already indicated that the arts, philosophy and religion caught my attention long before politics did. Certainly, it wasn't until the mid-1960s that I first became aware of politics as a site for moral evaluations, the notion that political arrangements might be fair or unfair. That meant that I had graduated from a tribal understanding of politics to an ideological one.

My first understanding of politics was that it involved loyalty to a tribe, usually based on inherited family attitudes to the Irish Civil War of 1922-23. Next, politics impinged on my awareness as an activity that could involve corruption. At this early stage, politics seemed to revolve mainly around the antics of colourful personalities. Then I realized that one could evaluate by rational criteria the policies of the competing political parties. A further stage involved moving to an evaluation of the fairness of the political *system*. By then I had reached my mid-thirties. Around the same time, I became aware of yet another layer of politics – the machinations involved in acquiring and maintaining power; in other words, the regular currency of realpolitik.

Finally, in my forties, I came to understand politics in yet another fresh guise. I became aware of politics as a major factor that (together with economics and culture) can help explain social change. So I was gradually learning that beyond the tribal, the ideological and the Machiavellian understandings of politics lay yet another layer. That other layer consists of seeing politics as one of the key factors that accounts for social change. Another way of expressing this is to say that politics is an important component in the philosophy of history. That understanding came to me as a result of prolonged exposure in the early 1980s to the ideas of the great social theorists from Marx and Weber onwards to contemporary thinkers like Ernest Gellner and Ulrich Beck. Politics could now be seen as a significant factor in understanding social change, but so too could economics and culture. I could see that this was a useful three-fold analytic framework for looking at both the past and the present. Determining which of the three factors was pre-eminent in effecting social change is an empirical matter: you have to look at the data. The problem is that the necessary data are thin on the ground because of the time-scale involved and the number of relevant variables. For Marx, a compound of economic interests and technology was of paramount importance in the mix, Weber kept his options more open, but on balance they veered towards ideas, towards culture. As far as the chronology of my own life is concerned, cultural interests had preceded those of a political or economic kind. From my late forties onwards, I had access to a framework for integrating all three perspectives.

This was not strictly speaking a *theory* of social change, of course, just a useful analytic tool. Besides, one had to distinguish between the straightforward factual question as to whether economics, politics or culture is the primary driving force in social change at a particular period, and the question as to what elites *believe* is the most influential of these factors at any given period.

I should add that the ordering by me in this book of these various ways of understanding politics (as a tribal phenomenon, as a site of corruption, as a policy-oriented process, as ideological in character, as power-centred, as partly explanatory of social change) is prompted not by any philosophical doctrine, but by the order in which these different understandings occurred in my life. In a word, the listing was determined solely by chronology.

If I were pushed to say which of those layers is the most foundational one, I would reply that the most basic layer has not yet been mentioned. It was the layer that was to impinge on my awareness last. What I am referring to is an understanding of politics that is grounded in the realization that reasonable people disagree. To that extent, it is an approach to politics that accommodates the ideological but that ultimately has to transcend it if we are to live together with our differences.

The fact that reasonable people disagree about crucial matters like the meaning of the common good appears to be one of the key features of the modern age. As a result, the first task we have as citizens is to try to agree to a framework that can accommodate the working out of our differences: this entails subscribing to agreed procedural rules before matters of substance are tackled. In other words, the ideological horizon cannot be the ultimate one in such discussions because it is a substantive horizon not a procedural one, unless you want to insist that devising a framework to accommodate differences is itself an ideology.

The political philosopher John Rawls in *Political Liberalism* (1993) has such high hopes for agreement at a substantive level that he seems to take for granted the kind of groundwork necessary at a procedural level. The reason for his optimism is that the substantive terrain which he has chosen for consideration he believes to be a relatively manageable one. Rawls has arrived at that sanguine position by distinguishing between those substantive disagreements that he considers relatively solvable and those that are not. So while he accepts that, in the matter of fundamental religious and philosophical worldviews, we are confronted with intractable disagreement, he believes that when it comes to an issue such as the main principles of justice, we *can* reach agreement. Such agreement is described by him as an 'overlapping consensus'.

Much as I admire the egalitarian moral intuitions that gird this philosopher's work, I feel he may be underestimating the difficulties involved in securing the overlapping consensus he talks about. By way of dealing with objections that his particular consensus is utopian, Rawls proposes one way in which that agreement might come about. The problem is that others will have different ideas both about the components of the consensus and as to how it might come about. Such dissenting views will have to be accommodated.

The broadly egalitarian character of much of the western world for over three decades after the Second World War was set in motion by President Franklin D. Roosevelt in 1933. That was the world I grew up in. John Rawls was to become its most eloquent philosophical voice. Following FDR's New Deal initiatives, government intervention became widely accepted as a rational way of ensuring that the basic needs of the community, particularly those of the less well off, would be taken care of. That principle was honoured to varying degrees in most western countries, including Ireland, neighbouring Britain and much of continental Europe. Roosevelt had set the tone by acting decisively in the wake of the Wall Street crash of 1929. The new system would last for fifty years. Significantly, Dwight Eisenhower in 1953 endorsed the kind of social order entailed by the New Deal, as indeed did later Republican presidents. Only with the advent of Ronald Reagan in 1981 did the old order begin to change. The world of deregulation and suspicion of big government, inaugurated by Reagan, is the one we still inhabit as I write in 2016.

I have worked for most of my life as a broadcast journalist in public affairs, the arts and religion. I had the good fortune to observe the world from three countries: Ireland, on the western edge of Europe, Britain to the immediate east, and North

America to the far west. The key vantage points available to me were three contrasting cities: Dublin, on the Liffey, London on the Thames, and Cambridge, Massachusetts on the Charles. However, my first view of the world was from the town of Clonmel on the river Suir in County Tipperary, where I spent my childhood and early teenage years. By 1957, I had settled in Dublin, where within a few years I would become a radio news-reader, and soon after that, a news anchor with the country's first television service.

Dublin has been my main base for half a century; Cambridge, Massachusetts has been my second home for over thirty years; London was the city where I recorded most of my book-based radio conversations over a period of thirty-five years. Dublin is home and so in its way is Cambridge, but London is the city that has been most rewarding for theatre, concerts, opera and art shows. Clonmel has the kind of place in my affections that only one's birthplace can have.

In the matter of books, Cambridge takes the honours, thanks to its scholarly bookstores and the Widener library. Since 1980, I have spent up to a third of each year in Cambridge. The city of Cambridge has been aptly described as Boston's Left Bank. It has no more than one-tenth of Dublin's population, but as home to leading universities like Harvard and MIT, can reasonably claim to be one of the world's leading academic capitals. The traffic of intellectual capital between Cambridge and Washington must be the busiest of its kind in the world.

Today much, if not most, of our travel is in virtual space: nowadays, even when we *do* travel, the first thing we do on arrival is turn on our computer. Not that we have altogether abandoned the jet for the internet, but it is in cyberspace mostly that we now navigate the globe. In my childhood in Clonmel, the family radio was the most advanced item of communications technology we owned. Not just the most advanced: the radio was the only piece of communications technology we had in the home. Manufactured by a company called Murphy, it carried the names of far-flung stations like Hilversum and Droitwich alongside Athlone, which is where our national station, Raidió Éireann, was located on the dial. Compared to today's disposable radio sets, this unignorable piece of furniture in the sitting room corner had an air of permanence. That station-crowded dial opened out on to a world of which I knew nothing. We had no contact with that world, apart from reminders of its existence in the post-war years when Clonmel's emigrants returned periodically from London or other British cities to spend much of their savings in the town. Some of these returning emigrants would show up at Christmas or summer time in our family pub in the Irishtown district. The cities of Britain, where many of my own townsfolk had found work, were something of a mystery to me, and yet I never asked any of those who returned about their experiences. My immediate environment, apart from having been the locus of a short-lived scare that accompanied the false threat of a German invasion during the war, was a secure and stable one, in which I felt confident that my needs would be taken care of and that I would somehow be looked after. Not even my father's death when I was eight years of age affected that as much as one might expect.

My father is listed in a Clonmel business directory for 1925/1932 under the heading of 'grocers and spirit dealers'. To me he seemed more spirit dealer than grocer, more publican than general merchant. I didn't begin to take much notice of customers until my adolescent years, when I began to become more aware of what was called 'the back room'. That was a special room reserved mainly for male members of the St. Mary's Choral Society, a musical organization founded in 1940 as an outgrowth of St. Mary's parish church choir. This disciplined cohort of tenors, baritones and basses enjoyed their favourite drinks and performed there the songs of Stephen Foster, various operatic choruses and assorted church music. They also sang popular songs of the period like 'On Moonlight Bay', 'Oh Genevieve' and 'Let the Rest of the World Go By'. It was an era of spontaneous vocal harmonizing in barber-shop style. Simon Denny, unofficial chronicler of the St. Mary's Choral Society, said memorably of bass-baritone Tom McGrath that 'he could harmonize to a creaking door'. Among the tenors in that group was a teenage Frank Patterson, destined to become the most acclaimed Irish tenor since John McCormack; also in the group was the dark-voiced Paddy Hickey from the Old Bridge, who had one of the finest baritone voices I have ever heard. On many occasions, the singers were joined by James White, the society's musical director, and by Brendan Long, who directed its theatrical productions.

Those choral sessions are events I associate more with my mother than with my father: I suspect that those sessions hadn't got off the ground in his lifetime. My parents enjoyed no more than a decade of married life together. My father was twenty years older than my mother, but died relatively young. Both of them came from the Cashel area of County Tipperary. Andy was born in 1881 in Lagganstown in the parish of Knockgraffon; my mother, Nora Collins, in 1902 in Mocklershill in the parish of Dualla. I am not too sure what prompted them to put down roots in Clonmel beyond the fact that it probably offered more business opportunities than nearby Cashel.

On a recent visit after an absence of many years, I approached the town of Clonmel from the Cashel Road side. I crossed Queen Street, turned left and then right on to Gladstone Street. From this vantage point – St. Peter & Paul's Church is on the right and the town's main Post Office on the left – the unfolding townscape took me by surprise. The pleasing visual effect created was due to three things: the nearness of the hills overlooking Gladstone Street, a well-proportioned streetscape, and a side-long glimpse of the Main Guard, one of the country's finest examples of seventeenth-century architecture. Even though I grew up in Clonmel, it was as if I had never seen this vista before. And perhaps, the truth is that as a child and adolescent, I never had.

How could I not have noticed the magnificent sweep of that street named after William Gladstone, a street framed by low-lying hills reaching down to the quayside. It is probably the best view of the town. There were so many of the town's features I had forgotten, among them the fact that the narrow strip that is Mitchell Street, between the Main Guard and Gladstone Street, is an urban gem. In my childhood, the town had a population of 10,000; now, it is heading towards double that.

My parents' business premises and residence were at 25/26 Irishtown in the parish of St. Mary's. They were located next door to the Catholic presbytery, which among other things sported a fine orchard at the rear. A few doors down from the presbytery stood the residence of the local parish priest. All these fine houses, which once graced the space between my old homestead and the parish church, have been demolished. St. Mary's Church itself, a building constructed in the second half of the nineteenth century in a style that accurately reflected the burgeoning Catholic self-confidence of that era, is still, thankfully, to the good. To us children, it was simply 'the chapel'.

When my father died of pneumonia, my widowed mother had little option but to take over the business. Not merely that, she had to care for five children as well. All that meant hiring extra staff, including some home help, who lived in. Freud is forever quoted as saying that there is little fear for a man who is loved by his mother. I suspect that my lifelong intellectual curiosity is traceable in large part to the security conferred by her affection.

Sunday mornings in the O'Mahony household in the late 1940s involved a three-part ritual for me, consisting of early Mass, a leisurely breakfast and reading the *Sunday Independent*.

(Beginning in 1952, I added *The Observer* and *The Sunday Times* to my weekly list.) Three modes of sustenance: spiritual, physical and cultural. The newspaper reading part of it was a solitary activity, the most private part of the ritual. It was confined to an upstairs sitting room that overlooked Irishtown. In those post-breakfast hours the seeds were sown for a lifetime of reading and reflection. In addition to the Sunday newspapers, I would also re-read the local newspaper, the *Clonmel Nationalist*, which was published on Fridays.

My newspaper reading in those childhood years was allo-cated to Fridays and Sundays, and to Mondays for the sports results. There were also forays into book buying: second-hand volumes for a couple of shillings at Bulbert's across the street in Irishtown. It was the latter practice that set in train my lifelong passion for buying books. It may be that the act of reading for me has always been unconsciously framed in the context of that enriching three-fold Sunday morning matrix of spiritual, physi-cal and cultural nourishment.

One clear recollection I have from that first whirlwind bout of reading in late adolescence is a piece by the great Victorian art critic John Ruskin from a second-hand tome purchased at Bulbert's. Ruskin said something that struck me intuitively as true at a first reading, and which has been constantly confirmed throughout my reading life. It is the suggestion that the most exhilarating aspect of learning occurs not at the point at which we have mastered something but at the point at which we sense we are on the *verge* of really learning something. As with so many pleasurable activities, the nature of which need not detain us here, it is to do with anticipation.

In Ireland in the 1930s, the country's energies were focused more on political than on economic stability. The country had enjoyed political independence only since 1922. The main con-cern was ensuring that the successful transition to a native par-liamentary democracy was maintained. As for developments in the wider world in the 1930s, there were three main responses to the global economic crisis: in America, the New Deal, and in Europe, communism and fascism.

Of those three responses, the only one to be replicated in 2008 on the occasion of a comparable crash was FDR's interventionism. That took the form in the United States of a large-scale rescue package first launched by President George W. Bush and completed by President Barack Obama. That leaves fascism and communism as untried options this time around. Despite the rise of the right-wing Freedom party in Austria, the anti-immigrant True Finns party in Finland, and the Golden Dawn party in Greece, fascism does not seem to be really shaping up today as the kind of threat it was in the 1930s. As for communism, its heady days seem to be over.

In the immediate aftermath of the 2008 crisis that necessitated extensive state intervention, nobody had a good word to say for unfettered markets. But even left-leaning economists like the Nobel Prize-winner Joseph Stiglitz, no more than Keynes in his day, had no wish to see the end of the capitalist order: they didn't want to throw out the baby with the toxic bathwater. As I have already indicated, that is broadly where I situate myself, despite mounting evidence that it is a posture becoming harder to sustain.

I am deeply distrustful of those who say regulations inhibit growth. At the same time, the most intriguing aspect of the capitalist order is the manner in which it allows free play to spontaneity, and therefore has an inbuilt energizing agent. When you think about it, a powerful feature of the capitalist system is that it is capable of embodying two principles that are central to successful functioning of any kind: planning and spontaneity. That tension between the spontaneity of markets and the regulatory activities of states appears to be the actual source of the energy of the system. That same tension, however, can be destructive as well as generative, if the balance between the two components goes seriously awry. The widespread social inequality that has been experienced recently in western countries is a clear sign that it has. There are at least two possible reactions at this juncture to the breakdown of the existing system: a creative reformist response from the pragmatists of the hour (those individuals, regardless of ideology, who realize more than most that things aren't working); and if all fails, a revolutionary response (which will probably involve more than cancelling your subscription to *The Economist*). Either way, we may well look back on the late twentieth and early twenty-first centuries as a major turning point in economic and social history.

Politics understood as a conflict between left and right, between those who speak for the less well off and those who represent the interests of the rich and powerful, was never part of my childhood, adolescence or early young adulthood. What *was* part of my childhood was the politics of the Irish Civil War of 1922-23. That war was set in motion by differences over the Anglo-Irish Treaty of 1921. On one side of the conflict were those who accepted the Treaty negotiated with the British; on the other side, those who saw it as betrayal. What caused the civil war though was not so much differences over the Treaty but a dispute about whether the Irish should be obliged to take an oath of allegiance to the British monarch. The main legacy of the civil war was that the issues that drove that conflict sidelined economic and social matters for almost four decades. Politics for me in my childhood years meant listening to veterans relive in their public utterances both the Irish Civil War and that which preceded it, the war of independence from Britain. The broad political map consisted of two main parties still defined in terms of the civil war of 1922-23: Fine Gael, which had been the pro-Treaty party and Fianna Fáil the anti-Treaty party. A third party, that of Labour, was identified exclusively with neither position.

One of the local political figures most identified with civil war politics was Dan Breen, who had opposed the 1921 Treaty with Britain. Breen had famously taken part in the first incident in the Irish War of Independence in 1919 at Soloheadbeg in County Tipperary. In the 1940s, as a local Fianna Fáil member of Dáil Éireann, he used to address the public from the steps outside the Denis Lacey Hall on the mall in Clonmel. The author of *My Fight for Irish Freedom* (1924) would tell us in every speech he made that his body was 'riddled with bullets'. As children we had no context for understanding what he was saying. And yet the events he spoke about had occurred little more than a quarter of a century earlier. But I remember that as we moved into early adolescence, and began in time-honoured fashion to feel smarter than anybody older than ourselves, we mocked Breen's gunman bravado talk and, by implication, that of his contemporaries.

Were we young brats who had no grasp of the sacrifices many of our elders had made or were we just hungry for real politics? I would later learn that the Great Depression of the 1930s had radicalized significant sections of society elsewhere, but Ireland seemed still mired in civil war politics. I didn't really begin to understand politics in the more customary European registers of left and right until the 1960s.

Two factors contributed to that: the first was when I learned in my early thirties that my inherited Catholicism was not only compatible with socialist thought but was arguably a natural bedfellow of it; the second was the widespread student revolution of the late 1960s. Ironically, the latter development came about in the wake of postwar economic prosperity in the western world. It began as an American campus phenomenon but it also spread to Europe, mainly to France, where Paris 1968 became shorthand for the politicization of students, which was occurring worldwide. University College Dublin had its own campus revolt: it was called 'the gentle revolution'.

One particular analysis that helped clarify matters for me at the time was *The Making of a Counter Culture* (1969) by historian Theodore Roszak. This author's central claim was that the student revolt was more a 'psychological' revolution than a political one. This was not meant as a 'put-down', but as an attempt to specify the precise nature of what was occurring. In other words, the new stirrings were more a matter of changes taking place in how certain young people thought than changes in institutions themselves. The key idea was that whatever about changing society itself, we can at least change the heart of man.

In that same spirit, Herbert Marcuse, the leading guru of radical student thought at the time, was someone who spoke more of altering awareness than of changing institutions. His influential book *One-Dimensional Man* (1964) encouraged critical, oppositional thought. He was a member of the Frankfurt School, whose main members had emigrated to California in the 1930s. His marriage of Marx and Freud in an earlier book had instant appeal for the campus radicals.

As much a follower of intellectual fashion as the next, I ordered a copy of *One-Dimensional Man* from the Eblana bookshop in Dublin's Grafton Street around 1968, but didn't make much sense of it. The reason for that was that I didn't have an adequate context for fully understanding it: my level of political awareness was quite undeveloped. In *Hitch 22: A Memoir* (2010), I note that Christopher Hitchens describes Marcuse as an intellectual fraud. However, that may be a hindsight assessment. It is not clear that he took that view at the time.

Precisely because I *did* have a context for understanding two British theologians who spoke in Dublin, what they were saying resonated much more with me than what Marcuse was saying. That context was a religious one, namely that of my childhood Catholicism. Around 1966, two Dominican priests visiting from Blackfriars in Oxford addressed a theological discussion group in Dublin, known as 'Flannery's Harriers'. It was a revelation to discover that the religion I grew up with could be seen through a political lens, in this case a socialist one. Admittedly, the Catholic social doctrine I had learned at boarding school was *tacitly* political in that it absolutized the rights of private property, but that doctrine didn't seem political at the time.

That particular sobriquet of 'Flannery's Harriers', which was used to describe our study group, was an affectionate tribute to Austin Flannery, an Irish Dominican priest who founded the group. It consisted of Catholic, Protestant and agnostic intellectuals and met every month or so at various venues to discuss matters religious and theological. It was a direct outgrowth of the second Vatican Council of 1962-65. Among those who attended regularly were the architect Richard Hurley, broadcaster Seán Mac Réamoinn, theologian Enda McDonagh, historian David Thornley, television producer Jack Dowling, Tom Stack, a notably well-read young Catholic curate, and Ray Carroll, a sculptor.

Of the two visiting English Dominicans, deeply influenced by Marx and Aquinas, Herbert McCabe was the more theologically subtle, Lawrence Bright, the more overtly political. It was from their lips I first heard talk of a 'religionless Christianity', the notion that Jesus's mission was to transform the world and in the process rid it of all irrelevant cultic accretions. These visiting theologians argued persuasively that not merely were Catholicism and socialism compatible, they were natural bedfellows. It was the kind of thinking that would later characterize the work of liberation theologians in South America. Their argument was that, given the thrust of New Testament teaching, the only credible political option for a Christian was to favour a socialist solution of some kind.

I wasn't at all alert to the institutional complexities involved in translating that into practice, but at least I now had a new starting place: being a Christian was a matter of redressing social inequality. In those days, we took the welfare state for granted; the struggle today is to hold on to it. It was as clear in the 1960s as today that efforts to promote social justice did not exhaust what being a Christian meant. But without it, other components, such as preoccupation with the transcendent, would ring hollow.

Had the visiting Dominicans been singing the praises of a socialist perspective divorced from a Catholic context, I probably wouldn't have listened. I felt safe integrating a political perspective into the religious framework with which I had grown up. But once that door to radical political thought was opened for me, the original religious foothold became less relevant. The Roszak book was a helpful overview, the Marcuse more polemical, but it was the Dominican theologians who politicized me, in however tentative a manner.

My newly developed political awareness never transcended the armchair variety. I was not one for meetings, let alone barricades. Oscar Wilde captured the milk and watery disposition of many attracted to the left, when he famously said the problem with being a socialist is that it would take up too many evenings. As I sat on my reclining couch in Dublin, whether in the neighbourhoods of Blackrock or Baggot Street, I was aware even then of the mild absurdities of what was called 'drawing room Che Guevaraism'.

The writer Tom Wolfe, after attending a party that Leonard Bernstein threw for the Black Panthers in New York in the 1960s, alerted the world to the high comedy of 'radical chic', which consisted of upper middle-class elites embracing political radicalism as a kind of fashion accessory. The celebrity Third World activism of rock stars and actors which came decades later did not have the same satiric potential, but was freighted nonetheless with puncturable inconsistencies.

By the early 1970s, I was, however tentatively, beginning to see the world in a new way, even though the contradictions that seemed to accompany the new politics multiplied. For example, in the early 1970s, let alone in subsequent decades, there was a rash of cynical commentary pointing out that many of the protesting radicals were moving on to lucrative positions in corporate life. The general line of criticism was that dissent had been commercialized, co-opted by the established powers. David Foster Wallace in his posthumous novel *The Pale King* (2011) applies the same kind of cynical analysis to what remained of American 'counterculture' in the 1980s: big corporations, he suggested, will always make money out of products that make dissenters feel they are being different. The commercialization of dissent goes on.

However, I now believe that, for all the flaws at the heart of the 1960s' counterculture, something of significance did happen: many of the youth of the day and some not so young did experience a genuine shift in awareness. The sixties era has had its eloquent critics but I believe there was a real shift in consciousness at the time. There was a move away from acquisitive materialism in favour of non-materialist values. Those who did experience such a transformation began to imagine what a new society might be like.

Such a newly imagined society tended to be a fairer one, but in the 1960s my impression was that the energies of many reformers were devoted to the kind of freedoms they themselves would enjoy within that more equitable society. That roughly was where I had positioned myself. I was particularly interested not so much in what a transformed society might look like, but, more precisely, what a transformed *individual* would look like.

In the summer of 1969, I recall airing that obsession at a party at the family home of the writer Maeve Binchy in Dalkey, County Dublin. 'What does it mean to be fully human?' I intrepidly asked as I sipped Dubonnet and soda outdoors that Sunday morning on a well-kept, south County Dublin lawn. Maeve's sister Joan punctured my balloon by asking me if I had been spending a lot of time with animals. It was a good line; it also revealed at least two possible understandings of the word 'human', a minimal one and an optimal one.

As to the issue of social unfairness, my concern was more ritualistic than real. In the matter of personal transformation, I was a natural convert to the notion that fulfilment lay not in owning things but in heightening one's awareness. That amounted to a realization that 'being' was more important than 'having'. In a word, it was more important to expand one's consciousness than to possess things. That line of thinking dovetailed with Aristotelian notions of a leisured, contemplative life, to which I had been converted in my late teens and early twenties by reading John Henry Newman, Jacques Maritain and Josef Pieper. Now in the 1960s that approach would take on a more political coloration. At the time one heard the slogan 'the personal is the political'. To some extent that is true, but I felt my own sense of politics was quite fragile: I still veered more towards the psychological than the political.

It was Erich Fromm, another Frankfurt School émigré, whom I first saw make that particular distinction between 'being' and 'having' in a political context. For many, 'expanding consciousness' meant drugs, and while I drank a fair amount of alcohol in the late 1960s, I was equally amenable to the simple joys of heightened perception, whether the delight of simply looking intensely at the world or listening to classical LPs.

However, I should add that merely to move to a point where one came to realize that expanding one's awareness was more important than owning things could be a purely selfish concern if divorced from the issue of the wider state of society. After all, Aristotle's idealization of the contemplative life coexisted in ancient Greek society with slavery. In the modern world it is reasonable to ask whether individuals could acknowledge Erich Fromm's privileging of 'being' over 'having', but do so in a state of wilful ignorance as to the underlying level of inequality and deprivation in the wider society. In so far as the counterculture stopped short at that point, it was markedly deficient.

If left/right politics did not really figure in my childhood and adolescence, religion did. No, religion didn't so much 'figure' in our lives: it suffused them. It took the form of a Catholicism of a markedly devotional kind. Local church ceremonies structured our lives: daily Mass, Confession, evening Benediction, baptismal rites and the removal of the dead to St. Mary's church in Irishtown.

One particular Sunday in the mid-1940s, I decided to take Holy Communion on the spur of the moment at a late Mass. Ever eager to please my mother, when I got home from that Sunday Mass I proudly announced that I had received the Sacrament of the Eucharist. Her reaction was one of undisguised fury because she knew that I had already eaten my breakfast before that particular late Mass. I had broken the relevant fasting requirements. I do remember how angry she became on that occasion. Such rules were not taken lightly in our household.

The annual Corpus Christi procession in the month of June, which ended with a military guard of honour at the Main Guard in Clonmel's O'Connell Street, was the liturgical highpoint of the year. The Main Guard and the West Gate were the principal architectural landmarks in the town: these buildings book-ended O'Connell Street. The Main Guard has been restored under the supervision of local architect Margaret Quinlan. In my youth, because of its association with the Corpus Christi procession, the building had a quasi-religious as well as an architectural significance. The West Gate had to make do with merely secular connections: it used to house a billiard hall on its top floor as part of the CYMS club.

Apart from the annual procession, the other main event was a church mission conducted by visiting Passionist priests or Redemptorist fathers. It was one of those visiting Redemptorist priests who asked my mother if she had a son who might consider the priesthood as a way of life. Among the Passionist preachers was a Father Hillary Barry, a 'local boy', it was said. In other circumstances this might have undermined his status as an authoritative dispenser of spiritual wisdom, but in 1940s' Ireland, it actually seemed to enhance it.

The kind of Catholicism I inherited as a child was decidedly ultramontane in character. It was a highly centralized, Vatican-controlled Catholicism, cemented in Ireland by Paul Cullen (1803-78), the Archbishop of Dublin and first Irish cardinal. The fact that the O'Mahony family in Clonmel lived so close to St Mary's parish church and presbytery in Irishtown reinforced this Cullenite world-view: we felt we were living in an outpost of a larger Rome-centred ecclesiastical empire. The church's chief local representative, the parish priest, Canon Dan Walsh, whose private orchard stretched all the way to the banks of the river Suir, struck the fear of God into all us schoolchildren. 'All eyes on the altar' he would bark at us as we sat in the pews of St. Mary's parish church. 'Now, all genuflect together'. We were heirs to what the historian Emmet Larkin has called a 'devotional revolution'. It was a mixture of Vatican loyalty and Victorian piety. And how loyal and devout we were. We were quite unaware that in the previous century there was another side to the Irish Church: prelates like Daniel Murray, Archbishop of Dublin, had stoutly resisted the kind of Vatican-controlled, centralised Catholicism we then practised.

In the early to mid-twentieth century, we seemed to have inherited only one side of that divide, the side represented by Cardinal Cullen. I should add, however, that we inherited little or nothing of Cullen's sectarianism, his deep contempt for Protestants as wandering souls hopelessly in error. One day in school, a fellow pupil took it on himself to fill me in on the minutiae of religious difference: 'the Ralstons are Protestant; they tell their sins to the wall, you know'. That piece of unsolicited liturgical/theological information neatly captured the innocent, non-adversarial character of inter-faith relations in County Tipperary in the 1940s.

The nineteenth-century conflict between Ultramontanism (which emphasized papal authority) and Gallicanism (which played it down), between centralized and decentralized visions of Catholicism, would be acted out on a global stage at the Second Vatican Council in the years 1962-65. An overwhelming majority of the bishops at that council opted for a more collegiate, less Vatican-dominated church; they hoped for a greater acknowledgement of the local church, and a greater emphasis on freedom of individual conscience. Essentially, the Second Vatican Council strove to envisage the world less as a threatening enemy and more as a potential ally in its mission to transform that same world. That vision has collapsed somewhere along the way in the last forty years, though in another five hundred years, who knows how things will look.

In Ireland, as elsewhere, the old ecclesiastical, institutional hulk resisted change in the postconciliar era, and by the twenty-first century had collapsed into near irrelevance. The clerical child abuse scandals actually masked the decline because they were wrongly cited as the main cause of it. The real cause of the breakdown was that whereas heretofore the Catholic Church was the sole dispenser of moral values, it was no longer the only source of moral guidance. People began to pay more attention to competing voices. On that score, the title of sociologist Tom Inglis's excellent book *Moral Monopoly* (1998) says it all.

In the years of my Catholic childhood, religion was essentially a matter of devotional practices. How good a human being you were was largely a matter of how faithful you were to these practices, and also a matter of living a chaste life. That was the size of it in the 1940s and 1950s. I made valiant efforts to try to achieve a deeper understanding of what a good or holy life might mean, but rarely got further than that until the late 1960s.

After the Second Vatican Council, things improved in that for the first time theologians and others began to talk about the role of experience in religious life. Irish theologians like Enda McDonagh and James P. (Jim) Mackey were particularly helpful in that regard. Eventually, I began to see that a person who had difficulty making sense of their inherited religious tradition had three options: to deny the tradition, to deny their experience, or to reinterpret the tradition in the light of their experience. For years, I tried the last option, before eventually moving to a position of agnosticism with regard to the existence of God.

It is not easy to identify the point at which I became an agnostic, because many people who subscribe to religious beliefs have agnostic moments. Nonethless, there may come a point for them when the agnostic moments outnumber the believing ones. If we envisage some kind of cognitive/credal continuum in this matter, there may come a further point in which religious belief is abandoned. Because of the subtle gradations involved, it is difficult for me to identify when such a moment occurred in my own life, but if we take desisting from church-going as a rough guide, I was in my mid- to late fifties.

My agnosticism pertains to two separate matters: whether or not God exists; and (if He does exist), whether and how He has made or continues to make contact with the human race. Alternatively expressed, there is first the question as to whether or not there exists a dimension that transcends human sensory experience, and secondly, if there is such a dimension, how it impinges on our lives. As a cradle Catholic, I believed that God did exist and that he was mediated through Jesus Christ and the Catholic Church. Today, I am agnostic as to both questions, but whereas in the matter of God's existence I am a 'weak' agnostic, I would describe myself as a 'strong' agnostic in the matter of whether and how such a God is mediated to the world. Let me clarify.

I am a 'weak' agnostic in the matter of God's existence because I believe that the question 'why is there something rather than nothing' is one that makes sense. Not everybody does: for some it is a meaningless question. Once you acknowledge that a question is meaningful, that it *does* make sense, you accept that it may have an answer. For me, it is perfectly rational to posit the notion of some kind of self-subsisting source, namely God, as a possible answer. As to the second matter of whether and how such a source might be mediated to the human race, I am a 'strong' agnostic. In other words, when it comes to the claims of Divine Revelation, I am at a loss, but nonetheless am open to the possibility that Jesus may represent a unique avenue to the Divine.

It may surprise you that someone like myself, who is a weak agnostic as regards God's existence, and a strong agnostic in the matter of whether the Christian tradition offers us a direct line to God (should such exist), should still be interested in the project of integrating his own experience with the religious tradition he inherited. I am disposed to do so for the following reason. First of all, a genuine agnostic has to be open to the possibility that he may one day acknowledge the existence of an 'ultimate source' and even that the particular tradition that he accidentally inherited is the correct one. If he is open to these possibilities, then it is not unreasonable for him to go on examining his inherited tradition in that agnostic state. If he is not open to the possibility of one day reaffirming an ultimate source or of affirming the truth of one particular tradition that claims to mediate that source, he can scarcely call himself an agnostic.

Whole libraries have been written about the two concepts already referred to of 'experience' and 'religious tradition'. But let me add one footnote about religious tradition. All too often it is distorted to mean an unchanging body of doctrine. It was the great Dominican theologian Yves Congar who alerted us to the perils of that view when he pointed out that Archbishop Marcel Lefebvre, who had rejected the Second Vatican Council, had a defective understanding of tradition. For Lefebvre, tradition represented that which was unchanging: he had no understanding of the *development* of doctrine. His view persists in some Catholic circles.

As far as experience was concerned, as a young man I did my best to try to make sense of Catholic teaching in the context of my lived experience. The first inkling I got that concrete meaning could be assigned to terms like 'good' and 'holy' was when I was introduced in the 1960s to the idea of a natural fit between Christianity and socialist thought: being good was a matter of subscribing to the kind of order that protected the weak and vulnerable. Before that, my reading in both psychology and philosophy had helped put flesh on notions of the good in different ways.

Philosophy, in introducing me to the debate about whether the good was rationally groundable or was simply a matter of individual preference, provided me with a foundational framework in which to discuss these matters. Psychology was helpful in alerting me to the fact that a virtue such as open-mindedness has resonance in both psychology, morality and religion. But it was my political education that brought home to me that probably the most fruitful way of giving concrete meaning to Christian values is in the notion of a transformed society that is fair and socially just.

I cannot emphasize enough the void I found at the heart of my religious formation in the matter of what living a good life meant. There was so much emphasis on church observance and on living a chaste life that one was at a loss as to what one should do. Be kind to your neighbour is a good start, but that injunction needs more precision, more content. And that is where a newfound political awareness came into play. One further way I tried to give meaning to my Catholic upbringing was to reframe my curiosity as implicitly God-oriented. In other words, the strategy was to interpret my desire for knowledge and wisdom as implicitly a desire for an ultimate source of some kind. That was another way of assigning meaning to the Christian life. It was a way of integrating the life I was actually living with my religious formation.

Of the three options facing me (deny the tradition, deny my experience, or re-examine the tradition in the light of my experience), the most disastrous one would have been to have denied my experience, that is to say, deny the experience I had of not finding that tradition (as mediated to me) something to which I could relate. It was a real option though: the result would have been two unintegrated lives in which one simultaneously lived an outward conformist life and an unresolved inner one. It is called 'playing the game' and is a perennial risk for members of any institution. At least, I avoided that option.

Chapter 3

THE MOST BEAUTIFUL TOWN
IN THE WORLD

THE BRITISH ECONOMIST JOHN VAIZEY may not have been the first to claim that the most important thing to know about a person is the year in which he or she was born, but his making of that claim certainly registered with me. The great Napoleon Bonaparte insisted that what you really need to know is the state of the world when that person was twenty. We can see an element of truth in both those propositions. And yet both claims overstate the influence of outside forces on a life. They tend to minimize what we as individuals can contribute.

After all, we do have a capacity to change both ourselves, and, even on occasion, however marginally, things around us. Or at the very least, like the protagonist in Kingsley Amis' *Lucky Jim* (1954), we can change our socks. Quite an achievement, though, is the capacity to recognize the things we cannot change. That very recognition, paradoxically, confers on us a certain freedom.

It is something of a cliché to say that while there is not much we can change about what happens to us, what we *can* change is the way we respond to what happens. I don't think we should dispense too precipitately with that hoary old adage. I have become something of a convert to an axiom that one might call the defining one of cognitive therapy; namely, 'things could be

51

worse'. The capacity to reframe the situations in which we find ourselves is a crucial survival tactic. Some years ago, I was afflicted for about two months with sixth nerve palsy, which causes the temporary onset of double vision. I complained to a friend who asked me if *both* eyes were affected. No, only one. Point taken. Before we reframe things, though, we have to understand them. This is a brief chronicle of one man's attempt to understand his changing world.

Understanding the world involves familiarizing yourself with a variety of contexts. The choice of contexts is up to each of us. For some it is their family and social environment, literature, politics, perhaps economics; for others, it is religion, philosophy or science. If we're lucky, as we move through life, we will expand the range of contexts in which we explore the world.

But for some people, understanding their world is either not of interest to them or they are under such pressure with work and family obligations that it is seen as an unaffordable luxury. Aristotle would presumably say to both groups that the desire to understand is irrepressible. Whether he is right or not is an empirical question: you have to ask people.

The Irish poet Michael Hartnett insisted that there is nothing sadder than people going to their grave without them ever knowing who they were. In his poem 'The Purge', he says:

To die without knowledge of yourself
Is the worst darkness, the worst hell:
To bequeath your truth to humanity is the only immortality

To get to know yourself means getting to know the world. Paradoxically, it is through understanding the wider history of your family, community, country, continent and species that you get to grips with your own personal identity. We begin our explorations tentatively but gradually realize that there is great delight in expanding the range of contexts in which we explore the world. It took me a while to recognize fully the relevance of history to personal identity.

Very often what underpins our exploration of the past is an attempt to expand the range of contexts in which we can find an answer to the 'who are we' and 'who am I' questions. So, after (or contemporaneous with) the Irish history voyage, there are the British, European, American and global ones, followed by an investigation of the human species itself. The ultimate contexts of inquiry are religious and philosophical. Yet also local.

The town in Ireland where I was born is in the southern part of County Tipperary. Clonmel is, by any standards, a town of striking physical beauty. That is mainly a matter of setting. In fact, the setting is everything. That is true the world over of places we admire, regardless of size. It is true of urban centres as different as Florence, Kyoto or Santa Fe. It may sound impertinent to mention what the guidebooks used to refer to as a thriving 'market' town with a population then of 10,000 in the same breath as some of the most beautiful cities in the world, and yet what they have in common is an appropriateness of setting.

Clonmel is set in a valley at the foot of a non-threatening mountain range overlooking the river Suir. That sounds like guide-book talk I know, but Clonmel is that kind of town. The river sneaked past the bottom of our back yard, framed by a reassuring low-lying mountain range. We had a perfect view of the Suir and the mountains from an upstairs window. Even the foothills were remarkably free of private houses. One tall house dominated the field of vision: a modest architectural landmark. I checked every morning to make sure it was still there. I find that my memory is such that I tend to recall thoughts and conversations in conjunction with the original physical location in which they occurred.

Most of my thoughts in the early school years would have been about sport or pocket money; in particular, whether an afternoon shower would mean that a football game arranged for the sportsfield that evening would be cancelled, or whether my mother would give me money for chocolate or ice cream. Those expressed concerns were not acute enough to be associated with specific locations, but I do recall that it was looking out of that upstairs window at about the age of twelve that I was gripped by a sudden apprehension of the world about me that really stopped me in my tracks.

Only many years later did I discover that the experience carried an implicit metaphysical question, and that the asking of that question had a respectable intellectual history. I had this sudden awareness of the world about me being in some way contingent: it wasn't just those low-lying hills that might not have existed; nothing at all might have existed. I tried to imagine what it would be like if nothing at all existed.

The realization that the very *fact* that things exist is something we take for granted recurs in my daily life from time to time but not often. But that initial wish to imagine what it would be like if nothing at all existed tends not to recur. There is a risk that once you learn to put words on these experiences through discovering how such experiences have fed into the western metaphysical tradition via Aquinas, Leibniz and Heidegger, you lose the intensity of the initial experience.

At one level, learning to locate one's private experiences within a philosophical tradition authenticates those experiences. At another level, such a discovery can easily occlude the intensity of those foundational experiences themselves. I suspect many children have the same jolting experience and ask themselves in inchoate form the celebrated 'Why is there something rather than nothing?' question.

And yet I'm not sure. It may be that what defines an experience of that kind is that you *don't* forget it. I had no idea at age twelve, of course, of the significance of the metaphysical question implicit in my puzzlement. Nor had I any idea of the dense scholarly ancestry of the question from Aquinas to Heidegger.

These days, I am inclined to the view that once you regard the question 'Why is there something rather than nothing?' as one that makes sense, you are an implicit subscriber to the notion of God, however that term is eventually unpacked.

At any rate, the precise moment of the foundational question that girds all that speculation I still remember, and where I was when it occurred. That reflective event is forever linked in my mind with that childhood view from our house in Irishtown, Clonmel: a view of the low-lying hills that frame the river Suir. It was a landscape that seemed to have only one large house in it. We lived in Irishtown in the parish of St. Mary's. Our particular townland designation 'Irishtown' was a reminder that that this had once been a British garrison town. Cromwell had forced Clonmel to surrender almost three hundred years before. This was one of the first things we learned at school about our past.

There were scholarly components in that story of our home town as well as soldierly ones, but little attention was paid to them in our schooling. No surprise there: history was usually cast almost exclusively in military and political terms, particularly in the 1940s. All we heard about was Cromwell and courageous local resistance to him. Not a word about a local seventeenth-century scholar, who became one of the great humanist figures of the day. Bonaventure Baron, Franciscan friar, and nephew of Luke Wadding, made his mark later in life in Rome, as a theologian and philosopher of distinction. Nor do I recall being told that another theologian, the illustrious John Wesley, credited with founding Methodism, paid three visits to our town in the middle of the eighteenth century.

The Franciscan church in Clonmel, which Bonaventure Baron would have first known as an adolescent, was built on a medieval site. As indeed was St. Mary's Protestant Church. All that meant a rich multi-layered past on our doorstep. Our awareness of that distant history was patchy, and we were even less aware of our recent past. Even though County Tipperary was once home to the Anglo-Norman Butler family among others, we had little real sense that a mere twenty years ago or so, our home town and its environs were part of the British empire: it didn't register with me as a child and adolescent that the southern part of Ireland had enjoyed political independence only since 1922, a mere twelve years before I was born.

As far as I was aware, the British presence in Ireland had to do with the distant past; the town I grew up in had always had its current complexion. The truth is, of course, that it hadn't, as local historian Seán O'Donnell's reminds us in *Clonmel: 1900-1932* (2009) with the following telling detail: there were at least seven British army bands stationed in the town before 1900. I hadn't the slightest inkling of such a past on our doorstep. It is true that the history I learned at school tended to cast the Irish story exclusively in terms of a British-Irish conflict, but my sense of myself had little to do with that particular internecine story. My identity was primarily Roman Catholic: Rome was my capital, rather than Dublin. The Vatican was more real to me than Dáil Éireann.

Nineteen twenty-two witnessed the election of Pius XI as pontiff of the Roman Catholic Church. Despite my seeing Rome as the centre of the universe, the Pope made no impact on me at all. Perhaps because he was eclipsed by his successor in 1939, the aloof Pius XII. The rimless glasses and once-off photographic pose of the new pope were ineradicable emblems for me of the 1940s and 1950s. It was Pius XII who eventually was to define my childhood and adolescence. He was the quintessence not just of ecclesiastical authority but of any kind of authority.

Another defining feature of my early life was a fervent allegiance to my home County Tipperary in the inter-county hurling championships. Tipperary winning the All-Ireland in 1945 eclipsed for me the news of the second world war's ending. Stakelum, Maher and Kenny were names that meant much more to me than Montgomery, Eisenhower and MacArthur.

The dropping of the atomic bomb had scarcely registered with me. Uppermost in my mind in 1945 were two things: the fact that the Tipperary senior team had beaten Kilkenny in Croke Park and that its minor team had lost to Dublin.

So the Catholic Church and the Gaelic Athletic Association (GAA) constituted the twin institutional poles of my childhood and burgeoning adolescent identity. The realization of what happened in Europe and Japan between 1939 and 1945 has not fully sunk in even to this day. When I read now about the loss of fifty million lives, it's scary to reflect on how little we knew. And yet it would serve no purpose here to pretend that we felt and thought other than we did at the time.

The main threat that Ireland faced a decade after independence was global in character: the Great Depression. The Wall Street Crash had occurred in 1929. As children in the 1930s and 1940s in an Irish inland town, we had no sense of what was happening in the wider world. Nor, I presume, did many of our parents, at least not in any comprehensive way. It appears there was a dearth of both information and analysis for them to peruse, compared with what happened after the financial/economic crisis of 2008. And yet one can ask if we *understand* our economic environment any better today.

If the grown-ups in the late 1930s and early 1940s were starved of financial/economic information and analysis, what chance did their children have? Yet, even as children, we had our own inchoate economic and political intimations. We knew deep down that poverty and prosperity were relative terms. Even within the narrow confines of an Irish market town, there were relativities. I would say mainly differences of wealth and income, rather than class, though there was an identifiable social hierarchy. The most socially privileged group lived in the deservedly famous fertile countryside outside the town. It consisted of a handful of wealthy landowners, like the Bagwells and Hely Hutchinsons. These were descendants of seventeenth-century Cromwellian settlers, who had prospered sufficiently through trade to acquire extensive estates, which they bequeathed to those who succeeded them. Next came the descendants of a Quaker influx, a century and more later: families like the Malcolmsons, who over the previous few centuries had made small fortunes in activities like shipping. Within the town itself, the professional classes, bank managers and senior clergy had a privileged status: they were the local haute bourgeoisie. Though a handful of retail merchants might qualify for the foregoing status, most of them belonged to the petite bourgeoisie. This category would have been ranked informally in terms of the numbers employed, and how long the various stores had been established. The broad category of workers could also be ranked in terms of income and/or in terms of white collar/blue collar categories.

In the 1940s and 1950s most people in my home town of 10,000 people would have had no more than an elementary education. Secondary or high school education was not at all common, let alone university education, which was rare; graduate education, rarer still. I recall only one person in the Clonmel community in the early 1950s with a doctorate: Philip O'Connell, head of the local Technical Institute.

The poet Patrick Kavanagh has rightly said that the essence of poverty consists of existing below a certain level of consciousness. In other words, the absence of material things is not as damaging as deficiencies in our level of awareness. Obviously, we need the basic necessities for a decent living, but beyond that no amount of material possessions will make up for an undeveloped awareness of ourselves and the world around us. Richard Wilbur in his poem 'A Summer Morning' takes Erich Fromm's distinction between 'being' and 'having' a stage further by suggesting that if you intensify your state of being by means of expanding your consciousness, paradoxically, you transcend mere *ownership* and arrive at a state of true *possession.* For Wilbur, possession is a deeper state than ownership. The irony expressed in Wilbur's poem is that the deeper state of possession can be achieved despite a lack of ownership. Perhaps it is achievable *only* through a lack of ownership.

In the poem the cook has the house to herself because her young employers have got in late the night before and so will not be coming down to breakfast. She makes a quiet breakfast for herself and 'breaks an egg into the morning light'. Outside, the gardener straightens himself to enjoy a view of the big house. What is being suggested here is that both servants are able to savour the full reality of the morning moments in a way that eludes the owners. Ownership is irrelevant to the capacity for heightened perception. The poem's concluding stanza is speaking first about the gardener:

> His young employers having got in late,
> He and the cook alone
> Receive the morning on their old estate,
> Possessing what the owners can but own.

In Ireland 'having' tended to matter more than 'being'; possessions more than the expansion of consciousness. To that extent, it was no different to other countries at the time. Ireland's firm attachment to Catholicism made little difference in these matters. The Republic of Ireland had secured independence from Britain in 1922, but close ties with the Vatican remained unaltered. A Eucharistic Congress, which was held in Dublin in 1932, was emblematic of the constancy of relations. John McCormack sang César Frank's 'Panis Angelicus' on the occasion and our elders spoke about that June day for decades.

Eamon de Valera, leading political figure of my youth, always seemed to be photographed in the company of Catholic bishops, so the papal flag carried more resonance for us than the national one. The Corpus Christi procession with full military honours at the Main Guard in Clonmel was the public highlight of our year. All life revolved around a liturgical axis, with mothers in the parish ensuring that all our religious obligations were regularly fulfilled. My own mother was called on to do much more than that. She had to take over the family business and rear five children on her own when my father died in March 1943. Even then I realized what a burden she had to carry. At eight years of age I was the eldest. My mother considered the transmission of Catholic practices and values to be central to the process of child-rearing. My father had died, but the religious liturgies on our doorstep offered a measure of stability.

Ours was not a household of books, though my mother was remarkably encouraging of my earliest efforts to buy books at Bulbert's across the street. Again, when it came to music she seemed more interested in ensuring that her children had access to music than in indulging her own tastes. The only exception I recall was that she enthused so much about 'In Happy Moments', the great baritone aria from Wallace's *Maritana,* that I bought her a 78 rpm recording of it at Belynda Cashin's music store opposite the Friary.

My mother's religion was the principal solace of her life. It informed everything she did, and in the process inevitably conveyed to me the idea that the main way to please her was through the consistent practice of Catholic devotions. Even though she spoke to me more than once about an unexpected change in her own family's circumstances which had deprived her of the kind of boarding school education she coveted, I don't think that deep disappointment affected her religious faith in the slightest.

The most distinctive feature of local culture in Clonmel was its musical character. St. Mary's Church choir introduced us to a tradition of sacred music under the direction of James White; St. Mary's Choral Society presented regular productions of operetta, mainly Gilbert and Sullivan. St. Peter and Paul's

Church, under organist Scott Minchin, also had a useful choir, but we in St. Mary's thought our own choir to be superior.

The broader cultural environment was framed essentially by the Catholic Church. Even as young kids we thought of ourselves as part of a wider ecclesiastical empire, whose headquarters was in Rome. The appointment of a new curate or canon had far more significance than the election of a politician to office. Of course, we attended the great political public meetings, which were addressed by the leading lights of the day such as Eamon de Valera, but in the main we viewed the political arena as a secondary, silhouette one: the real action was in the parish church and its environs.

That emphasis was reinforced by my schooling. I grew up thinking the church's view of the world was the only one that mattered. The church possessed the truth, and that was that. This conferred enormous security at first: no matter what the subject under scrutiny, be it art, politics or business, all you had to do was to find out the relevant Catholic principle and then apply it.

The risk was that, in exchange for that security, one sacrificed independence of thought. And that I certainly did. There is, granted, some measure of thinking involved even in the grasping of and application of given principles, but serious thought has to do with a critical scrutiny of the principles themselves. John Henry Newman taught us with good reason that it was perfectly rational to accept *some* things on trust, but the tendency to accept everything on trust from a central authority eventually undermines confidence in your own capacity to adjudicate.

Chapter 4

LATIN AND GREEK;
GILBERT AND SULLIVAN

My EXPERIENCE OF SCHOOLING UNTIL 1941, when I reached the age of seven, was at a convent school run by the Presentation nuns in St Mary's parish, Clonmel. Among our instructors were Sister Augustine and a Miss McEllistrim, the sole lay teacher in the school, but my main teacher was Sister Stanislaus, a family friend. As a result, she took a particular interest in my progress. She told me in later life that she was struck by the fact that I seemed determined to make my First Communion as soon as possible, and that I attached a high priority to the ceremony.

I have no recollection of that particular display of liturgical determination, but apparently that is the way it was. First Communion and Confirmation, like the Bar Mitzvah in the Jewish religion, are foundational rites of passage in the Catholic dispensation. What I do remember is my embarrassment and annoyance at my mother for insisting that I wear a frilly cream blouse with my First Communion suit, when all the other boys were wearing plain white shirts and ties.

After infant school under the tutelage of Sister Stanislaus, I went to St. Mary's Christian Brothers Primary School on the Western Road. I regard the influence of Brother Paddy Kelly on me at the age of ten or eleven as one of the most significant in my life. He awakened me to the treasures of theatre, painting and good writing. He was later laicised and married. Brother Kelly's main influence on my intellectual development occurred, surprisingly enough, in geography classes. This inspiring young teacher asked us to draw a map of the island of Ireland in simplified outline. We were instructed not to worry about the detailed eddies of the map, but simply to focus on the broad, if crude, outline. The result was that we could soon draw a map of the entire island with ease because we had concentrated on 'the big picture'. The pedagogical transfer value of Brother Kelly's teaching in geography classes to other subjects was extremely valuable. It meant that you realized the importance of grasping a topic in broad outline before concentrating on details.

It was during those primary school years at St. Mary's that my father died. In the final days of his life, I must have sensed from my mother that the end was near. I was told he had pneumonia, which these days is highly treatable, but was usually fatal at the time. On my way home from school in those anxious days in March 1943, the minute I turned the corner at St. Mary's Place and Irishtown, I used to look at the upstairs blinds. If they weren't down, I knew my father was still alive.

On a Saturday morning towards the end of March, my mother came to my bedroom and said: 'Your father's in heaven, child.' The male members of the Condon family, who lived directly across the street from us, were enlisted that morning to help us children get dressed. Death seemed to usher in a kind of familial helplessness: one *expected* to be momentarily looked after. The increased level of activity in the house was a reminder that something highly unusual had happened. A particular image of that morning fixed in my mind is that of Paddy Condon having difficulty attaching a pair of braces to the buttons of my trousers. He needed a penknife to solve the problem, an implement he quickly found. I have always been intrigued by the fact that this image has remained with me so vividly down the years.

There was something about Paddy Condon's resourcefulness at that moment that was reassuring: I felt I was in the hands of an all-powerful guardian. Another image was seeing my father laid out in what looked like a Franciscan habit. An eight-year-old cannot possibly understand what the death of his father means, but for the moment you feel old beyond your years. It is not altogether true that you can't put an old head on young shoulders.

Another recollection from that time was the sympathetic response of Brother O' Dwyer, one of my teachers at St. Mary's. When I returned to school he asked me to step outside the classroom and said quite simply, 'You poor fellow.' I also remember relishing whatever sympathy came my way; one of the few advantages of bereavement was that people tended to be nicer to you than they might otherwise have been.

Because my father died when I was only eight, I got little chance to know him. My overriding memory is of a very impatient man. I felt I didn't grasp the intricacies of clock reading quickly enough for him, nor for that matter the detailed rules of Gaelic games. He used to take me to the High School Sports Grounds for inter-college hurling games. I sensed Gaelic games were a passion for him. As indeed they were for me until my late teens, when I lost the intense interest of the earlier years. Dick Walsh of *The Irish Times*, writing at the end of the twentieth century, used to say there were three pivotal institutions in Ireland: the Fianna Fáil party, the Catholic Church and the Gaelic Athletic Association. As I write in 2016, the first two are mere shadows of their former selves, but the GAA is, if anything, going from strength to strength. Because of the close interlocking that always existed between the three institutions, that asymmetric outcome is something of a mystery. Perhaps because of my father's early influence, I never took to rugby, unlike my younger brother, Eddie, who got hooked on the game with the Holy Ghost Fathers at Rockwell College.

I can detect only one hint in my early childhood as to why I might have turned to a career in broadcasting. My father, while shaving one morning, insisted on teaching me the correct pronunciation of the American town Schenectady. In fact, I think he got it wrong because he put the emphasis on the penultimate syllable, whereas the stress should be on the second syllable. It is possible, of course, that my memory is faulty here in misattributing the error to him. However, the significance of the exercise for my subsequent development was that I was alerted early in life to the role of syllabic stress in pronunciation.

As to the kind of man my father was, the evidence I have is slight, but I suspect there was a marked element of the teacher in him, even if an impatient one. I recall no words of advice from him as to how I should behave, no dispensing of life maxims, but my memories of his explaining how to read time, what a parallelogram was, the pronunciation of words like Schenectady suggest a true pedagogue. All in all, not many memories of my father, but when he died, I do recall older people saying: 'Andy was so young', though sixty-one seemed to be ancient to a child of eight.

My mother lived on until 1975, to the age of seventy-two, but I could sense that her life immediately after my father's death was a crushing burden. She was then forty-one with five children aged between eight and two. Every so often she would cry in my presence, which I found disconcerting because I didn't know what to say. Because I was the eldest, I suspect that mine was the shoulder she wept on most, though I can't be sure of that. My determination to perform well at boarding school was rooted in a sense of obligation to do what I could to make her feel that her eldest child was doing well despite the setback in the family's fortunes.

I gradually took on the role of man of the house. Certainly by the time I reached my teenage years, I had developed a sense of adult responsibility for the affairs of the family. I am convinced that the reason I never married was that I took on that role so young. But it was a role I felt comfortable in. In return, I got preferential treatment from my mother, especially when, later on, I would come home on holidays from boarding school. Because it looked at that stage as if I would eventually become a 'man of the cloth', I was never asked to do household chores. To my shame, I took advantage of the privilege, much, I'm sure, to the annoyance of my siblings, Charlotte, Maureen, Nora and Eddie. To their credit, none of them ever raised the issue with me.

Each of my siblings settled down in turn to their own way of life, with Charlotte, the second eldest, being the second to leave the homestead after me. She became a member of the nursing staff at St. Mary's Hospital in London in the mid-1950s. In 1958, she married a Welsh engineer, Jeffrey Davies, and settled in Canterbury, England. They moved in later life to Germany, where Charlotte died in 1993. Maureen, who became a member of the Presentation order of nuns in the mid-1950s, was based all her life in Cork, where she taught at the North Presentation Primary School. Maureen (Sister Perpetua) died in 2003. Nora worked for the Bank of Ireland in Dublin where she met her husband Gerry Rawson, also a member of the bank staff. They have both been retired for many years and live in Blessington, County Wicklow. Eddie retired in 2001 from Peter Owens Ltd., an advertising and public relations firm, of which he was managing director and chairman. Married to Bernie D'Arcy from Bray, County Wicklow, they commute between Tramore, County Waterford and Paphos in Cyprus.

When I had completed primary school education at St Mary's in 1946, I spent the first year of my secondary education at the High School in Clonmel, which, like St. Mary's, was also run by the Christian Brothers. Because the High School was situated at the other end of the town, my mother bought me a Hopper bicycle at Bartlett's in O'Connell Street. That purchase symbolized a new stage of life for me. Even more symbolic of the change occurring at that point in my life was getting hold of a Latin grammar, *Elementa Latina*. Our Latin teacher was Brother 'Bon' Moynihan, who dispensed the kind of sarcasm that can bewitch those students not under immediate pressure. *Elementa Latina* was of pocket book size, with a navy cloth cover and red lettering. I would soon discover Latin was a subject I really liked.

In addition to mathematics, Latin, Irish, geography, English literature and history, I studied chemistry with Brother 'Moses' Burke; I got private tuition in French on Saturday mornings from Brother Ling. Among the lay teachers were 'Bags' Cleary, who taught geography to my own class and Latin to others. 'Bags' was alert to every imaginable student ruse. It had become part of school lore that, suspecting a student of having memorized a translation of Virgil's *Aeneid*, he asked the student, to the sound of growing mirth, where he got 'love's pestilential influence' from. Alfie Sullivan, who taught from an anthology called *Flowers from Many Gardens,* conveyed a weariness at having to awaken a group of twelve-year-olds to the subtleties of English verse, but he was a gentle soul.

Later in that school year 1946/47, my mother went to confession to a visiting Redemptorist missionary priest in our parish church. When she had completed her part in that particular liturgy, the priest, Father Leo O'Halloran, asked her about her children. Would the eldest like to go to a boarding school in Limerick? There would be annual fees, but of a manageable kind. I was consulted and expressed delight at the prospect of a new learning environment. There is little doubt but that when a visiting Redemptorist missionary raised with my mother the prospect of her son going to a school that encouraged vocations to the priesthood, she was enchanted. The idea of a priest in the family was one of the most cherished motherly aspirations of that time. No doubt about that. As for her eldest son, he was attracted by the idea of a new school with accompanying brochures advertising a library, a college dining hall and various sports facilities. But he also wasn't averse to the security of a career in the clerical priesthood. I was now fatherless and deeply insecure. I felt scared of having eventually to choose a career in the highly competitive world of business and the professions. The priestly option offered a way out and was entirely congruent with my religious upbringing. So both mother and son were momentarily happy.

Before formally committing to a period at this secondary boarding school, my mother and I travelled to Limerick city to meet the Director, Fr. Tom McKinlay and, of course, to see the college, Mount St. Alphonsus. That same evening I was due back in Clonmel to take part in a Gilbert and Sullivan operetta, *The Gondoliers*, at Magner's Theatre. Jack Griffin, who was directing this production, had asked me to play the drummer boy. It was a non-speaking part, which consisted of walking on stage, sticking out my tongue at the Duke of Plaza Toro, and running off again. Clearly any twelve-year-old could have gone on stage in my place, had I failed to make it back. I can still recall how chuffed I was to be invited to play this small role.

At a certain point in the interview proceedings at the school in Limerick, I nudged my mother to indicate that we had to make sure I was back in time for that evening's performance. The reverend director's response had a definite edge to it: 'Oh, we can't have him late for that.' That remark captured what I came to recognize as a key feature of the man, a tendency to nip in the bud any hint of self-importance.

Mount St. Alphonsus was a secondary boarding school run by the Redemptorists. It was not an actual seminary, but nonetheless the school authorities hoped to *foster* vocations to the order. A secondary school of this kind ensured a pool of students from which vocations might be expected to emerge. It was called a *juniorate*. The Redemptorist order, a congregation of Roman Catholic priests, was founded in Italy in 1732 by St Alphonsus de' Liguori, a Neapolitan lawyer. He was formally declared a Doctor of the Church in 1871 and is regarded as one of the leading Catholic moral theologians of the last one hundred and fifty years.

Father Tom McKinlay was a remarkably gifted man: he had a fine baritone singing voice, directed plays, designed scenery and taught mathematics. In fact, his range was amazing: he gave us extra classes in the visual arts, including architecture, speech training and New Testament studies, and on Sunday nights presided over a music appreciation class.

Because of the shortage of tenors in the school, Father McKinlay seemed to want to convert as many baritones as possible to the rank of tenor. Perhaps, more accurately, he wanted his baritones to reach for notes with which they weren't comfortable. Such was the case with one of the choruses in Wallace's *Maritana*. I will never forget 'Angels that around us hover'. My throat still hurts whenever I hear it. Eventually he accepted I was a baritone and cast me as Giuseppe in *The Gondoliers* and Strephon in *Iolanthe*, two regularly performed Gilbert and Sullivan operettas. I enjoyed the praise attendant on these performances and may have shown it because one evening during the run of *Iolanthe*, I went to the director's office for medication to cope with a sore throat. I stood in the doorway as he examined the medicine cabinet. He found something for me and then suddenly said, 'It's great to feel important, Andrew, isn't it?' Any sixteen-year-old would feel bewildered. Father McKinlay seemed conflicted in the matter of striking the right balance between praise and censure, but, in general, I felt affirmed by him.

The school was particularly concerned with meeting the requirements of the Department of Education in the matter of Intermediate and Leaving Certificate examinations. In the run-up to these, we occasionally worked for five or six hours a day. You couldn't but do well. The only deficit in the curriculum was the absence of physics and chemistry. In their place, Latin and

Greek reigned supreme. Bringing up the rear were mathematics, history, English, Irish and French.

I seemed to have had a particular aptitude for Latin and Greek, and really enjoyed the classes and homework. In the teaching of both languages, the emphasis in those days was on grammar and composition. This was the era of *North and Hilliard,* a classic text of the period. Among the Roman authors we studied were Livy, Horace and Cicero; among the Greek writers were Xenophon and Thucydides. As was probably the case in many secondary schools in Ireland in the late 1940s and early 1950s, little attention was paid to conveying a sense of the distinctiveness of Greek or Roman civilizations, let alone conveying an understanding of these ancient worlds as staging posts in the evolution of human consciousness.

Father Willy Murphy, who tended to address less responsive students as 'plaster', confined himself to grammar and composition, and some Greek political history. On the other hand, you could argue that mastering the languages was what ultimately mattered: that linguistic control was a precondition of whatever subsequent conceptual acrobatics one might get up to.

The Irish Christian Brothers are often accused of displaying a nationalist bias in the teaching of Irish history. I didn't spend long enough with them to find out: apart from primary school, I spent just one year with them in secondary school in Clonmel. Certainly, Brother Paddy Kelly in primary school was, as far as an eleven-year-old could make out, a model of scholarly detachment. The Redemptorists seemed to me free of bias in the teaching of Irish history. Father Paddy O'Donnell alerted us to the destructiveness of the Saxon conqueror in Ireland in the sixteenth century, but not in a manner designed to arouse feelings of bitterness. For me, the most cogent testimony to lack of bias in the teaching of history at this Limerick boarding school is the fact that since leaving school I have nurtured no animus towards Britain or the British people. Where there have been lapses on the British side, I am inclined to focus on those responsible for these particular lapses, rather than condemn all and sundry. What I remember particularly of that class in which Father O'Donnell spoke about 'the systematic destruction of a native Gaelic culture' was the sense of a conflict within the man himself. The way he moved his teeth as he spoke suggested to me that he was deeply upset personally by the thought of that destruction, but wanted to pass on the information in as detached and scholarly a way as possible. Either that or he needed new dentures.

When I look back on some anomalous incidents at that Limerick school, I have to remind myself that the late 1940s and early 1950s had a much different climate – moral, religious and educational – to today's. I find it hard to categorize the first incident, but this is what occurred. On a Sunday morning in 1950, Father McKinlay addressed us en masse in the study hall before lunch. We were due to go that afternoon to an early round of the Munster Hurling Championship between Cork and Tipperary. This was a golden age for Tipperary, which won three hurling All-Irelands in 1949, 1950 and 1951; it was the era in which the great John Doyle first came to prominence, at the age of nineteen.

We were looking forward on that particular Sunday to our excursion to the Ennis Road grounds. To our amazement, Father Director told us he had decided not to let us go to the game that afternoon. The reason he had so decided, he informed us, was that he wanted us to learn early in life how to deal with disappointment. He was *deliberately* disappointing us so that we would (a) experience disappointment *early* in life, and, (b) learn how to cope with it. On that sunny May day, we had no option but to comply. Since Father McKinlay was an intelligent man, it seems not unreasonable to conclude that he seriously believed that what he was doing had a legitimate role in character formation. At this distance, his decision seems absurd.

The second and third incidents are related: they pertain to Hollywood films. One year before we left college for our regular summer holidays, Father McKinlay told us not to go to the cinema because, on the whole, the films available were 'sentimental and debasing'. That struck me even in the late 1940s as quite a sweeping generalization. The third related incident involved the school going to the Lyric Cinema in Limerick for a matinee performance of a 1948 film called *The Emperor Waltz*, directed by Billy Wilder and starring Bing Crosby and Joan Fontaine. We had not been sitting down all that long when suddenly we were summoned to our feet, and the director ushered us all out of the cinema. Why? we wondered.

The particular incident that prompted our departure was this. It was a scene in which the camera panned between the male and female leads who were being affectionate at one end of the room, and two little puppies who were expressing affection for one another at the other end of the room. The logic of Father McKinlay's decision is intriguing because presumably had he not so decided, we wouldn't have noticed. The fact that I remember the scene to this day indicates that it was probably imprinted on our minds through subsequent discussion, rather than through direct awareness of it at the time.

I think the most likely explanation for the director's action is that it took little to inflame his existing distrust of a medium that he told us was to be avoided. In fairness to him, film in general was viewed in Irish clerical circles in the 1940s as profoundly inimical to the Christian life. Francine Stock, in her book *In Glorious Technicolor: A Century of Film and How it has Shaped Us* (2011), makes it clear that suspicion of film was widespread at the time. In the 1930s the Film Production code (formerly the Hays code) in the United States insisted on elegant dance duets between the romantic leads, instead of close-bodied clinches. In Britain, Richard George Burnett in *The Devil's Camera* (1932), saw movies as heralding the end of western civilization. Father

McKinlay was a man of his time. I should add that the most memorable of all film experiences for me in those years was seeing Laurence Olivier's *Hamlet* (1948) at the Savoy Cinema in Limerick.

There were other visits to the Savoy Cinema to hear the Raidió Éireann Symphony Orchestra play Britten, Dukas and Prokofiev. After the resignation of Michael Bowles as this orchestra's conductor in 1948, there were a number of guest conductors. Perhaps for that reason, it is solely the name of the orchestra's *leader*, Renzo Marchionni, that has remained with me. In the same theatre we attended Sunday night concerts by leading Irish tenors of the day like Michael O'Duffy and Frank Ryan. The tenor voice, it seemed was the voice to have. For most of my life I have preferred the baritone and bass voices, but at that time everyone wanted to be a tenor.

It was at boarding school that I began to realize that I had an aptitude for reading in public. This awareness was reinforced during our weekly speech class when the Father Director gave an encouraging reception to my delivery of Murellus's famous 'Wherefore rejoice?' speech in Shakespeare's *Julius Caesar*. I recall his correcting my two-syllable pronunciation of the word 'block' in 'You blocks, you stones, you worse than senseless things'. I had unconsciously introduced an extra syllable before the 'l' consonant to prolong the short 'o' vowel for dramatic effect. I can see as I write that by adding an extra syllable to the word 'blocks' I was perilously close to enunciating the word 'bollocks'. This is something I was unaware of at the time. On the other hand, it may well have been a source of great private amusement to the Father Director, something he couldn't wait to pass on to his colleagues at their morning break.

During lunchtime and evening meals in the refectory, the students took turns reading the assigned books of the day from an elevated lectern. These books tended to be mainly religious if not outright devotional in character. There was a biography of

Bishop Shanahan, renowned for his work on the African missions. But we also had more intellectually stimulating fare like Canon Patrick Sheehan's novel *Luke Delmege* (1901).

Father McKinlay made use of these readings to instil in us the rudiments of effective public speaking. I remember one student being put through his paces because he was doing less than full justice to the word 'stimulate'. Whether because of tiredness or indifference to the phonetic subtleties involved, the student managed both to stress the last syllable and to drop the consonant 't' at the same time. He made the kind of sound that if one were deliberately trying to produce it for a bet or as a display of vocal versatility, might cause one permanent physical injury. The Father Director instructed the student repeatedly to 'hop it off the back wall'. Not the most felicitous of injunctions you will agree, but we concluded in the interests of general propriety that it was the consonant 't' the reverend superior was referring to.

I made no close friendships at boarding school. My best friend and for a good five years afterwards was Richie (Dick) Condon, whom I first met during my year at Clonmel High School in 1946/47. Apart from his obvious academic ability, Richie was a gifted actor and one of the wittiest people around. He had sharpened his capacity for good lines by listening regularly to radio comedy shows on the BBC Light Programme, featuring the likes of Ted Ray, Tommy Handley and Kenneth Horne.

We took quite a precocious interest in the work of Raidió Éireann news announcers in the late 1940s and early 1950s. One such announcer was nicknamed 'Hohenstaufen' by us because of the way he pronounced words like 'nation'. That deployment by us of the name of a medieval royal German dynasty suggests that our classes in European history weren't entirely going to waste. There were regular arguments between us over the proper pronunciation of words. Imagine disagreeing over the pronunciation of the surname 'Burke', but we did. Under the influence of Father McKinlay, I insisted it was pronounced 'Berk'.

And so on it went: from chat about broadcasting to music to films. We thought we were so smart when we discovered we could enjoy films that didn't have clear resolute endings. After our school years Richie and I saw less of each other, and then eventually lost touch. He died in April 2012 in Tipperary town; he had retired from his post as principal of a primary school in Raheny in Dublin. Richie Condon played a highly creative role in my teenage years, a fact for which I remain eternally grateful.

My school years with the Redemptorists deepened my interest in music, painting, film, theatre and architecture. These were interests I pursued with great satisfaction for the rest of my life. Before going to Limerick at the age of thirteen, I had already developed an interest in theatre and music. My introduction to music was listening as an altar boy to the choir of St. Mary's parish in Irishtown under the direction of James White. James hailed from Belfast and taught Latin at Rockwell College, Cashel; he lived in nearby Anne Street and was always known simply as either 'The Professor' or 'Mr. White'. One sensed that was the way he wanted it. I still recall the plaintive sounds of pieces he conducted: '*Illuminare his qui in tenebris et in umbra mortis sedent*' from the Tridentine plain chant version of the Dies Irae.

The Mozart 'Ave Verum' was a special treat. It was also in St. Mary's that I first heard Handel's 'Hallelujah Chorus' in the mid-1940s. Every Christmas morning, Tom Hogan, who had a tenor voice of incomparable sweetness, sang the solo part in 'Adeste Fideles'. The way Professor White spoke was noticeably different to the way his choir of shop assistants, tradesmen, clerks and factory workers spoke. Even more noticeable was the respectful silence with which each of his pronouncements was met. The choir members were in awe of him. And it was clear he that enjoyed that. He had an indifferent bass voice himself, but he worked magic on the choir.

While it is true that I developed a number of cultural interests, including music and theatre, in my boarding school years, I was otherwise very much a passive piece of flotsam responding to powerful forces around me. I wanted to please everybody, whether my mother, my college superiors, or the Catholic church itself, everybody except myself. All that sounds quite sad at this distance, but that's the way it was. I gave way completely to others. I was seeking refuge from a forbidding competitive world. It meant that I was spared having to make a real career choice. More than that, I sensed that, from now on, all that was required of me was compliance with the wishes of others. All that underpinned my decision to join the Redemptorist order. My memory is that only a handful of my Leaving Cert class in Limerick decided to go to the novitiate, which was the first stage of the journey to ordination.

The novitiate was housed in Esker near Athenry, County Galway. The night before I left for the novitiate in 1951, I called to see some first cousins of mine in Clonmel. Only John O'Mahony, a few years older than myself, was in. It was a sunny Sunday evening in August. He had just begun his evening meal and had propped up in front of him a copy of Thomas Merton's *Elected Silence* (1949), which was one of the fashionable books of the day. Merton was an American Benedictine monk whose account of monastic life had enormous appeal for thousands of readers. It seemed a highly apposite book for my cousin to be reading on that particular evening.

Because the custom in those years was that when you joined a religious order, you didn't come home again until after ordination, saying goodbye to someone had a poignant resonance to it. If I was expecting sympathy from John, it wasn't forthcoming. 'They tell me the first ten years are the hardest,' he said, with the air of a young man who disdained sentiment of any kind. The remark alerted me to the element of sacrifice involved in my decision. It brought home to me the fact that I hadn't really given much thought to the practical consequences of my decision. Or perhaps, that after some reflection, I had minimized the importance of such consequences. The remark made me feel both proud of my 'bravery' and also wary of what lay in store. Little did I realize that I would be back home in six months.

My brief experience as a novice from August 1951 to February 1952 was steeped more in pious devotions than in any kind of intellectual or spiritual exploration, though it did allow me pursue my interest in music. The kind of formation dispensed in the Redemptorist novitiate was not unlike what I imagine one encounters in the army. The main idea was to generate deep conformity to the prevailing monastic culture. Independence of thought or action was not encouraged. This was the early 1950s, when Catholic culture was even more authoritarian than in post-Vatican II times: the church then hadn't changed since the Council of Trent in the sixteenth century.

There was a half-hearted attempt to crush whatever egos the young novices had: humility was the order of the day. I say 'half-hearted' because, even at the time, some of the attempts at ego-bruising were laughable. After our first day of football, the novice master, Charlie McNiffe, said to me: 'Have you played football before, Brother O'Mahony?' 'Yes,' I eagerly responded. 'You wouldn't think so,' he said. I felt the novice master's efforts at 'humiliation' were quite ritualistic.

A highly recommended spiritually charged practice of the time was 'modesty of the eyes', meaning that one's eyes should not be too prying or predatory. Another desirable practice was 'mortification', which implied depriving oneself of legitimate consolations and pleasures for the sake of spiritual advancement. A Redemptorist spiritual writer of that era, named Father John Carr, said wittily of someone or other: 'He wasn't one of those who believed the essence of spirituality was the mortification of *other* people.'

The system was not so crass as not to allow us to minister to our particular cultural interests, assuming we had any. I was put in charge of the music collection. That modest library featured many recordings by Leopold Stokowski, one of the leading conductors of the day. He was more celebrated than his colleagues not least because of his work in Hollywood: he had featured as himself in a number of feature films. In addition to a generous slice of the standard symphonic repertoire, we had pieces like Vaughan Williams's 'Fantasia on Greensleeves'. That piece has stayed with me because the novice master one evening asked me to identify it. My reply that it was a traditional folk air elicited the response: 'Down from the wilds, is it?' He went on to say that the music was composed by Vaughan Williams. In asserting that, he was only partly correct: Williams had composed a set of variations on a tune but not the tune itself. Béla Bartók once mischievously suggested that a *nation* creates music, a composer merely arranges it. It would have taken a brave man to argue matters of that kind with the novice master, even if I had had the requisite skills. The important point is that I was building on the groundwork done in boarding school in developing an interest in classical music.

One of the surviving images for me of my six-month novitiate experience of 1951/52 was a devotional practice that used to take place on the 25th of each month in the oratory. The idea on those occasions was to honour the infant Jesus. What I recall was the odd manner in which the vulnerability of the infant was juxtaposed with his capacity to induce fear. The hymn we used to sing went like this: '*Benedicat nos Deus, Deus infans, benedicat nos Deus, Et metuant eum omnes fines terrae.*' As you can see, the baby Jesus of this hymn inspires fear: 'all corners of the earth fear (*metuant*) Him'. It does sound odd that a baby, even the infant Jesus, even the Divine infant, is spoken of in this way. However, there is a sense in which all infants wield enormous power even if they don't necessarily inspire fear:

their helplessness allows them to control the adult environment about them. That is not what the hymn was about, but the juxtaposition of infancy and power is a fertile one. As for the early 1950s, fear was a constituent component of Catholic spirituality. Commonly invoked was the biblical reminder that fear of the Lord was the beginning of wisdom.

When I left the novitiate, the general understanding was that I would take a degree and then, if it suited me, return to religious life. The Redemptorists accurately assessed my need for 'more experience of life'. It became gradually apparent to them that my vocation had been more a matter of responding to various pressures than a truly independent decision. At any rate, I did not return to the congregation, though it would take another five years before I embarked on a degree. Once I returned to a regular life and got a job, it didn't take very long to realize that I never *did* have a vocation to the priesthood. In so far as I did have a calling, I would discover that it was to a life of reading, reflection and learning.

It was on my return journey home in February 1952 that I became more aware of what was happening in the wider world of popular music. On the train journey between Athenry and Limerick Junction, two American soldiers on holiday in Ireland were talking about two young film stars, Dean Martin and Jerry Lewis. It was the first I had heard of the famous American duo, though that partnership had been first formed in 1946. I remember feeling that I was in at the birth of something and felt privileged to be getting access to the latest entertainment news from two American servicemen.

My experience of school plays and operas whetted my appetite for theatre-going. In an inland town in the early 1950s, theatre-going was limited to seeing the productions of travelling companies. One such was the Longford Players, founded by Edward Pakenham, Sixth Earl of Longford, and former chairman of the Gate Theatre. This company tended to perform plays by Wilde and Shaw along with surefire pot-boilers, but by far the most celebrated of the touring companies was that run by Anew McMaster. A much-lauded Coriolanus at Stratford in the mid-1930s, McMaster was now bringing Shakespeare to rural Ireland. I saw his *Hamlet* and *Lear* in Magner's Theatre in Clonmel in 1952. I regret to say that he played to an almost empty theatre.

I heard McMaster's daughter, Mary Rose, say on radio recently that the midland town of Athlone in those days was notorious for poor theatre attendance, but Clonmel was not much better in the early 1950s. We learned subsequently that Harold Pinter toured Ireland with McMaster in 1952. So, in all likelihood, I saw Pinter on stage at the time. Two things I remember from *Hamlet*: someone 'drying' at an awkward moment; and McMaster's even then over-the-top delivery of the line: 'Take him for all in all, I shall not look upon his like again.'

I gather that the great Beckett interpreter Patrick Magee was also on that 1952 tour, but that was long before I began to keep theatre programmes. On the night McMaster died in August 1962 I was presenting a live television programme on RTÉ called *The World This Week.* Hilton Edwards, co-founder of the Gate Theatre in Dublin in the 1930s, and now in the 1960s head of drama at RTÉ, came in to studio to pay a tribute to McMaster. I still recall the calculated way he hesitated before the word 'prince' as if he were searching for the *mot juste* as he spoke. It's an old trick, but Hilton carried it off superbly: 'Mac was a a ...*prince* of the theatre.'

For most of my life, despite my addiction to books, I have probably been more influenced by people than by the written word, but in those early years I read a handful of books that gave my life direction. Three books in particular gave shape to my emerging sense of who I was. In late adolescence, I knew that owing to family circumstances I had to earn a living straight-away, but I saw doing so primarily as a way of paying the rent while meantime I pursued my scholarly interests in whatever leisure time I had. In those early years I tended to the view that my personal identity should be based more on my own intellectual and cultural interests than on whatever I did for a living.

That idea was consolidated when I read *The Intellectual Life* (1948) by A.D. Sertillanges in 1953. I bought the book at Devlins in Gladstone Street, Clonmel, a bookshop then run by the late Jim Binchy, member of a prominent legal family. Sertillanges, a French Dominican priest, had written this work in 1921. It was translated into English in 1947 for Mercier Press by Mary Ryan, Emeritus Professor of Romance Languages at University College Cork. I was amused to learn recently from Peter Hebblethwaite's biography of Pope Paul V1 (1993) that the Italian translation of the book in 1925 had a notable influence on the young Giovanni Montini. Sertillanges quotes Disraeli's dictum, 'Do as you please, provided it really pleases you', in the context of discussing the meaning of the term 'vocation'. For Aquinas too, Sertillanges notes, discovering that which pleases us reveals our vocation, particularly if it corresponds with our aptitudes.

The second book that helped shape my emerging sense of who I was and what I wanted to do with my life was a collection of essays by Cardinal John Henry Newman. I bought this collection in O'Mahony's bookshop in Limerick in 1952. The key idea of Newman's that caught hold of me was excerpted from his *Idea of a University*: namely, the idea of learning for its own sake. Psychologists call this *intrinsic* motivation, as opposed to the kind of extrinsic motivation that consists of learning in order simply to do well in an examination or to get a job. A few years later I had many debates wth my good friend, the late Tom Naughton, who simply saw no point in the idea of learning for its own sake. In arguing that line, Tom was much more in tune with the educational philosophy of the upcoming half-century than I was.

The third book was *Leisure: The Basis of Culture* (1952) by Josef Pieper, a German neo-Thomist philosopher. I bought it in

Parsons Bookshop on Baggot Street Bridge in Dublin in 1957. The key idea of this book is that the goal of the reflective life is not intellectual activity itself but arriving at some kind of contemplative state that is the *fruit* of reflection. Pieper cautioned against becoming too absorbed with simply being intellectually active, and not adverting sufficiently to acts of contemplation: there was value in just doing nothing from time to time. In this sense, Pieper's thinking represented an advance on that of Sertillanges. The French Dominican had pointed out that the heart of the intellectual life was not reading but reflection; Pieper was now insisting that reflection itself was but a step on the way to contemplation. It is as if having worked towards a conclusion, we should now relish the contemplation of the conclusion. Clearly that is not the only route to a contemplative state. If one chooses not to go the discursive, intellectual route that emanates in a conclusion of some kind, there is always the option of simply looking at the world in the manner of, say, an attentive painter or sculptor. Art is really about *looking*.

Sertillanges first alerted me to the fact that it was possible to define oneself as a person devoted to the pursuit of knowledge; Newman to the importance of conducting that pursuit in a disinterested way. Pieper, echoing Aristotle, presupposed but then transcended both those perspectives, in that he was championing not simply the search for knowledge, in however disinterested a fashion, but the act of contemplation itself. The progression was from reading to reflection to contemplation; from intellectual activity to stillness. Soon afterwards I grappled with Bernard Lonergan's *Insight: A Study of Human Understanding* (1957), which had the effect of endorsing Newman's emphasis on the importance of a disinterested approach to knowledge. Only recently have I become aware that the great English essayist William Hazlitt, too, was a prominent champion of intellectual disinterestedness. And in our own day, the

American poet Louise Glück endorses the approach in a brief but persuasive essay in *Proofs & Theories* (1994).

To put this in a wider context, thinkers like Hazlitt, Newman and Lonergan are all powerful advocates of an attitude that was challenged by Marx, Nietzsche and Freud, who from different perspectives question the very possibility of disinterestedness, of approaching things in a detached way. There is merit in what these sceptics ('the masters of suspicion' Paul Ricoeur calls them) have to say about the way that economic interests, the will to power and the unconscious mind can *undermine* the likelihood of disinterestedness as a human posture, but I tend to the view that these qualifying factors, while quite potent, do not altogether destroy it.

The most important practical feature of my early reading was that it resulted in my knowing early on what I wanted to do with my life: I now had an identity as a potential lifelong learner. I knew I could combine hours of study even with a job I didn't find all that congenial. I need not have worried on that score, because by the age of twenty-six I found a career that really suited me, that of a broadcaster. Much of the reading I did over the years was carried out in a formal university setting, whether at Trinity, UCD or Harvard, but the bulk of it was done in the comfort of my own library, built up over a lifetime.

The reason I had enough money in late adolescence to buy books was that I spent a year clerking with Clonmel Foods Ltd. from 1952 to 1953 and a further seven years with the Bank of Ireland, which I joined in early 1954. Given the peripatetic nature of bank life, the result was that during that period I had to get used to the idea of regularly moving my books. Even when I finally took up a career in broadcasting with RTÉ in 1961, that pattern persisted until I finally settled for one particular living quarters in Donnybrook in 1989. So, until that year, my personal library was housed for no longer than six years in any one location.

Chapter 5

BUILDING A PERSONAL LIBRARY

IT WAS IN CLONMEL IN THE EARLY 1950S that my life-long interest in book-buying first surfaced. Bulbert's was a second-hand books outlet in Irishtown, not too far from where I lived. Here was a store that sold everything from sweets, chocolate, confectionery and household goods to magazines and books. 'Ma' Bulbert presided over this diversified retail operation. I don't recall seeing a husband around, but she did have a daughter and a son; he was a Carmelite priest.

The first major purchase I made there as a teenager was a second-hand set of the Rev. A. D'Alton's six-volume history of Ireland (1925). How well I remember the delight with which I salted away those large green-backed volumes, embossed in gold. I dipped into them rather than read them: what they represented was concrete evidence that I was now a book collector. Subsequent purchases I *did* read. Not all of them, I should add, and when I did read them, it was often long after the time of purchase. What tends to happen regularly is that I ignore many of my books until a particular interest of mine is ignited. At that point, I seek out every related book on the subject in my library.

My collection covers philosophy, religion, history, literary criticism, literary theory, the social sciences (economics, sociology, politics), literature and the arts. My broadcasting colleague, the writer Aidan Mathews, once surmised on the basis of our past conversations that the largest category was religion. I wasn't sure myself until the reorganizing of my library was done, but he was right. A strange outcome that for an agnostic.

There's one obvious trap attached to a life devoted to books and learning, and that is the danger of becoming puffed up with it. I recall Brendan Kennelly talking to me decades ago about Beckett's reference in a poem of his called 'Gnome' to the 'loutishness of learning'. It's an intriguing phrase, all the more potent because we think we know what it means, but are not sure. It has the kind of fruitful ambivalence that characterizes good poetry. Nor am I sure what Aquinas meant when he said that, having had a brief intimation of the Beatific Vision, all his work in philosophy and theology 'was as straw'. Nor indeed do I know if there's such a thing as the Beatific Vision or glimpse of the Divine, but it would be churlish not to be open to its possibility.

It will become clear to the reader of this book that for long stretches of my life I devoted more time to research and study than to broadcasting. The process of education is so inalienably linked with the classroom that it badly needs emancipation from that sole mooring. I have already pointed out that not until I reached the age of thirty-seven did I reduce my workload in a manner that facilitated to my satisfaction a life of reading and rumination. More to the point, I have been able to sustain that energizing rhythm for forty years, thanks to a mutually agreed arrangement with my long-time employer, RTÉ. In 2013 I was in a position to withdraw from even the most minimal programme obligations to concentrate exclusively on writing this book.

'Book collector' sounds a tad too grand for what I have been up to. When, in the early 1980s, I worked on a radio series with producer Donal Flanagan about book collectors, most of them collected rare books. These major collectors told me that I had what's called a 'reader's library', that is to say, a library with books that were meant to be read by me, rather than sold on at some point to a dealer. The world of rare books holds no particular appeal for me. Nor do first editions matter to me. The world of rare books is a comparatively small one: all the dealers and collectors know one another. I enjoyed the stories that emanated from that world. One that regularly surfaced was about a dealer entering a house, spotting one book he deemed of value, and then offering to buy the entire library rather than draw attention to the particular book in which he was interested. The dealer figured that if he showed his hand, a smart owner might refuse to sell on the grounds that he had something of value he could get more than one dealer to bid for.

That story reminds me of a minor variant of it that involved my own purchase of a book in a 'used' bookstore in Cambridge, Massachusetts. One afternoon many years ago, I spotted a copy of a book by J. P. Mahaffy about the history of ancient Greek culture. When I realized I had no cash on me at the time or at least didn't have enough to pay for the book, I asked the owner to put it aside for me. In so doing, I couldn't resist showing off a bit by asking the owner if he knew that Mahaffy had taught Oscar Wilde. When I returned the following day, he couldn't find the book. It is quite possible that he had a client interested in anything by or about Oscar Wilde. I'll never know. Perhaps I appeared too eager.

There's a highly rarefied zone of book dealing confined to the very well-off. I've learned something of that world from an American scholar friend who lives in Edinburgh, and who buys very expensive rare books and manuscripts. This is a small market within the rare books market itself. Even though the prices he navigates are in the telephone number category, he is, because of his scholarly credentials, a far cry from the type who sees books and manuscripts purely as merchandise. I am undeniably envious of those buyers who can swim comfortably in these waters, but in truth neither the promise of ownership nor the thrills of dealing have as much appeal for me as reading itself.

That habit of not reading my purchases, at least not straight-away, persisted to a certain extent. Some books I have tended to devour on the spot; others often come into play only when I begin to research the particular subject to which the books belong. Some titles have just been browsed through; others not touched at all. In the course of a radio interview in the mid-1980s, my broadcasting colleague Mike Murphy asked me if there were any books in my library I hadn't read. On that oc-casion, I cited Werner Jaeger's *Paideia*, about the nature of education in ancient Greece. I bought this three-volume set at Heffers in Cambridge in 1978. At that time, I was particularly interested in the interplay between the Graeco-Roman and the Judaeo-Christian worlds.

Earlier this afternoon, I took a book from my shelves un-opened for over forty years, despite its being a classic of its kind. A 1972 paperback version of Karl Popper's *The Logic of Scientific Discovery*, first published in 1934, was purchased at the old APCK bookshop on Dawson Street, Dublin in the mid-1970s. Verdict, some hours later: I've never read anything as lucid on the great physicist Werner Heisenberg (including Gino Segrè's *Faust in Copenhagen* (2007)) or as forbidding on prob-ability theory. I don't mind being made feel 'slow on the uptake', provided I get something from a book in the end, which, in this case I did. More and more, I use indices and dip in here and there.

My first shelving area in my earliest home in Clonmel was none too impressive: the bottom of a press in the family 'clothes room'. That's where I put the D'Alton history, and early purchas-es like Evelyn Waugh's *Brideshead Revisited* and L.P. Hartley's *The Go-Between*, Joyce's *A Portrait of the Artist as a Young Man* and Jacques Maritain's *Art and Scholasticism*. There was also a second-hand Italian grammar with a faded hard blue cover.

Eventually my budding collection was transferred to a small mahogany press of my own with four spacious shelves in the sitting room.

I used to look admiringly at my little collection in those early days, as it was slowly added to. Mostly, new Pelicans on music, art and philosophy. Among these were *The Meaning of Art* by Herbert Read; *The Symphony* by Ralph Hill; *Mysticism and Logic* by Bertrand Russell; *Spinoza* by Stuart Hampshire. Noel Annan in *Our Age* (1990), a survey of the mind-set of his own generation, informs us that Stuart Hampshire's 1951 paperback on Spinoza sold 40,000 copies. The books of G. K. Chesterton, including *Aquinas* and *The Everlasting Man*, were among my earliest purchases. Also, I got Bernard Shaw's brief life of Chesterton, available then in paperback for a shilling.

In the Penguin series I got a collection of essays by Aldous Huxley, poetry and prose by Gerard Manley Hopkins, and poetry by Keats. In the Everyman series, I bought Aristotle's *Poetics & Rhetoric* (1955) and his *Politics* (1959); and also in the Everyman series plays by Ibsen which included *The Wild Duck* and the plays of Sophocles. It was a heady time, facing into the treasury of world literature and philosophy. It is a moment that never reoccurs, the point at which you're setting out on the journey. The Penguin and Pelican series were a godsend because of what they offered me for half a crown each. When I recall that my first earnings were in the region of three pounds a week, I was relatively well off and could afford to buy books.

When I moved to Listowel, County Kerry in 1954 in the early stages of my brief career in banking, I decided to bring my small book collection with me. Judging by the number of tea chests that required, I realized that it was a much bigger collection than I had thought. That is what happens with books; they creep up on you. In Listowel itself, I don't remember buying that many books. One book I recall getting in nearby Tralee was Colin Wilson's *The Outsider* (1956). Wilson examined the role of the social outsider in literature and philosophy. It was a publishing sensation of the year. I gather it has never been out of print. Critics like Philip Toynbee and Cyril Connolly, who first lauded it as a masterpiece, later regretted doing so. As so often happens when we buy books because everybody is talking about them, we don't read them. All I recall after a cursory glance was a reference to Henri Barbusse's novel *L'Enfer*, in which the protagonist confesses to desiring all women who pass him by on the street, an impulse I assumed at the time was common to all young men of my age.

It wasn't until the 1960s that my book 'fever' really took hold. Though not making a fortune, I was now earning more as a broadcaster than I had been in my job at the bank. By the time I moved into a flat on Mount Merrion Avenue, Blackrock in early 1965, my collection had grown to the point of being noticeable to visitors. I had bought from Parsons, APCK, Hodges Figgis and the Eblana Bookshop. Many of the books were occasioned by my reading for a degree in philosophy and logic, but also by a need I felt to keep up with literature, criticism, religion, history and politics. Though my collection between 1965 and 1970 was modest enough, it was beginning to grow. It aroused the curiosity of my landlord's son, Michael Moriarty, then a law student in his early twenties, and later a High Court judge who would preside over the Moriarty Tribunal. I was quite flattered when Michael asked to see my collection. The approving noises he made on that occasion were welcome to an embryo collector.

Bill McCormack, former Professor of Literary History at the University of London, and Head of the English Department at Goldsmith College, used to work for Hodges Figgis in his student days in the 1960s. I was quite impressed to discover recently that he remembered a book on aesthetics by the American philosopher of art Monroe Beardsley which I had ordered from him in those years. Hodges Figgis is a really well-stocked bookshop at the bottom of Dawson Street in Dublin, with a well-informed staff. I can't leave the topic of that particular store without recounting a story told me about it by a friend. A shy customer walks in and whispers something to a member of the staff. This staff member then turns around and shouts the length and breadth of the store: 'Has that book on deviant sexual practices in the Tropics come in yet?'

In the 1970s Vincent Deane was a particularly well-read manager of the APCK bookshop on Dawson Street. He was willing to risk stocking material that did not have obvious commercial appeal. It was Vincent who introduced me to the writings of Harry Wolfson. Wolfson was a remarkable Jewish scholar, who taught at Harvard. He had command of Greek, Jewish, Islamic and Christian sources. Such was the nature of anti-Semitism even in academic circles in the 1920s that it is said his book about the Jewish philosopher Hasdai Crescas was publishable only if Wolfson could link it in some way to the Greek tradition. Hence the eventual title: *Crescas' Critique of Aristotle* (1971).

In the early 1970s I began to buy in Dillons in Malet Street in London and in the Compendium Bookshop in Camden Town. Foyles in Charing Cross Road and Better Books were other favourites. As were the Oxford University Press outlet and Zwemmers, both also in Charing Cross Road. It was in the 1970s that I first noticed that I tended to buy a lot of books on my way to various holiday destinations.

Paris in 1975 represented the peak of that book-buying phase when I spent a few months at the Cité Universitaire, and bought furiously at La Hune and Presses Universitaires France. The first book I got on that trip was *Anthropologie de la Mort* (1975) by Louis Vincent Thomas; the second was Lacan's *Écrits*. The Lacan purchase was a classic case of the kind of book one feels one *should* read but never does. However, since the purpose of that visit was to improve my French, I had a go, but didn't do very well.

It was in the following year, on a visit to Athens, Georgia and New York, that it became clear to me that I had morphed from being a lover of books to having become something of an addict. I could sense a mildly pathological component. The first book I bought in the university bookstore in Athens, Georgia was Paul Roazen's *Freud and His Followers* (1975). Many years later I recorded two programmes with Roazen in London about his work on Freud. Roazen came to prominence in Freudian circles as a revisionist: he took a noticeably less hagiographical approach to the master than Ernest Jones, Freud's official biographer.

In New York I paid my first visit to the now defunct Gotham Book Mart, where I bought a collection of poems by Delmore Schwartz. In John Guare's play *Six Degrees of Separation* there is a reference to 'those pricks at the Gotham Book Mart', which remark seemed to me unjustified with the exception possibly of one staff member. The Gotham featured new publications, but had an even bigger collection of 'used' books, especially fiction. The Strand Bookstore in Greenwich Village was *the* centre for used books. To my knowledge, it is still going strong, but I haven't been there in years. In those days, it was not air-conditioned, which meant you were at the mercy of electric fans, which just blow hot air around the room.

There was a bookstore on Third Avenue, managed by Liam Gaffney, a former Gate Theatre actor. I bought a copy there in 1976 of David Tracy's *Blessed Rage for Order: The New Pluralism in Theology* (1975). Tracy was familiar to me as the author of *The Achievement of Bernard Lonergan* (1971). Also in New York was Books and Company, beside the old Whitney art gallery. A block or two down from Madison Avenue was a bookstore, no longer with us, called 'The Paraclete', which specialised in theology and philosophy. One day I was arranging that a handful of books be mailed to Dublin. It tells you something about the restricted nature of the readership of theology books in the late twentieth century that the manageress, solely on the basis of my choice of books, asked me: 'Have you got a parish back in Ireland, Father?'

Between 1970 and 1974 I lived in Wilton Place, close to Baggot Street bridge. Because I was now closer to Parsons Bookshop than heretofore, my collection began to grow. When I lived in Shelbourne Road, Ballsbridge between 1974 and 1980, my library expanded even more. I housed the collection by stacking numerous bookshelves, which I'd bought quite cheaply in 1970 from a local supermarket. However, eventually there was a considerable overflow, which I vowed to have accommodated when I next moved.

In recent weeks, I found on my shelves a copy of Hans Küng's book *Infallible?* (1970) with an inscription by him dated 16 January 1977, which says: 'the truth in truthfullness [*sic*]'. I recorded a *tour d'horizon* style interview with him in Dublin on that day. My prime recollection of our conversation is that, for all his theologically liberal leanings, he was wary about Christianity being identified with the political left. In that regard, I notice that in the second volume of Küng's memoirs *Disputed Truth* (2007), he gives quite a revealing account of a conference at Notre Dame University in May 1977. At that conference of theologians and social scientists, Johann Baptist Metz and Gregory Baum, both of whom championed political theology, were at loggerheads with Charles Curran and Andrew Greeley, for whom *church reform* was a top priority. Küng himself took the same view as Curran and Greeley, but on that occasion, in order to keep his various friendships intact, decided not to get involved in the dispute. The first two volumes of Hans Küng's autobiography, a very recent addition to my library, show him to be quite vain, but, nonetheless, a good man, and, in the end, that is all that matters.

In 1979 I bought a house on Strand Road by the sea in Sandymount. I hired de Blacam and Meagher, at that time an up-and-coming firm of innovative architects, to transform my house. I asked them to design a library within the house that could store up to 7,000 books. Earlier generations would regard that as paltry pickings: Isaac Foot, father of Michael, the former leader of the British Labour Party, had a library variously estimated at upwards of 50,000 books.

Both Shane de Blacam and John Meagher got involved, but assigned responsibility for the project to Paul Gilligan. Shane and John were particularly interested in the library component. One of their first suggestions was to construct a separate unit at the back of the house. Another was the more conventional one of simply shelving most of the walls. And then, they came up with what seemed to me an irresistible proposal. The idea was to take out the staircase and shelve the vacant stairwell space from top to bottom through all three floors. They would install a spiral staircase close to the stairwell, so that occupants of the house could get from floor to floor. For cost reasons, the architects' idea that we should use steel and glass was abandoned in favour of wood. There were separate entrances to the library from each floor. In order to render each floor as light-filled as possible, it was decided to put in slatted flooring on the two top floors. This meant that you had a clear view of the entire three-storey library from both top and bottom. The final touch was to put in a long window on the back wall of the house which ran the full length of the stairwell. It was a truly excellent piece of design.

From 1980 until now I spent almost a third of each year in the United States. This meant that because of the feverish pattern of my book-buying in Cambridge, Massachusetts, my library was being added to considerably. In addition to the formal library, I retained most of the single bookcases that I'd had before moving to Sandymount. I got rid of books that I decided I didn't need. In the autumn of 1982 I spent a full academic year in America. That represented quite a wrench in the matter of leaving behind my private library. It sounds an absurd concern, given that I now had access to the Widener and other Harvard libraries. Still, you can get very attached to something you have assembled yourself.

When I arrived in Cambridge, in 1980 for the first time, this city of 100,000 people was generously endowed with book-stores, the main ones being the Harvard Bookstore, the Co-op, Wordsworth, and the Harvard University Press bookstore. Thirty years later, Wordsworth has gone, as have the Harvard University Press bookstore, the Thomas More bookstore, Man-drake (which specialized in architecture and psychoanalysis), Reading International, Paperback Booksmith, the Asian Book-store and Pangloss (used or second-hand books). Pangloss, pre-sumably owing to increased rents, moved from Mass. Ave. to Mount Auburn Street.

Over the past two decades, I have availed of summers in Cambridge to catch up on books, mainly fiction, I hadn't yet got around to. Usually mainstream, but occasionally quirky work like that of the Austrian novelist Thomas Bernhard, many of whose books have been translated into English. The authors ranged from Trollope and Hardy to Proust and Flaubert, from Dante to Dostoievski and Tolstoy. When I told Aidan Mathews that I read several Trollope novels from the Barsetshire Chronicles one summer in the late 1980s, he remarked that that was very 'combative' of me in such a venue and at such a time. Richard Ellmann tells us in his biography of Joyce (1959) that the author whom Yeats chose to read alternately with *Ulysses* was Trollope. My friend Adrian Moynes, former managing director of RTÉ ra-dio, said to me recently that Yeats would probably have enjoyed Trollope more than Joyce.

I recall surprising parallels between Tolstoy and Proust: both equally adroit at shifting gear almost imperceptibly from the microscopically personal and psychological to larger social canvases. It is impossible to deny a certain feeling of virtue when we have read those books we feel we ought to have read. We are never comfortable with such an admission, but that's how it is. Nonetheless, I know I am never going to read *War and Peace*. I may read Proust's *Remembrance of Things Past* again, but not Tolstoy's *Anna Karenina* or *The Death of Ivan Ilyich*.

If I were to comment adversely on my book collection, I would concede that there are too many books about books in it. It would probably have been wiser to have concentrated more on those books that *generate* commentary than on the commentaries themselves. It is always a good idea to have full sets of seminal authors, be they novelists, poets, essayists or playwrights. That is equally true of historians, psychologists, philosophers, social theorists, theologians and economists. Well-informed friends tell me that one would do well to choose say Gibbon, Macaulay, Collingwood and Braudel for one's history section; Freud, Jung, Rank, Adler and Maslow in psychology; Plato, Aristotle, Aquinas, Descartes, Hume, Kant, Rawls and Rorty in philosophy; Marx, Weber, Durkheim and Luhmann on your social theory shelves; Barth, Rahner, Congar, Küng, von Balthasar and Lonergan if you collect theology books; and Adam Smith, Keynes, Kalecki, Polanyi and Schumpeter in your economics collection. Nonetheless, it is never easy to resist the fashionable, say the latest Slavoj Žižek. Speaking of whom, in giving us *The Fragile Absolute* (2000) (a reference to the Christian legacy), Žižek has devised one of the best titles of the last two decades.

Another important category is that of reference books of various kinds. The last reference book I purchased was *The Oxford History of Western Music* (2004) in five volumes, plus an additional volume replete with appendices. This history was written by Richard Taruskin, author of *Stravinsky and the Russian Traditions* (1996). It is an unusual set, not least because of Taruskin's combative style. We have grown accustomed, mistakenly perhaps, to reference books of this kind being more neutral and less provocative.

Given the song and dance I have been making in this book about how for me the notion of expanding consciousness has always been far more important than expanding possessions, one might well stop me in my tracks by pointing to my life-long book-collecting. What is that, if not a prime example of prizing possessions. Yes, it would be, he said defensively, if I had bought books primarily for speculative purposes or even as objects in themselves. As to the first, unless one is dealing with rare books, dramatic depreciation is the order of the day. As to the second, very few of my books qualify as beautiful objects.

On airline flights I notice that people are now mostly reading electronically. To date, I myself have read only one book in such a form and, even at that, the Kindle belonged to someone else. I don't have strong views on this either way. For someone of my age, I have an understandably sentimental attachment to Gutenberg values, but there is no stopping technological progress in this domain, as in others. Robert Darnton of Harvard University Library has probably judged this matter correctly in predicting the survival of the book side by side with other comparable devices. His tone seems just right: let's not get too excited about this, so long as people continue to read.

As I look at my library now, I know there are books in it that I will never read, even were I blessed with the kind of gene-defying longevity given to few. That thought disturbs me not. I have always known I would never read them all. It's the fact that they were always readily to hand that mattered. I notice that, instead of diminishing, the pleasure I get from perusing my collection is actually growing. In February 2015, I donated my present collection of over 7,000 books to the Glucksman Library at the University of Limerick.

For the moment, I am holding on to more than half the collection to facilitate browsing. My earliest book purchases favoured philosophy, religion, critical essays, theatre and music. Not that I ignored fiction or drama, but there was a definite bias towards nonfiction. Two people who helped me redress that early imbalance by recommending good fiction were the journalist and local historian Margaret Rossiter, who was an office co-worker of mine in Clonmel Foods in 1952/53, and the writer Bryan MacMahon, whom I first met in Listowel, County Kerry, where I worked as a young bank clerk from 1954 to 1957.

My first efforts at formal study came about in my final four years with the Bank of Ireland: I enrolled at Trinity College, Dublin in 1957. Then, with the kind of synchronicity one longs for but rarely experiences, I landed a job as an announcer/newsreader with Raidió Éireann in 1961, a few months after completing my Trinity Finals for a commerce degree. The next chapter will give the reader a flavour of those Trinity years, the last of which was particulary busy, including as it did a day at the office, classes from 5.10 pm to 7.10 pm, and the occasional newsreading stint at the national radio station. In those years I was living in 'digs' in Percy Place, an attractive location overlooking the Grand Canal between Baggot Street and Upper Mount Street. These lodgings run by Josephine Hardiman (Miss 'H') became home for countless Bank of Ireland staff in the late 1950s and early 1960s, including Pat Molloy, a future chief executive and chairman of the bank.

Chapter 6

TRINITY COLLEGE DUBLIN IN
THE LATE 1950S

IN THE AUTUMN OF 1957, WHILE STILL WORKING for the
Bank of Ireland, I began to attend lectures in economics, statistics and the history of political thought at Trinity College;
it was part of a two-year Diploma in Public Administration
course. I spent a further two years taking courses in commercial
law, economic geography and German to qualify for a degree
in Commerce. At that time, Trinity required all its students,
whether in commerce, medicine or law, to complete an arts degree as well. When it came to the arts degree syllabus, it was a
pleasant surprise to discover that I could take History of Music,
a welcome relief from the grind of matters mercantile.

There was one unusual hurdle I had to overcome at that
time. As a Roman Catholic, I had to get a bishop's permission to
attend a Protestant university. It seems difficult to believe now
but in those days a Catholic who attended Trinity without such
permission was deemed guilty of grave sin. The rule wasn't re-
voked until 1970. I decided to play the permission issue as craft-
ily as I could, by applying not to the hard-line archbishop of
Dublin but to the bishop of Waterford and Lismore, the diocese
where I had grown up. Although technically I now belonged to
the Dublin archdiocese, since that was where I was currently
domiciled, I was happy to avail of any loophole I could find.

One didn't need a background in theology to see that the fact that what was treated as a grave sin in one diocese might not be so heinous in another cast doubt on the actual gravity of the offence. However, I was brought up as a dutiful member of my church and wanted to follow the rules, even if in a devious way. There was one amusing but revealing phrase in the response I got from the secretary to the bishop of Waterford. The letter gave me permission to attend Trinity and said it hoped that, as a result of my Catholic upbringing in County Tipperary and my schooling at the hands of the Redemptorists in Limerick, I would acquit myself well at college and that I would 'edify others'. Those were the days: I have rarely, if ever, encountered the verb 'edify' since.

Even in the 1950s, the Roman Catholic church ban on its members attending Trinity was regarded by Catholics themselves as quite anomalous. Having had a stricter religious upbringing than most, I was more obedient than others. A much more pressing matter in those days was how to fund oneself at university. I approached my employer, the Bank of Ireland, for a loan. It tells us something about the bank's attitude at the time to financing higher education for its staff that before it would make a decision to advance me £56 a year to cover the fees, I had to present my case in person to the chief executive, J. M. Harkness. Having listened to my presentation, he agreed to my request, but not before reminding me that in so doing he was conscious that he was thereby 'setting a precedent'.

The main reason I opted for Trinity rather than its main rival, University College Dublin, was that the practical side of my nature was won over by the idea of completing two degrees (arts and commerce) and a diploma (public administration) in four years on a part-time basis. The lectures lasted from 5.10 pm to 7.10 pm. Those were very suitable hours. The best that UCD had to offer was the choice of either an arts or a commerce degree in three years. Besides, the UCD lecture hours of 6.30 to

9.30 pm were much more inconvenient. Essentially, I saw the four years at Trinity as a way of ensuring that were I to leave the bank, I would have something to fall back on. What I would really loved to have done was either classics or philosophy, an option not open to someone who had to earn a living. So, given all that, it was no surprise that I did not derive much intellectual stimulus from the Trinity experience between 1957 and 1961.

It took about ten minutes to walk from the Bank of Ireland in College Green to the lecture hall in the Museum Building in Trinity. Entrance to the university on College Green was via the college's narrow Front Gate. The façade itself, opening out on to College Green, is called the Main West Front, and sports a small bright blue clock on its forehead. That clock is one of the city's unchanging landmarks and is featured in James Joyce's short story 'Two Gallants'. The Campanile at the other end of Front Square was the first thing I saw when I emerged from Front Gate. That is, if I were looking. Remember, after a day at the office, I was now rushing to classes. I headed rightwards in the square, scurrying past the Examination Hall, the 1937 Reading Room and the Long Room Library until I reached the Museum Building. I never noticed the ancient Rubrics Building on my left, at right angles to the Museum Building. There was only one objective: the auditing of the mandatory lectures. Afterwards, I left the campus via College Park on to Nassau Street and Merrion Square, home to my 'digs' at Percy Place at the corner of Northumberland Road. It was as if the bank centre, the college campus and my lodgings were all elements of one elaborate streetscape.

These degrees in commerce and public administration were geared specifically to equip staff working in the civil service, state-sponsored bodies and banks with the kind of administrative and commercial knowledge they needed. In fairness, the arts degree that one was obliged to complete, in conjunction with the commerce degree, had a much broader remit than catering to strictly professional needs. Moreover, it should be acknowledged that these courses represented Trinity's attempt to make university education more widely available.

Rarely did we part-timers stay around to talk after class. Home and supper was foremost on our minds. We seemed to be permanently on the move. Ours was not the Trinity of the May Ball or the Hist. and the Phil. or endless hours in the Buttery. At best, a quick drink in O'Neills or the Old Stand. The carefree college of the post-war years was changing anyway: there were fewer signs of sub-Brideshead glamour. There was still a considerable intake in the late 1950s from public schools and grammar schools in England and Northern Ireland. But that trend was beginning to wane, especially the influx from public schools: there were fewer Old Etonians who had narrowly failed to get into Oxford. I did meet a Radley alumnus, who hailed me excitedly one day in Front Square. It was my tie that had caught his attention. 'You were at Radley, I see.' Before I could clarify, he went on: 'There's quite a few of us here, you know.' I had no idea that casually purchased neckwear would ever create such a stir.

A different Trinity then, but that was over fifty years ago. In the college's long history, half a century is nothing. Less than a century before that again, one might have seen Oscar Wilde in Front Square; almost three centuries before that, Jonathan Swift. I find it interesting to reflect that very few in the late 1950s would have spoken of Samuel Beckett gracing the campus a mere thirty years before: the university's most distinguished twentieth-century alumnus was still relatively unknown. It used be said of post-war university life that what Oxford once was, Trinity is. Meaning, lots of fun. Not for those of us who had to earn a living. My classmates, like myself, were hoping to escape from the drudgery of junior clerical posts. To what positions we might migrate, we weren't too sure. We worked in banks, the civil service, the Electricity Supply Board, the Dublin Port and Docks Authority, and the Central Bank. In fact, it was a Central

Bank staff member, Pat Murphy, who usually led the field at examination time. Then a young civil servant of notable charm, Pat would subsequently distinguish himself in the commercial world both at home and abroad, and also become one of the country's leading art collectors.

Louden Ryan was the most gifted and academically distinguished of our teachers. He had been a pupil of the Trinity economist George Duncan and had completed a doctorate at the London School of Economics. His book on *Price Theory*, published in 1958, was extremely well received and is still in print. He lectured to us on 'economic principles'. The use of the term 'principles' was very much of its time. One questionable consequence of framing a discipline in terms of principles was that it tended to convey the impression of economics or whatever as a fixed body of knowledge to be mastered and applied, rather than as a discipline to be structured through inquiry. 'Inquiry', after all, underlined the provisional nature of the enterprise; 'principles' tended to suggest the opposite.

For some reason not clear to me now, I took an optional course in penology as part of the Diploma in Public Administration. Lectures were dispensed by a soft-spoken, fair-haired man who sighed in a manner that signalled either a troublesome respiratory condition or unspeakable boredom. Professor Eldon Exshaw talked to us at length about Cesare Lombroso. Why all I recall of that course is the name of a now discredited nineteenth-century Italian criminologist, I have no idea. He was the one who believed that criminals had identifiable anatomical features. I suspect it was Lombroso's melodious name rather than his ideas that accounts for the long-lasting nature of the impression he made on me. Who could not but be enchanted by a name like Lombroso. The surname 'Exshaw' doesn't have quite the same legato air to it, though it does have its own abrupt staccato appeal. Lombroso had authored the mellifluously sounding

L'Uomo Delinquente. These were sounds vibrant enough to revive anyone after a day at the office.

I had become alive to varieties of intonation, accent and voice quality among the lecturers: Amory Pakenham-Walsh on aspects of monetary policy; James Byrne talking about economic organization. Pakenham-Walsh sounded very Foxrock or Carrickmines; Byrne's accent was of indeterminate rural origin. Different accents, but what these men had in common were voices that, in singing parlance, were not altogether comfortably 'placed'. Louden Ryan had a more resonant, free-flowing voice than his colleagues. The vowel sounds were part Portadown, part London School of Economics. He would give the word 'now' that duo-syllabic value that only citizens of Northern Ireland can manage without doing themselves a permanent physical injury. It always sounded like 'noya'.

I was alert to voices and accents perhaps because I wasn't totally engaged by the content of the lectures. That lack of full engagement was partly my fault but also attributable to something else. With hindsight, it seems to me that we students weren't sufficiently made aware of the variety of contexts we needed to familiarize ourselves with, before we could understand economics. Understanding anything involves familiarizing ourselves with all relevant contexts. Even mathematics and logic have a history and a method. You may not agree with the historian John Lukacs that the history of physics *is* physics, but he has a point.

It was only after I had studied logic later on at UCD and, later still, the history and philosophy of science at Trinity, that I began to reflect seriously on method in economics. Most beneficial of all was my encounter at the Jesuits' Milltown Institute in the late 1960s with the highly illuminating work of Bernard Lonergan on scientific method. And then when I began to read the history of economic thought, I came to realize how essential that particular context was for understanding economic theory itself.

At an eightieth birthday party in early 2009 for Tom Hardiman, former Director-General of RTÉ, I had the pleasure of meeting my former professor Louden Ryan, who was then eighty-seven. Recalling my days as an economics student with him, I remarked that I had come to the conclusion that it was very difficult for a student ever to understand economics unless he had some familiarity with the two contexts already mentioned: the history of economic thought and the nature of scientific method. He responded with the air of a man, who, however animated he might have become by such matters in the past, had now lost all interest. 'I haven't opened a book on economics since I retired from Trinity. These days, what really preoccupies me are the intricacies of the Nicene creed.' There is, as the late, great Eric Morecambe would say, no answer to that.

Our teachers were, presumably, familiar themselves with these larger contexts, but didn't feel the need to share them with us. As for method, the discipline of economics occurs in the context of the human sciences at large. These disciplines have a method. Within that general framework of method, economics is likely to have a method specific to itself but still sharing some common structural features with other branches of human inquiry. One then can read Marshall, Keynes or whomever in the light of such a methodological framework. Familiarity with this context of method (like exposure to the context of the history of economic thought) is essential to grasping what one is doing when studying economics.

In Trinity in the late 1950s I felt an outsider. I never became integrated into college life: it was simply a place where I attended lectures. I must say that my years at UCD in the early 1960s were no different. In both cases, lack of involvement in college life was a consequence of trying to combine a full-time job with lectures. I rushed into Earlsfort Terrace to catch a lecture in philosophy or logic and then scurried back to the radio or the television centre. It wasn't until the early 1970s, when, freed from the demands of a daily newsreading job, I returned to Trinity to do a doctorate in psychology that I had the freedom to relax into student life. Not that I had any interest then in college societies or the like, but I did want to lounge for much of the day in the Berkeley library, or the Buttery or in Bewleys of Westmoreland Street. Evidently there was something I felt I had missed out on: a work-free life replete with leisure time for three or four years. What I finally engineered was a compromise: close to a decade of study in which I supported myself by means of a very light workload.

It was in Bewleys coffee house in the early summer of 1975 that I recall talking to Brendan Kennelly about my growing obsession with the value of permanent intellectual revision. As I grew more and more animated, the Ballylongford poet and professor of English developed a twinkle in his eye. The paradox of someone absolutizing the notion of permanent revision was too much for him: he roared with laughter. We both did.

Those were the days. I lived the life of a student for a decade. It wasn't altogether a student life in the accepted sense, of course: I still had to support myself. But my relatively undemanding broadcasting commitments paid me enough to sustain a life of scholarly leisure and exploration. In a reference to that phase, my broadcasting colleague Mike Murphy once said to me, 'You opted out', and, in truth, I did. Apart from research at Trinity, I studied French at the Sorbonne and German in Bavaria. The late Dick Hill, erstwhile director of television at RTÉ, told me at that stage that I was living out the fantasies of many of my colleagues. I am certainly glad I did what I did at that point in my life. I was thirty-seven when I embarked on that phase: not old, but not young either.

In conjunction with academic studies, I had always maintained an interest in singing and voice production. So during my sojourn in Cobh, County Cork in the summer of 1954 as a member of the Bank of Ireland's relief staff, I managed to get to

Cork Opera House to hear visiting singers. One of these was the English baritone Dennis Noble. I don't remember much of the programme except his rendering of 'Fair Provence' from *La Traviata*. Little did I realize as I listened to him that evening that I would study singing with him for a few years beginning in the late 1950s. Noble was born in 1899 in Bristol and made his debut at Covent Garden in 1924. He sang there regularly until the outbreak of the Second World War. I had got to know his work first through his 1947 recording with Heddle Nash of Elgar's *The Dream of Gerontius*.

My interest in singing began when I played in Gilbert and Sullivan operettas at school in Limerick. Sometime in the mid-1950s I spoke to the baritone Michael O'Higgins about taking singing lessons from him, but nothing came of it, because I was living in County Kerry at the time. When I returned to Dublin in early 1957, the matter arose again. One evening at the interval of a performance of Benedict's *The Lily of Killarney* at the Olympia Theatre, I ran into a former school mate, Dermot Horgan, who had an outstanding tenor voice, and who reawakened my enthusiasm for voice classes. Dermot had just returned from London, where he had studied singing with the Italian tenor Dino Borgioli, one of the leading teachers of the day. Dermot spoke like an evangelist about the value of singing lessons. 'I could whip out a top C', he said at one point, in a manner that indicated that he was quite willing to do so on the spot if I wanted a demonstration. We arranged to meet. The result was that I registered with Jay Ryan, an elderly Dublin baritone, who had teaching rooms in the centre of the city, not far from the Olympia Theatre. When did singing standards collapse, I asked Jay one night. 'After the war, son'. He meant the *First* World War.

Dermot Horgan used to organize practice sessions in his family home in Raheny, where he and I and other singing student friends of his used to gather. Like all groups of this kind, there was a sense of 'the one true faith' of voice production.

This understanding of vocal 'truth' did not emanate from Jay Ryan but to a large extent from Dermot, whose gospel text was *The Voice of the Mind* (1953) by Edgar F. Herbert-Caesari. This particular book, as the title indicates, lays more stress on the psychological than the physiological aspects of voice. Both Beniamino Gigli and Lauri Volpi were contemporaries of Herbert-Caesari's as students of the famous baritone Antonio Cotogni. Gigli, in fact, wrote an introductory lesson for *The Voice of the Mind*.

Dennis Noble, the distinguished British baritone, had a less gentle approach than Jay Ryan, but equally cautioned against 'forcing'. Noble taught at the Royal Irish Academy of Music in Dublin in the early 1960s. His favourite injunction to students when he wanted them to open the larynx as widely as possible was to ask them to imitate the physical posture that accompanies 'getting sick'. It is not the most edifying of images, but there's merit in the idea. I used to walk to the academy in Westland Row during my lunch break at least once a week from the Bank of Ireland head office. At that stage of his life, Dennis had become 'partial to the drop'. One of his favourite requests was 'Have you got ten bob, old-boy?' If you had, he would vanish after the lesson to Kennedy's across the road.

If it is not too presumptuous or far-fetched a thought, it is interesting to reflect that, in taking lessons from Noble, I could be seen as positioned in a line that had a rich ancestry. Noble himself had studied with the Algerian baritone Dinh Gilly, who was one of Emmy Destinn's lovers in the early part of the twentieth century. Gilly in turn was taught by Antonio Cotogni, who died in 1918. And, as I have already mentioned, Cotogni taught Gigli.

I had no interest in pursuing a singing career, even part-time, but, as a budding broadcaster, it seemed to me to make sense to try to improve my vocal foundations. The singer whose speaking voice impressed me most was the soprano Margaret Burke-Sheridan. Coincidentally, when she experienced technical problems with her singing voice later in life, she turned to the author of *The Voice of the Mind,* Edgar F. Herbert-Caesari.

At Trinity I was enjoying 'commercial' German. The precise force of the qualifier 'commercial' was never clear to me, but that didn't matter, because it meant that I got an introduction to the basics of the language anyway. I also bought a set of Lingua-phone recordings to try to master the sounds of German. By a curious coincidence, something emerged in a German class that had a strong musical connection. It wasn't a prescribed text, but was written by the author of one of the prescribed texts. The drift of the passage was that the only authentic way to develop musical taste is to build on a foundation that consists of hon-estly acknowledging your likes and dislikes. There is nothing as crippling as feeling you're *supposed* to like anything. If that outcome isn't an unpredictable feature of 'commercial' German, I don't know what would be.

It was in 1959 that I first applied to Raidió Éireann's music department with an idea for an evening concert programme. There wasn't anything original about my proposal: what I was really angling for was an announcing/newsreading job. Anyway, originality in the matter of programming is a very rare occur-rence: a former colleague, the late John Skehan, was told by a senior executive in BBC radio that the last original idea submit-ted to them was *Desert Island Discs.* In due course, I got the customary acknowledgement, saying that my suggestion was now on file, ready for possible use should the occasion arise.

In early 1960 I applied for an audition with Raidió Éireann as an announcer/newsreader. I knew that were I to get a part-time job, I would be juggling three balls in the air: a 9.00 to 4.30 job with the Bank of Ireland, a degree programme at Trinity, and part-time evening work with the national radio station. Still, I was so eager to make tentative moves towards leaving the bank that I pressed ahead with the audition application.

Chapter 7

RAIDIÓ ÉIREANN ON THE EVE OF TELEVISION

IRELAND IN THE SECOND DECADE OF THE twenty-first century, like countries the world over, is littered with radio stations, but in 1960, the year I began to broadcast, the country had only one. Raidió Éireann had been founded by the Irish government in 1926, four years after national independence. The new station was modelled on the lines of BBC radio and was funded by licence fees. Although it would soon become partly dependent on advertising revenue, it continued to subscribe to a BBC Reithian ethos (first articulated by Sir John Reith in the 1920s) that enjoined broadcasters to inform, entertain and educate.

The Raidió Éireann I would eventually begin to work for in 1960 still reflected the values of official post-independence Ireland: it was recognizably Gaelic and Catholic. As for the Gaelic component, it was quite common at that time for both administrative and production staff to use the Irish language version of their names. Prominent among bilingual broadcasters of the period were Seán MacRéamoinn, Proinsias Ó Conluain and Ciarán MacMathúna. The use of the Irish language both on air and in the work environment declined over the years, in line with the relative decline of the Irish language in the culture at large.

The country's Catholic identity was proclaimed twice daily on air with the broadcasting of the Angelus, a distinctively Roman Catholic devotional practice. The new television service continued the practice when it opened in 1961. From time to time, this has been denounced as sectarian, an example of the national network favouring one particular denomination over all others and none, but the custom continues to this day.

In those days Raidió Éireann was the only outlet in the entire country for an aspiring broadcaster. Moreover, it was a tight ship: notoriously difficult to get a job there. Many assumed that to do so, you needed political influence or personal connections. One job, though, that seemed to float above such considerations was that of announcer/newsreader: vocal suitability was all that mattered. In March 1960, I was invited to an audition not long after I had made an application to the station.

Because the radio station was administered by the Department of Posts and Telegraphs, the studios were housed in a building that also contained the General Post Office. The GPO was renowned as the launching site for the 1916 Rising against British rule in Ireland. When I arrived at the Raidió Éireann studios in the GPO, I took a lift to the top floor. The first person I saw in the reception area was a rival candidate. He was a young man of about my own age who was listening intently to the radio monitor in what was, by any standards, a modestly proportioned reception area. There was something arresting about this aspiring young broadcaster who had chosen to sit so close to the monitor. I noticed the remarkably focused way he was listening to the evening's radio output: as he leaned forward, his right shoulder was elevated, his left ear was hugging the monitor in the manner of someone who was not just listening casually but actively assessing the merits of what he was hearing. What I had no way of knowing that cold March evening was that this young fellow job-seeker in a grey-white, herring-bone overcoat, and who probably drove a Morris Minor carefully, would define

Irish broadcasting for the next forty years. That was my first sighting of broadcasting *wunderkind* Gay Byrne.

The audition went well: I wasn't particularly nervous. Even phonetically treacherous words like 'plebiscite' didn't stop me in my tracks. I recall thinking that the insertion of that particular word was a trap, overlooking the fact that the primary purpose of the audition was to assess vocal quality and general reading fluency. All that remained was Raidió Éireann's assessment of my efforts. It was an anxious enough time awaiting the outcome, but I got word within a month. The result of those March auditions was that Gay Byrne and I emerged as the successful applicants.

In less than two months, we underwent a training course conducted by Denis Meehan, the chief announcer. At our first meeting in Denis's office in May 1960, he asked his two trainees what we thought the most important quality was in a radio announcer/newsreader. A wide arc of possible replies crossed my mind afterwards, ranging from fluency in Aramaic to good personal hygiene, but I couldn't think of any at the time. Gay opted for relaxation as the quality to be prized the most. We then both waited to hear the 'correct' answer. Announcers, we were told, must above all else be 'pleasant'. I thought Gay's was the better answer: the injunction to be pleasant, after all, is open to misinterpretation. Besides, who can say that a bad-tempered presentation of a symphony concert wouldn't occasionally make for interesting listening.

Denis Meehan's assistant on that training course was another staff announcer, Liam Devally, whose fine tenor singing voice led to a subsidiary career as a concert and recording artist. Denis's key contribution to that early summer course was the manner in which he alerted us to that most insidious of broadcasting habits known as a 'speech tune'. What a 'speech tune' consists of is a tendency to read every sentence with the same fixed pattern of cadences, regardless of the *sense* of the sentence.

There is a related notion, but not at all as irritating, which is observable mainly in American network television news. This is what one might call the 'in-house voice' phenomenon, in which reporters and anchors deploy an on-air tone that they believe to be in tune with the network's authoritative news tradition. That tendency is less apparent in the early twenty-first century, but you can still occasionally hear the 'in-house' baritone cadences of former news broadcasters like Walter Cronkite, Eric Sevareid, Harry Reasoner, Chet Huntley et al. in the news broadcasts of the main networks. When former network reporters/anchors migrate to cable news channels they stick out like sore thumbs, for that reason. Chris Wallace, formerly of NBC and later with Fox News, is a classic example. So too is Martin Savidge, also a former NBC reporter, now with CNN. You can hear in their cadences echoes of the great American news broadcasters of the past.

After that month-long training course, Gay Byrne and I were invited to join the announcing/newsreading panel. At that point, we were both much given to discussing broadcasting styles and techniques of voice production. The BBC radio news-reader whom we spoke most about was Frank Phillips, who was particularly associated with wartime broadcasts. His delivery sounds quite mannered today, as indeed most BBC newsreading voices of the wartime and post-war period do, but it was a superb instrument and, unusually for a news announcer, it was a tenor voice: most are baritones.

The first radio news bulletin I read was at 6.30 pm on Monday, 11 July 1960, and it was an unqualified disaster. On that debut occasion I experienced a bout of truly enervating microphone fright. How I survived that opening mishap, I have no idea. When someone as congenitally diplomatic as that long-serving radio and television newsreader Don Cockburn said to me later that I wasn't myself on that occasion, I knew it had been pretty bad. All I remember of the news content that evening is that developments in Africa dominated: the turmoil in the Congo was at that time a major international story. I checked recently to discover that on that particular news day, Moise Tshombe, a Congolese politician, had declared the Congo province of Katanga independent and had applied to Belgium for help. Patrice Lumumba, the prime minister of the Congo, asked the United Nations to intervene. That piece of research brought me back half a century. Those sonorous, erstwhile newsworthy names: Tshombe and Lumumba; those faintly menacing 'm' and 'b' sounds: the beating of distant drums. Not a great chapter, incidentally, in Belgium's imperial history.

In order to minimize 'first night' nerves, Denis Meehan had concealed from me until late that Monday afternoon the fact that he wanted me to read the evening's news bulletin. Denis pretended that what he had in mind for me was the far less onerous 6.20 pm compilation of station announcements that preceded the news. Maybe that was the problem: had I been worrying about it beforehand, I might not have been quite as terrified. In effect, I think the supervisor's tactic backfired.

Between the station announcements and the bulletin itself, the continuity announcer on duty, Brigid Kilfeather, played Eric Coates's *The Dambusters March.* For my highly strung debut, it was an unfortunate choice. That particular piece of music reinforced in me the feeling that I was embarking on a quasi-military escapade from which I might never return. My breathing was slowly slipping out of control, and there was no escape.

So I had a very shaky start. Shortly after I began my broadcasting career, I met a former school classmate in Henry Street, close to the studios. In the course of our conversation, he began to tear some new radio announcer to shreds. An obvious invitation to a joint bout of *schadenfreude*, until it dawned on me that the apprentice broadcaster he was talking about was myself! I received enough criticism in the first few months to alert me to the need for instant improvement. Then eventually I began to get the hang of it. After several months, I finally settled in, so much so that by the autumn of the following year, 1961, Denis Meehan offered me a permanent staff job. Gay Byrne, a committed freelance by nature, pointed out to me the advantages of not taking a staff job, but having known only the security of bank employment, I discounted his advice.

Denis Meehan also offered a job to another former bank clerk, Terry Wogan. Two lucky lads: we had landed permanent posts for which, according to our boss, thousands had applied. On 1 November 1961, Terry and I joined the announcing/ newsreading staff of Raidió Éireann on a salary of £750 a year. Terry had been with the Royal Bank of Ireland; I had been with the Bank of Ireland, earning £600 a year.

After we joined Raidió Éireann, young Wogan and I developed a routine of meeting every other morning for a cheese sandwich and a Bovril in Mooney's of Middle Abbey Street. You can just imagine the unbridled excitement of it. In those days the radio service was off the air between 10.00 am and 1.00 pm and again between 3.00 and 5.00 pm. Come to think of it, those breaks were fraught with risk for anyone inclined to have a few jars. Frankly, this never crossed our minds, though, in general, the radio service had the reputation at that time of being an alcohol-saturated industry. In between broadcasts, Terry and I would occasionally go for a walk on Dun Laoghaire pier or perhaps in the Phoenix Park. Meantime, we sized each other up, wondered when we would get a break in the new television service, and couldn't believe our luck in escaping the tedious life of a junior bank clerk.

In the late autumn of 1962, I was about to enjoy my first holiday in years: for the previous four years I had forfeited holiday time to prepare for and sit for university examinations. Terry recommended I go to the Oktoberfest in Munich, which indeed I did, eager to try out my college German. He went to Ibiza, which, at the time, I thought was a ballet playing at the Gaiety. That trip to Munich, Innsbruck, Salzburg, Vienna and Paris in the autumn of 1962 was my first to the European continent. One of the highlights of the holiday was a production in Munich of Verdi's *A Masked Ball*. That was the first time I had seen a 'raked' stage, the kind that could accommodate royal courtiers standing in small groups that seemed to recede interminably into the distance. Before that, the only kind of staging I knew at Magners Theatre in Clonmel, the Savoy in Limerick, the Gaiety in Dublin or indeed at Covent Garden was essentially box-like in appearance, consisting of a modest backdrop with tenors and sopranos on the left, and basses and altos on the right. Among the whispering baritones with the Dublin Grand Opera Society at the Gaiety in the late 1950s had been a young Terry Wogan.

Of the three newcomers who happened to clamber aboard the national broadcasting omnibus in Dublin in 1960/61, Gay Byrne was the most disciplined, confident and single-minded. Terry Wogan, easy-going, amusing and charming, seemed more interested in a night out with his rugby friends than in building a career. Of the three novices, though, Terry had the greatest sense of others' strengths and frailties: he was the shrewdest psychologist among us. Also, more than anyone I had met up to then or since, he seemed perpetually in good spirits: Terry Wogan was someone you wanted to be with. Both Gay Byrne and I were of one mind on that.

Like Terry, I too was someone with unfocused broadcasting ambitions; above all else I was determined at that point to pursue a degree in philosophy. The way Gay and I would eventually turn out was reasonably consistent with those early assessments: the one becoming Ireland's most talked-about broadcaster for the next four decades; the other, a low-profile host of book-based discussion programmes. Terry's casual approach in those early apprentice years gave no intimation of the ambition that would eventually take him to the pinnacle of British broadcasting and the distinction of a knighthood. His talent was obvious from the outset; less so was his drive.

Ernest Byrne, a brother of Gay's who returned from the US to take up a senior position with RTÉ, interviewed both Terry Wogan and myself, together with many other hopefuls in late 1961, for a staff newsreading job in the new television service, but we weren't invited to audition. Neither of us felt we had shone in response to Ernie's opening, 'Tell us about yourself' question. To Charles Mitchel fell the honour of being Ireland's first television newsreader. Meanwhile, Gay had stolen a march on all his contemporaries by landing a television job with Granada in Manchester. None of us were then married, though Gay and Terry would find their spouses, Kathleen Watkins and Helen Joyce, within three years. I didn't get seriously involved for another six years; I met Maireóg Golden in April 1968, and even then didn't settle down to marriage. A footnote to Gay Byrne's marriage in 1964. Terry Wogan and I discussed it at length in the RTÉ make-up room the evening the story broke. Terry indulged my weakness for speculation until I had exhausted at least three elaborate hypotheses as to why Gay had decided to get married. Terry drew proceedings to a crushing close, as he picked up his script saying: 'Then, of course it may simply be that he *fell in love* with Kathleen?' Game, set and match to the future Sir Terry.

Among the part-time radio announcer/newsreaders I became friendly with at that time was the late Michael Herity, a young teacher who was studying archaeology at University College Dublin. He possessed an ideal broadcasting voice, but opted instead for what would prove to be a distinguished academic career in archaeology. I had many conversations with him down the years and have benefited from his insights. It was in his house in Sandymount circa 1971 that I first heard a then relatively unknown musical group called The Chieftains, and first met Seamus Deane, the most brilliant literary critic of his generation. Michael Herity died in January 2016.

What books were young Irish radio announcers reading in 1961? Gay Byrne was savouring Somerset Maugham's *The Moon and Sixpence*. What Terry Wogan was reading I don't recall, though, given his lifelong love of P. G. Wodehouse, it is a safe bet to infer that the work of the comic master was on his list at that time. As for my own reading, I was engrossed in a Pelican paperback, *The Organization Man* by William Whyte (1956). That book, together with David Riesman's *The Lonely Crowd*, co-authored with Nathan Glazer and Reuel Denney (1950), have turned out to be classics of the era. These books articulated powerful critiques of postwar American society. Both writers championed personal autonomy; Whyte was a journalist, Riesman a sociologist. Whyte's castigation of conformism appealed to someone like myself who was attracted to the idea of personal autonomy, but was still quite indifferent to larger political issues.

I am not sure what the station supervisor Denis Meehan was reading in those years. As to his erudition, no one had any doubts. By all accounts, the world lost a brilliant scholar in Denis. As a result, we were the beneficiaries of his skilful wordplay and wickedness. He was one of the station's great storytellers. There was no tale of his I cherished more than the one about the Raidió Éireann telephonist who one evening vacated his perch and headed for the Tower Bar directly opposite the studios in Henry Street. His sole objective was to inform Denis, then station supervisor, that at that very moment the director-general of the network was on the phone in the throes of an important conversation. Would Denis like to return to his office to listen in to that conversation? Denis used to say that if he had accepted the telephonist's invitation, and if it became publicly known that he had done so, it would have meant the end of his career.

Denis was remarkable in that he could switch from green room informality to BBC Home Service-style formality in seconds. The voice was a compound of the BBC's Alvar Liddell and rural County Laois. When Denis began his career, the prevailing style in broadcasting was such that an announcer's on-air voice was the equivalent of what is called 'the telephone' voice. Even at a time when formality was the order of the day, Denis was more formal than most: he brought a sense of importance not just to special occasions but to every broadcast he made. What added a certain irony to that was that he had a more mischievous sense of humour than most. In the early days of the BBC, the corporation's radio announcers read the news in dinner jackets. Raidió Éireann announcers in the wartime and post-war eras were moulded in the shadow of the old BBC Home Service tradition: you could sometimes hear the fine-fabric rustle of those dinner jackets in the voices of the briefless barristers who constituted the first cohort of Irish radio announcers.

The most important fact of life for a newly minted radio broadcaster in Ireland in early 1962 was that the new television service had just opened. Recently appointed radio announcers-cum-newsreaders could not have come on stream at a more propitious time. This was our big opportunity. We had cracked the radio side; now television beckoned. Luck was with us in that it was soon recognized that radio experience was a big help in making the transfer. Nonetheless, none of us knew if we would survive the move. One slip in the trial period and our chances would be blown for good. We saw it happen. The magic words aspiring television newsreaders wanted to hear were: 'Des Greally is looking for you'. Greally was editor of television news; he had joined RTÉ after many years at ITN in London, where, among other things, he was reputed to have selected the type of spectacles that would define for ever the television image of Robin Day, one of BBC's twentieth-century television greats. One evening in early 1962, the chief sub-editor on radio news, Frank Keane, uttered the magic words to me. I could scarcely believe that I had heard them.

Before being invited to read an evening news bulletin, I was asked to present a news feature programme, *Newsview*, about the Kenyan politician Tom Mboya, who was on a visit to Dublin at the time. What intrigued me was how relatively free of nerves I was, compared to my debut on radio two years before. Reaction to my first television appearances was reasonably good, but when Wogan got his television news break a few weeks later, I began to worry that I might lose my spot.

To begin with, Terry was more photogenic than I was, which is what we tend to say when someone is better-looking than ourselves. I was relieved to discover that when the initial excitement that greeted Terry's debut had subsided a little, I was still in demand. We all realized that we were vulnerable in the face of fresh talent: if you lost out early on, you might lose out completely. It was imperative to survive the initial chaos that permeated the television newsroom. Apart from reading the weekend news, Terry and I alternated as presenter of a weekly current affairs programme called *The World This Week*. This was a singularly unambitious programme; its principal function was to deploy international material that hadn't made the nightly bulletins.

Terry Wogan early on indicated that he was more interested in light entertainment than in news. He was a big hit on Irish television in the 1960s with a quiz show called *Jackpot*, but hadn't yet found the ideal television vehicle for his talents. He moved to London in 1969 and soon found success on BBC radio; a decade later he repeated that triumph on BBC television. On Irish radio, it was with a programme called *Hospitals Requests* that he first made his mark. In the originality of presentation style that the young Wogan brought to a weekly 'warhorse' programme, which consisted of playing musical requests for hospital patients, lay the seeds of his later blossoming. The direct engagement with the listener, the informality, the humour, even traces of skittish fantasy, were all there fifty years ago. When you think about it, it took the unique talents of a Terry Wogan to transform what is often regarded as the most humble rung on the broadcasting ladder, namely 'hospital radio', into something altogether wondrous, a significant first step on the road to stardom.

There was a neat complementarity about this remarkably gifted pair, whose entry into broadcasting in 1960/61 coincided with my own. If we can agree that planning and spontaneity are the two key coordinates of great broadcasting (as of much else in life), Gay Byrne exemplified the first, Terry Wogan the second. In time, Gay would become renowned as the most fastidious of programme preparers, while managing to convey the impression that events on air were unfolding in a casual, unplanned way.

Terry often waxed eloquent about the unimportance of rehearsal and preparation, and though said tongue in cheek, he probably meant it to some degree. And yet one wouldn't want to insist too strictly on those labels. Gay was no mean off-the-cuff responder; and some of Terry's best lines were probably planned. In fact, Clive James made the point in 2013 in the *Daily Telegraph*, when discussing Graham Norton's handling of the Eurovision Song Contest for the BBC, that the difference between Norton and his predecessor was that Wogan had his improvizations ready. I think Clive James is right. While Terry notoriously disdained rehearsals or mechanical run-throughs, what I suspect he did prepare for were the memorable one-liners and imaginative flights of fancy that could be deployed so casually whatever the programme format. One of my favourite Wogan lines is one that *sounded* planned, but perhaps it wasn't. He once back-announced a disc by a lamentably bad Elvis impersonator thus: 'Meanwhile, all over the Home Counties,

My parents posing for a photo in 1933

St. Mary's Catholic Church Clonmel, a major landmark in childhood

Gladstone Street, Clonmel offers one of the best views of the town

A boarding school production of *Iolanthe* in Limerick in 1950

A short walk from the Bank of Ireland to Trinity lectures 1957/1961

Front Arch, Trinity College Dublin

Brendan Kennelly, a permanent feature of
Trinity since the late 1950s

Dennis Noble, British baritone and
voice teacher

Denis Meehan, chief announcer,
Raidio Éireann

Gay Byrne had remarkable self-assurance in his mid twenties

Terry Wogan's talent was always obvious; less so was his drive

Michael Herity, archaeologist, announcer, was shrewd and erudite

John Bowman, an excellent editor of 'Who's News' and 'Topic'

David Timlin, a television newsreading colleague

En route to Berlin in January 1964 with an Italian journalist (right) and a German photojournalist (left) after a month-long seminar in Salzburg on mass communications

Denys Turner, now at Yale, was my tutor in moral philosophy at UCD

The playwright Tom Murphy, always scarily honest

At the lock gates near Baggot Street Bridge for 'Lookaround' series, 1974

Maireog Golden, central to my life from 1968 to 1973

The actor Donal McCann was in quest of being understood

aging colonels hide behind their copies of *The Times* and fight back the tears.'

On the last Sunday morning of January 2016, I was in the process of making final adjustments to this manuscript when I learned of Terry Wogan's death. I had just sat down to watch the Andrew Marr Show on BBC1 when I heard the news. Terry's death affected me to a surprising degree, given that we had worked together for only a few years in the early 1960s and had met no more than a dozen times since he moved to London. The truth, I suspect, is that the bonding that occurs between two young people setting out on a professional journey together is deeper than one might think. Besides, not everyone is given the privilege of starting a new job on the same day as a broad-casting genius. Terry was twenty-three years of age when we first worked together in Raidio Éireann in 1961; he was seventy-seven when he died.

By 1966, Gay Byrne and Terry Wogan were firmly perched on the glamorous ladder of light entertainment. I had had to make do with the more sober world of news and features. In late 1963 the Head of News, Pearse Kelly, had offered me one of three newly created posts of radio and television newsreader; the other appointees were Charles Mitchel and David Timlin. In 1966 I was invited by producer Gerry Murray to front a pio-neering television programme called *The Course of Irish His-tory*. I will discuss my involvement in that series in a subsequent chapter on the early days of Irish television.

By 1971, *The Late Late Show* had made Gay Byrne Ireland's leading television star. Terry Wogan was beginning to make his mark in BBC radio in London. As to the present writer's career trajectory, I was at that stage still working as a radio and televi-sion newsreader and, in addition, had begun to branch out into arts and religion programming. In fact, I probably then took on too much work. The *Irish Times* radio critic of the day, the late Paddy Downey, remarked in one of his columns that I was presenting programmes in all existing departments apart from agriculture and sport. It was rumoured that I was earning more than the director-general.

Then in 1972 I experienced something of a conversion. I decided that, although I was very busy, I wasn't really being true to myself. I had reneged on whatever impulse I had towards a life of learning, reading and reflection. It was becoming clear that if I wanted to make more time for that, I would have to quit the newsroom. What finally helped me make up my mind was discovering that the Controller of Radio, Roibeárd Ó Farachain, was not at all happy that I was presenting so many feature programmes in addition to my news duties. That meant I now had a second reason to leave news. Were I continue in that role, I had little chance of being permitted to do anything else outside the news department. All that led to a complete reframing of my life. I decided to abandon a time-consuming newsreading career, but earned enough from programme work in radio and television to sustain myself in the kind of bookish, scholarly life I wanted. I returned that year to Trinity College Dublin to pursue graduate studies.

I didn't realize it at the time but my change of direction in 1972 wasn't all that sudden and unexpected: it represented the working out of an impulse that had governed my thinking twenty years before. That is where my real vocation lay. The decision to comply with a deep longing that had been lying dormant since it first surfaced twenty years before was for me a life-changing one. I was now doing what I really wanted. Thereafter, the amount of hours that I would devote to broadcasting would be significantly reduced. I never worked as hard again as I had for the first twenty years of my working life. Indeed, I was once told with a fair degree of accuracy that I have been in semi-retirement since 1972.

I realized more than forty years ago that I had only one life to live: I had to make up my mind. It was becoming clear to me that what I really wanted to make the main project of my life (at least for the foreseeable future) was my own education, and that broadcasting would have to take second place. It wasn't as simple as that, of course: there would be brief periods when broadcasting got the upper hand (1984–89 and 1996/97) but, on balance, the attraction to learning would win out. At any rate, I spent the years between 1972 and 1983 in various forms of graduate study and research. I earned enough from broadcasting to support myself in that venture. During the academic year 1982/83, I took a sabbatical in the United States, and thereafter continued working regularly in broadcasting at a leisurely pace until 2013. In total, I was to enjoy forty years of that kind of life, working at half the pace I had kept up in the years 1952–72.

In my first three years in broadcasting, I had tried to combine my daily duties with formal academic study. The experience brought home to me how crucial free time is to conducting serious study. Nonetheless, I am so glad that within a year of joining RTÉ in November 1961, I enrolled for a degree in philosophy and logic at University College Dublin. Although, as was the case with Trinity in the 1950s, I was still combining study and a full-time job, the difference now was that I was prompted solely by an interest in the subject matter. Nonetheless, looking back on it, it was an extraordinary decision at that juncture. After all, why introduce a time-consuming distraction just as the new television service was getting underway? It gives you an idea how important that course of study was to me. Let me give a more detailed account of that transformative experience, which lasted from 1962 to 1965.

Chapter 8

PHILOSOPHY AT UCD UNDER CHURCH CONTROL

S INCE LEAVING SCHOOL, I HAD WANTED to study philosophy at university, but the need to earn a living ruled that
out. It wasn't possible to do so even part-time because the
relevant lectures took place during working hours, mainly in
the mornings. Yet one of the consequences of landing a job as
a radio and television news anchor is that I was now free to
attend those morning lectures. In September 1962, just when
the new Irish television service was getting into its stride, I
spoke to various luminaries in the philosophy department at
University College Dublin before embarking on a degree there.
Among them were Monsignor Feichin O'Doherty, Professor
of Logic and Psychology; Father Desmond Connell, lecturer in
metaphysics, and later to be Cardinal Archbishop of Dublin,
and Father Conor Martin, Professor of Ethics and Politics.

There was a reason why all the staff were clerics: the department was under the control of the Catholic Archbishop of Dublin, Dr. John Charles McQuaid. At that time, the common perception of philosophy in UCD was that it was a subject studied
only by clerics. Fifty years later, that situation looks singularly
anomalous, but at the time it was accepted as the natural order
of things: in those days, the Catholic Church's writ in Ireland
ran unchallenged. In line with Church thinking, the philosophy

courses were Thomist in character, and officially approved mainstream Thomism at that.

Let me make it quite clear that not merely did I at that juncture have no difficulty with the prevailing order of things, I was quite happy that the philosophy courses were inflected as they were. What I wanted was a philosophical formation that was in accord with my strict Catholic upbringing. If, as we had been assured by our teachers and elders, Catholic teaching was the sole repository of religious and moral truth, it seemed to me that one should apprentice oneself to a philosophy that was in accord with that religious viewpoint. My view of the role of philosophy would eventually change, but in the early 1960s that is how I saw it, as an intellectual foundation for my religious faith.

From the time I left the Redemptorist novitiate in 1952, I had been attempting to pick up what knowledge I could in the matter. I had borrowed the lecture notes of a friend, the late Tommy Cooney, who was studying philosophy at Maynooth College as part of his seminary education and who later became a secondary school teacher in Cork. In addition, I had bought Cardinal Mercier's two-volume introduction to scholastic philosophy, a book by Father C. N Bittle on ethics and by Father G.H. Joyce on logic. Now I would have an opportunity to tackle the subject more systematically.

The first person I spoke to about doing a degree in philosophy and logic at UCD was Professor Feichin O'Doherty. One of the university's best-known academics, he had an office on the Stillorgan Road opposite the RTÉ television studios in Dublin. I had first heard him speak at a public symposium on Greek tragedy at UCD in 1957; the guest speaker on that occasion was the American poet Robert Frost. O'Doherty seemed pleased to discover that late autumn day in 1962 that someone from the newly emerging television industry in Ireland was planning to audit his courses. He pointed out that a background in philosophy and logic at UCD would equip me for a role in shaping public opinion. The actual term he used was that I could become a 'kingpin' in moulding public opinion. I remember being intrigued by that remark, because wielding public influence was not on my agenda: I was more explorer than polemicist.

I had recently read the work of a Spanish philosopher named Julian Marias, who claimed that to benefit properly from the study of philosophy you needed to come to it in the first place with specific philosophical questions. O'Doherty's response to that was that, while it was true that the *professional* philosopher approached the subject in this way, there was no reason why a college student could not study philosophy like any other subject, such as economics or history. Certainly if you proceed to research work, it is important to be animated by a question of one's own. There is all the difference in the world between a research question assigned by someone else, and one of your own devising. The latter will be rooted in a more personal intellectual hunger. It has been well observed that the essential difference between an examination and a piece of personal research is that, in the latter case, you set your own questions.

According to the historian Tom Garvin in 'The Strange Death of Clerical Politics at University College, Dublin', an article in an issue of the *Irish University Review* (1998), Conor Martin and his junior colleague Father Fergal O'Connor were hoping in the early 1960s to set up a department of ethics and politics at UCD, which would be independent of the control of the then archbishop of Dublin.

Father Desmond Connell, lecturer in metaphysics, was cordial and encouraging. He was in those days over a quarter of a century away from his eventual career destination as Cardinal Archbishop of Dublin and confidant of Joseph Ratzinger (Pope Benedict XVI). What did Desmond Connell think of Bernard Lonergan, whose book *Insight* I had found quite difficult but inviting. 'A bit Kantian' was the reply. It was the fact that Lonergan had put human consciousness at the centre of his philosophical analysis that reminded the future Cardinal Archbishop of the thinking of Immanuel Kant. 'Kantian' in this context was code for 'Lonergan is not a mainstream Thomist'.

Philosophy as taught at UCD was considered the handmaid of theology. In effect, philosophy was regarded as a necessary preparation for theology. Again, I had no problem with that at the time. At this juncture, I would like to clarify further for the reader what my approach was in those days to the study of philosophy. I conceived of philosophy at that point, as I did other disciplines such as economics or sociology, as being structured in terms of basic principles rather than as a process of inquiry. The task in hand, I believed, was to master the principles of a particular discipline (as mediated by the prevailing consensus) and then to apply them rather than investigate the principles themselves. I would eventually discover that principles in any field are ultimately provisional; they are always revisable in the light of new data and new questions. So it is preferable to frame a discipline as a process of inquiry rather as something organized around a set of principles.

Before I had began to study philosophy, I assumed that in different schools of philosophy there were competing sets of principles based on different religions or on none. Philosophical expertise, I presumed, resided more in working out complicated supporting arguments for the agreed principles than in investigating those principles. So these upcoming university courses would articulate the basic principles that were in accord with my own religious upbringing, and also supply me with a supporting line of reasoning and argumentation if I needed it.

And yet my interest in a supporting line of reasoning was not borne of any interest in Catholic apologetics. I wasn't concerned with defending my inherited religious faith or with convincing others of its merits. As far as I was concerned, it was true, and that was that. It didn't need defending. What I wanted was to get a better understanding of the particular philosophical school that underpinned what I took to be the one true religious faith. Furthermore, I believed that once one had mastered the philosophical principles that were underpinning the Roman Catholic faith, one could apply them in many fields of life: politics, economics, science and culture. That meant, of course, that I was in disciple mode, but nonetheless I retained a certain curiosity even within that framework. That is what ultimately saved me.

My curiosity, such as it was, was firmly set within the framework I have outlined, but curiosity in any framework is potentially transformative. Whatever about my devout religious upbringing, I did have what one might call a philosophical temper or disposition, in that I gravitated naturally to questions about the *meaning* of this, that or the other. For example, I was much preoccupied at the time with the meaning of the term 'order', both in an artistic context and in a scientific one. So it wasn't a case that I was unreflective; merely that I was too dazzled by the notion of authority.

It gradually dawned on me that there is an intimate connection between independence of thought and the quality of one's intellectual performance. No matter how quick and alert a student is, he is still at a disadvantage until he begins to think for himself. Mind you, independence or originality of thought is itself a complicated variable. Alan Bennett, in his play *The History Boys*, cleverly lampoons the abuses to which an undue glamorization of originality of thought can lead. In that play, we find that some of the brighter Oxbridge-bound students, under pressure to be original at all costs, begin to question whether or not the Holocaust was a bad thing.

The philosophy on offer at UCD was presumed not to disturb one's inherited faith and church allegiance. The fact that I subsequently became an active interrogator of these same religious and moral traditions cannot necessarily be attributed to that course of study, if only because it is very difficult to specify with precision the causes of any one significant change in one's outlook. What I can say is that such study equipped me with the skills needed to examine critically the traditions I had inherited. So, in the jargon of the trade to which I was then apprenticing myself, such study was a necessary, if not sufficient, condition of a subsequent change of outlook.

From the beginning, I was impressed by that approach to philosophy which spoke of it as an activity that seeks to convert inarticulate certainty into something else. I latched on early to the central role that the exploration of presuppositions plays in philosophy. Within the department, some courses seemed less 'agenda-driven' than others, less bound by 'party line' considerations. This was particularly true of ethics and politics. Under Conor Martin and Fergal O'Connor, ethics was taught in a manner more true to the spirit of open inquiry than was the case with either metaphysics or even philosophical psychology. Ethics at UCD seemed less agenda-laden than the other branches of philosophy. Tom Garvin's claim in his essay that Conor Martin and Fergal O'Connor were actively trying to elude episcopal control is quite consistent with that hypothesis.

Even logic at UCD seemed agenda-laden, in the sense that the metaphics it assumed was Thomist in character. For example, Feichin O'Doherty tended to imply that logic *necessarily* presupposed a realist metaphysic of the kind endorsed by Aquinas. On the other hand, ethics (or more accurately meta-ethics) was taught in a less agenda-driven way. It appeared to be less bound to a 'party line' approach than other subjects. In moral philosophy we were exposed to a deeply thought-provoking problem, associated with the British philosopher G.E. Moore, namely: what is meant by 'the good'? First of all, there was the problem of whether 'the good' could be grounded rationally or was simply a matter of emotional choice, beyond the pale of rational analysis. Secondly, even if there was agreement that the good could be grounded rationally, how did one resolve the ensuing disagreements as to what it comprised. All that made me sceptical of any attempt by religious authorities to nail down in a dogmatic way what 'the good' meant. Heretofore, I was happy to accept that 'the good' is whatever the Catholic Church thinks it is.

After studying philosophy, it seemed to me that that particular religious viewpoint was just one more view that had to fight its corner in the broad human conversation. The Catholic view might well be right, and indeed its invocation of revealed truth in support of its position might be perfectly legitimate in theological discourse, but meanwhile the overarching social imperative was to try to live as best we can within a framework where people disagreed about these matters. Because, even if one concedes that there is ultimately one right answer as to what 'the good' is in a given context, the fact that people disagree about it is a social and political reality that has to be respected. In a modern democratic society, we have to live as best we can with our differences.

The political philosopher Charles Larmore reminds us in *The Morals of Modernity* (1996) of the fact that one of the cardinal experiences of modernity is the growing awareness that reasonable people disagree about the nature of the good life. Larmore fills in the historical background here: early liberal thinkers could not ignore a century of religious wars. He points out that Greek and medieval thinkers generally agreed that moral principle should shape the work of government, but in doing so they made the assumption that reasonable agreement about the good life was very much on the cards. As a result, Greek and medieval thinkers usually assigned to the state the task of implementing what they perceived to be easily agreed solutions. The key point here is that one cannot assume that reasonable people will agree about the meaning of the good life.

Catholic thinking in Ireland in the 1960s (and indeed in subsequent decades) reflected to perfection the aforementioned

Greek and medieval idea that moral principle should shape the work of government, on the assumption that reaching agreement about what was meant by 'the good' was a straightforward uncomplicated business. The Church was quite sure that it knew what the good life consisted of, and that this view merited enshrinement in legislation. If others disagreed, it was not uncommon for Catholic protagonists to say that they (the Catholic protagonists) were propounding such views not because the views were 'Catholic' views but because they had a rational basis and so should be obvious to reasonable people. Such an outlook overlooked the fact that even people who argue from reason will often disagree. At which point, we have to try to build what common ground we can, rather than retreat into an unyielding restatement of positions.

The star of the UCD philosophy department in those years was Feichin O'Doherty. He flounced into the lecture hall in a black flowing cape, his eyes directed solely at the podium. He exuded a cosmopolitan air in what was then a more insular academic world. His accent was part Derry, part Cambridge and faintly mid-Atlantic. The political philosopher Father Fergal O'Connor described O'Doherty to me as 'a philosophical artiste', by which I think he meant that the man was very much 'an entertainer', deeply conscious of his style of presentation in class.

O'Doherty had earned a doctorate in experimental psychology from Cambridge in the 1940s, at a time when Ludwig Wittgenstein taught in the university's philosophy department. I had always suspected that he attended Wittgenstein's lectures, but wasn't sure until I read confirmation of it in Tim Robinson's scholarly book *Connemara: The Last Pool of Darkness* (2008). In fact, it was to O'Doherty that Wittgenstein made the remark about Connemara being 'the last pool of darkness in Europe'. Robinson cites the source for that as *Portraits of Wittgenstein* (1999), edited by F. A. Flowers. I presume it was Wittgenstein's influence that partly accounted for Feichin O'Doherty's deep interest in the philosophy of logic.

Father Mike Nolan, O'Doherty's side-kick for many years, and a near neighbour of mine in Donnybrook, told me once that although Feichin O'Doherty was perceived mainly as a psychologist in UCD, his first love was logic. I believe Mike got that right. In the years 1963/64, on Saturday mornings at 9am in Newman House on St Stephen's Green, O'Doherty talked to us about Frege's *The Foundations of Arithmetic* (1953). He seemed to buy completely into Frege's view that since logic was more impersonal than psychology, it was therefore superior to psychology in the scientific pecking order: logic had been more successful in eliminating the intrusion of the human subject. For Feichin, the essence of logic was illustrated by the term 'implication'; psychology was captured by the term 'inference'. By 'implication' was meant the relationship that existed between propositions, regardless of whether we *grasped* that relationship or not. In contrast, 'inference' was a *psychological* act carried out by you or me; it belonged not so much to logic as to the natural history of thought, that is, to psychology. To get to the heart of logic, you focused on 'implication'. Years later, I began to suspect that Feichin, in the manner of Frege, had exaggerated the extent to which logic had eliminated the human subject.

On those early Saturday mornings, he also spoke about Wittgenstein's *Tractatus*. Gradually I began to think that his reading of Wittgenstein was skewed by a need to reconcile the Viennese-born master with Aquinas. Wittgenstein's metaphysics, in O'Doherty's hands, sounded quite Thomist. To that extent he was something of a gifted conjuror, a great reconciler whether of Wittgenstein and Aquinas or of Freud and Aquinas. He was more reconciler than inquirer. It was in such matters that one sensed a highly gifted man working in the service of a cause.

Since the end of the nineteenth century Thomism had been the officially approved philosophical position of the Catholic Church. Central to that philosophy was the affirmation of metaphysical realism. In explaining Aquinas to wider audiences, Chesterton famously said, 'the cardinal metaphysical principle is: there is an "is". One day in class I asked O'Doherty if logic *necessarily* presupposed a realist metaphysic, as he seemed to be implying. His reply was so convoluted that he lost me. I felt I had touched a nerve. Intuitively, I had no problem with metaphysical realism, with the idea that there was a reality independent of our thoughts: my difficulty was with the suggestion that logic *necessarily* presupposed one particular metaphysic rather than another. It seemed to me then and still does that the science of logic was as logically compatible with say metaphysical idealism as with realism.

Logic was for me the most exotic of all the philosophical disciplines I was then studying. It was the one I had had least familiarity with up to that point. This was particularly true of *mathematical* logic, which instead of ordinary language, featured a new, unfamiliar symbolic notation. The main lesson I learned from those three years of logic had little to do with mathematical logic and everything to do with the more traditional linguistic variety. That lesson was this: an individual's *motivation* for saying something is ultimately irrelevant to the truth or falsity of what he or she is claiming. You may be saying something about me because you don't like me, but that in itself doesn't invalidate *what* you're saying: it doesn't mean that what you're saying about me isn't true.

It helped to hear the American psychologist Percy Tannenbaum endorse that way of thinking at a seminar on mass communications I attended at Salzburg in 1964. At that time I was in the middle of my logic studies. Later I began to realize that it is possible to extend the principle in the following manner. One could argue that not just an individual's *motivation*, but also his *behaviour,* is irrelevant to the truth or falsity of his proclamations. Such behaviour is likewise irrelevant to the person's creative output. Thus, Eliot's anti-Semitism, however reprehensible in itself, does not undermine his poetry.

The poet Dennis O'Driscoll once put it to me graphically. If one were to learn that the discoverer of penicillin was guilty of the most heinous behaviour, that would not, in itself, undermine the value of his discovery. That it might undermine the moral reputation of the individual concerned is another matter. But neither the poetry in the one case nor the scientific discovery in the other are in themselves undermined. In similar vein, I heard the pianist Murray Perahia point out to Tom Service on BBC's Radio 3 that Alfred Cortot had betrayed Jewish friends to the Nazis, but yet remained one of the greatest pianists of all time.

Of all the books I bought for those courses fifty years ago, I have held on to mainly the ones about logic. Among subsequent purchases of books about logic, Susan Haack's *Deviant Logic* (1974), which explores the question as to whether the laws of classical logic are revisable, is the one that stimulated me most. I am not sufficiently up to speed in current developments in logic or the history of logic to know if those earlier books from my college days have stood the test of time, but I have a sneaking suspicion that after half a century they have held their own, particularly a book like *The Development of Logic* (1962) by William and Martha Kneale.

Politics in the UCD philosophy department was presented as a sub-division of ethics. It was the *moral* dimension of politics that was foregrounded. I was reminded of all this when recently reading *Philosophy and Real Politics* (2008) by the Cambridge philosopher Raymond Geuss. In that book he criticizes John Rawls and Robert Nozick, two giants of twentieth-century political philosophy, for tackling politics primarily as a branch of ethics. Geuss points out that Rawls, Nozick and many of those engaged in conventional political philosophy begin with a conceptual analysis, emphasize the moral dimension of politics, and scarcely mention what politics is really about, namely power.

What lends weight to Geuss's argument is that he is something of an old-style Marxist who can scarcely be accused of wanting to downplay the moral dimension of politics. Geuss made clear to me in conversation in Dublin in 2009 that he was not saying politics did not have an ethical dimension; merely, that philosophers shouldn't *begin* their analysis by focusing on the ethical. Only since meeting Geuss have I caught up with the Rawls of *Political Liberalism* who, though not any more focused on the realities of political power than in his *Theory of Justice* (1971), *is* more concerned with accommodating differences of outlook in a broad societal framework.

Whatever way the philosophy degree at UCD was structured in the early 1960s, Father Fergal O'Connor's lectures in political philosophy were not on my list. However, I did make a point of going to hear him, such was his reputation. He was very skilled at presenting the thought of Hobbes and Locke or whomever in a manner sympathetic to those thinkers, and then providing you with the tools to dissect the work in hand. He was less interested in offering his own position than in eliciting the positions of his students.

Patrick Masterson, later president of UCD, and later still president of the University of Florence, who taught me contemporary philosophy in my first year, was the youngest member of the UCD faculty. He was also the only lay person on the permanent staff. His lectures were models of lucidity. He had just graduated with a doctorate in metaphysics from Louvain University. His special interest was contemporary atheism and he was accordingly widely read in contemporary European philosophy. He had a different take on Wittgenstein's *Tractatus* than O'Doherty. Masterson's approach brought home to me the extent to which O'Doherty was determined to find points of metaphysical similarity between Wittgenstein and Aquinas. In mid-career, Paddy moved to administration and developed a reputation as a formidable university politician.

My impression of Masterson is that during the later years of university administration he lost his early appetite for speculative thought, but afterwards, as his well-received book *The Sense of Creation* (2008) clearly demonstrates, he recovered it. Academics who migrate to administrative pastures often lose their early scholarly passions. And, in an era when fund-raising has come increasingly to define the administrative function in universities, that is becoming more common. In 1999 when I recorded a conversation with the sociologist Anthony Giddens, then director of the LSE, I sensed that the pressures of the job were making clear inroads on his scholarly impulses. On the day following our encounter, he was due to fly to Hong Kong to help raise funds. I have not spoken to Giddens since, but Masterson has emerged remarkably unscathed from his brush with 'the suits'.

Denys Turner, like Masterson, was not a cleric. He wasn't then formally on the staff; he was a part-time tutor and my tutor in moral philosophy. We became good friends. He was then a member of Opus Dei and encouraged me to join. After a Saturday afternoon retreat at the organization's headquarters in Ely Place, Dublin, I decided that Opus Dei was not for me. Denys some years later left that organization and undertook an intellectual journey that would encompass Thomism, Marxism and mysticism. He now teaches medieval theology at Yale University, having previously held the Norris Hulse Chair of Divinity at Cambridge.

What really impressed me about Denys was his genuineness. He was the kind of searcher one expected more of in a university, particularly in a philosophy department. He was of great assistance to me because, in or around 1964, he gave me a copy of his master's thesis in moral philosophy, which he had just completed. It dealt with what for me was then becoming a central question, whether ethics could be grounded rationally. This was the famous question raised by G. E. Moore, who claimed that it couldn't. Conor Martin, in common with moral philosophers like Philippa Foot, argued that it could.

Proponents of the second view felt that Kant had driven too sharp a cleavage between facts and values. Turner's thesis, under the direction of the Dominican priest Fergal O'Connor, was in tune with the view that ethics could be given a rational basis. If I recall aright, central to Denys's dissertation strategy was the act of making explicit the particular theory of meaning that each competing view of the question presupposed. The idea that the good is rationally describable seemed to me then intuitively right, and still does.

The college lecturer I became most friendly with in later years was Father Paddy Bastable, who taught logic. In the matter of his understanding of life and learning, he impressed me more than anybody in the department. Paddy had a much less flamboyant demeanour than his fellow logician Feichin O' Doherty, but there was a depth to him, a wisdom, lacking in his more extrovert colleague. For one thing, Paddy was by far the more psychologically acute. His assessments carried a lot of authority precisely because of their disinterested character. He saw O'Doherty as essentially a supremely gifted advocate who could argue a case either way. It struck me that the Catholic church offered perfect career opportunities for such an advocate, who had no reservations operating within the system.

O'Doherty was clearly brilliant; what he lacked was a driving intellectual curiosity. I invited him in later years to do an interview about his intellectual interests, but he declined on the grounds that he had left all that behind. Even at my first meeting with him in 1962, I got little sense of a man passionately interested in ideas. Bastable, on the other hand, was not only fascinated by ideas, but maintained his scholarly interests to the end of his life. He was the first to alert me to the role of context in understanding. He said Einstein used to insist that it wasn't that he (Einstein) was cleverer than other physicists, but that he had made himself more familiar than they did with the context in which physicists worked.

Father Mike Nolan taught both scientific psychology and philosophical psychology at UCD. We tend to forget that psychology was part of philosophy until the end of the nineteenth century. The philosophical psychology Mike taught consisted of an exploration of the conceptual presuppositions of scientific psychology. He did so from a Thomist perspective, which meant that Aquinas's view of the human person prevailed. Mike had a double first from Cambridge in the Natural Sciences Tripos, majoring in experimental psychology. He also had a doctorate in theology from Rome. He did his best to breathe psychological life into Thomistic concepts like 'intellectus agens', and spoke more clearly than most about the idea of 'the soul'. Mike was clearly a thinker, no handicap in a philosophy department. There was also the quiet humour: a psychotic, he used to say, is someone who thinks that two and two are five; a neurotic is someone who *knows* that two and two are four, but is worried about it.

Mike had a deeply conservative cast of mind, which became more pronounced later in life. In fact, he amazed me on one occasion many years later by taking exception to the sexual content of a frivolous tabloid item I had presided over on a Sunday morning radio talk show. He wrote me a letter of complaint, saying the item had made him switch momentarily to the BBC. Also, I was surprised when I heard that he had prevented Richard Kearney, an internationally renowned expert in modern continental philosophy, from addressing the Psychology Society at UCD because of his 'liberal' views. These were inexplicable quirks in a man of such high intelligence.

Monsignor John Horgan held the chair of metaphysics. Although he was regarded by some as a tad dotty, he displayed an impressive clarity of mind in holding forth on the philosophical legacy of the early moderns, particularly Descartes, even though he did see him as engaged in a pointless and erroneous detour in the wake of Aquinas. Horgan seemed more pastor than don, and reputedly had little time for Feichin O'Doherty's flirtations with Freud and Frege. Rumour had it that the monsignor was the eyes and ears in the department of the Catholic archbishop, Dr. John Charles McQuaid. Whether true or not, he was a party line Thomist, but an excellent teacher.

Father Bertie Crowe was essentially a historian of ethical thought. He was a real charmer, and clearly knew his stuff, but his style of lecturing was not at all engaging. I was surprised when, just after the publication of John Rawls's major treatise on justice in the early 1970s, I asked Bertie if he had read it, and he said he wasn't aware of its existence. The explanation in all likelihood was that Bertie operated within an exclusively Thomist framework. Joseph de Finance, for example, whom he quoted regularly, is firmly rooted in that tradition. At Bertie Crowe's funeral Mass, Mike Nolan described him as a true humanist, with roots in the high scholasticism of the Middle Ages.

I discovered that my main interests focused on logic, ethics and politics. Metaphysics was a huge disappointment to me. I gathered later on that this was mainly because the teaching reflected what is called 'the manualist' Thomist tradition, rather than the writings of Aquinas himself. I skipped many of these lectures, partly because the timing didn't suit my changing broadcasting schedule, but more because I failed to get a sense of what key questions were animating metaphysics. The teaching methods of the lecturers didn't help. After all, as a child I had felt the pressure of what much later I came to know as the great Leibnizian/Heideggerian question: 'why is there something rather than nothing?' These lectures should have been more stimulating but, apart from hearing Des Connell on Malebranche, they weren't.

As I write, none of that early 1960s, UCD philosophy cohort is still alive apart from Masterson and Turner, both laymen. Of the ones who died, few got the attention they deserved by national media on the occasion of their passing. Inexplicably, neither Paddy Bastable nor Mike Nolan were accorded broadsheet obituaries. Feichin O'Doherty, who died in 1998, was. Not merely was he a key figure in Irish university life, he was also a significant one in the culture at large. Both Nolan and Bastable were outstanding teachers. Both retained early stirrings of inquiry longer than O'Doherty. They were conservative in outlook but with significant self-critical impulses.

In those years between 1962 and 1965 at University College Dublin, I was witness to the tail end of a highly intellectual clerical culture, nurtured in Oxford, Cambridge, Louvain, Maynooth and Rome. Not long afterwards, it would vanish from UCD for ever. It may have been legitimately lumbered with the reputation of a department under the thumb of a particularly hard-line Roman Catholic archbishop, Dr. McQuaid, but it was a department peopled by some of the most capable scholars of the time. The control that the archbishop sought to exercise over the department is regrettable, but, as I have already indicated, philosophy is such that, by definition, it doesn't ultimately lend itself to control. I registered for a degree, perfectly happy with the idea that the philosophy taught to that end had ecclesiastical approval, but I emerged from the experience as someone who wanted to cut loose from those same ecclesial moorings.

Most of my fellow students were attached to Clonliffe and other Catholic seminaries. Every day, en masse, they tied their bicycles to the railings of the UCD campus at Earlsfort Terrace. An orderly flock of black-suited, white-shirted adolescent clerics, eager or not as the case may be, to expand their intellectual horizons. I didn't get to know many of these students, because they tended to vanish quickly after lectures and seminars. I remember one particularly helpful student from Mount Argus seminary, who shared his notes whenever I missed an important lecture, but, like most of the others, Barnabas didn't hang around after classes.

One of the few clerical students who did stay around after class was Kevin Traynor, who was at Clonliffe. In addition, our paths tended to cross outside the college walls. He complained to me one day in Clare Street that Feichin O'Doherty was always talking *about* logic: Kevin wanted more straight logic. In fairness to Feichin, his brief was to concentrate on *philosophical* logic, which by definition takes you into a meta-logical terrain. Afterwards, Kevin went to Buffalo, New York to do a doctorate in metaphysics. I next met him a decade later at a talk on Blake at Trinity given by Kathleen Raine. Afterwards, Kevin and I adjourned for a drink to the nearby Lincoln Inn. Following up on Raine's lecture, we soon got to discussing matters like competing or perhaps complementary approaches to truth. He mentioned somewhat casually that he had actually found the truth, whereupon I may well have spilled my drink.

Kevin went on to say that this philosophy lark that he and I had apprenticed ourselves to was only two and half thousand years old. Before that you had the wisdom of the East, a tradition still alive. Kevin had met a Maharishi in New York, became converted to his way of thinking and was now converting others on Dublin's public transport. That was the first time I realized that an undue need for certainty is no respecter of intelligence: they did not come any brighter than Kevin. That occasion was the source of a simple but important insight for me: that the need for certainty is an emotional phenomenon, not an intellectual one. At a conference in Paris in 1981, Feichin O'Doherty told me that initially he had seen Kevin Traynor as his successor at UCD.

Eddie Hyland was another clerical student who stayed around after lectures. A remarkably clever young man from the north of England, he was then attached to Mount Argus seminary, run by the Passionists. He looked no older than sixteen. He first came to everybody's attention when the logic professor circulated an unsolicited paper that Eddie had written on 'logical form'. It was a stunning performance: nobody else was writing papers on such topics at the time. Come to think of it, no one was writing papers of any kind at the time. Eddie would hold forth on various topics with the kind of bewildering range of reference that indicated not just omnivorous reading but an exceptionally quick and retentive mind. After UCD, he studied at Trinity, was deeply influenced by Marx as a graduate student, and later wrote a fine book about democratic theory. He has been teaching in the Political Science Department in Trinity for most of his life.

John Dowling was a clerical student with the Divine Word Missionaries. I had more conversations with him than with any other student. Not merely was John a natural philosopher, he had the makings of a fine fiction writer and poet. A newsroom colleague of mine, Seán Purcell, remarked at the time that John's jottings reminded him forcibly of the poet Lawrence Ferlinghetti. There were expectations that he would write a philosophical novel à la Sartre. John became an academic and taught moral philosophy at University College Cork. I met him in the late 1970s. At that time I was reading Susan Haack's *Deviant Logic*, which addressed a question of great interest to me: whether or not the principle of non-contradiction was revisable. Well, said John: either it is or it isn't. Follow that.

So, for three years in the early 1960s I bused in from my home in Mount Merrion, an outer suburb on the south side of the city, to University College Dublin, which in an earlier incarnation had Cardinal John Henry Newman as rector, and later still James Joyce as a student. In the afternoon I made my way to the radio and television studios in Donnybrook. The time constraints meant the skimpiest of college lives: no time to read widely, let alone write term papers. What did help was post-class conversations with some very sharp students.

Little wonder that in due course I would lighten my workload to devote substantial time to further study. But for the next seven years, my workload would, in fact, become even more demanding. That change occurred straightaway because in late 1965, in addition to my newsreading duties, I was invited by producer Gerry Murray of RTÉ to present a six-month television series about Irish history.

Chapter 9

IRISH TELEVISION: THE EARLY DAYS

IRELAND DID NOT GET ITS OWN TELEVISION service until New Year's Eve 1961. Because of the close links between the existing radio service and the arrival of a younger sibling, it was quite a privilege to have begun to work in radio just as the new national television service was getting under way. One was ideally placed both to observe the new service and to be in line to work for it. The newsroom, which serviced both radio and television, was located in the new television building on the Stillorgan Road.

The new network attracted some outstanding talent from abroad but also some of the biggest chancers on the media planet. The staff canteen was home to a greater variety of dress and sexual orientation than had been seen in radio in over thirty years. Correction: than had been seen in *Ireland* in over thirty years. Gradually, a television uniform emerged, where the aim was to avoid as much as possible looking like an insurance agent or office manager. Even some of the reporters and sub-editors began to affect a sort of bohemian, fin-de-siècle appearance. But, within the decade, everything had congealed. Young directors who had once wandered around speaking only of Bergman, Fellini and *Cahiers du Cinema* now spoke of mortgages, pensions and life insurance.

The first television programme to make an impact at the beginning of the service was *Broadsheet*, a nightly magazine compilation, modelled on the *Tonight Show* on BBC. It was fronted by John O'Donoghue and Ronnie Walsh, and edited by P.P. O'Reilly. Among the programme's first directors was Jim Fitzgerald, one of the leading theatre directors of the day. John O'Donoghue soon became Ireland's first television personality because of nightly exposure from the inception of the new service. O'Donoghue had trained as a historian at University College Dublin and qualified as a barrister. He began as a radio announcer and around 1963 became editor of a Sunday evening radio current affairs programme *Newspoint*, to which he invited me to contribute interviews.

Broadsheet was a television programme that may well have attracted half the population as viewers. If so, the other half were appearing on it. Not as guests, I should add, but as interviewers. In the early days, the show must have featured every journalist working in Dublin. There was a reasonable chance that if you were passing by in the corridor and could string a few sentences together, you would be roped in to conduct an interview. No one could deny that the programme was innovative and experimental. Meanwhile, the two stalwart professionals fronting the show, O'Donoghue and Walsh, kept things on an even keel. Joining them were other regulars like the novelist Brian Cleeve, the radio announcer John Skehan and a young Guinness Brewery executive Al Byrne, older brother of rising television star Gay Byrne. Brian Farrell, an administrator at UCD and later an associate professor of politics there, was also one of these first television interviewers and would go on to become for decades RTÉ's main current affairs anchor.

Technical lapses in those frontier days were rare enough, but when they did occur they tended to be quite memorable. On one occasion, the composer Brian Boydell had been invited to interview the guitarist Julian Bream. The actual content of the piece has faded from my mind, but not the following sequel to their on-air conversation. When the interview ended, the sound, unfortunately, remained switched on. Unaware of that fact, Boydell, in his unmistakeable basso profundo, informed Bream that the interview was over and that they should both remain in their studio positions, while the camera panned silently over them. 'This is the part,' said Boydell, 'where we say rhubarb, rhubarb, rhubarb.' Quite.

One of the young television directors who had come to RTÉ in its very first year was Peter Collinson; he had been a television floor manager in Southampton. He learned his directorial trade in the new station and in 1969 directed *The Italian Job* with Michael Caine and Noel Coward in starring roles. In early 1962 he was a freshly minted television director assigned to *The World This Week*, a compilation of news stories, which I presented in alternate weeks with Terry Wogan. The opening months of television were quite treacherous: if you made a mistake in front of camera, you might never be heard of again. I saw it happen.

One particular Saturday night in either late 1962 or early 1963, I realized how close to the wind I had sailed. The programme was running short. Collinson instructed the floor-manager to tell me to keep talking for two to three minutes. Luckily, I had read a news feature article that day in *The Times* about President Kennedy's recent conversion to deficit spending and, with a few years study of economics behind me, felt confident enough to waffle to order. The point here is that to talk for a minute on television when you have to depart from a tightly scripted programme (which it was) is quite long; two or three minutes is an eternity.

When I emerged from the studio, quite shaken, I confronted Peter, who dismissed me with a wave of his hand. 'They all do it: Cliff Michelmore, Richard Dimbleby,' he said, rattling off the big BBC names of the day as broadcasters who would have taken a problem of that kind in their stride. This was heady stuff for a young lad who just two years before had spent his time poring over a bank ledger. What all that brought home to me is that the front of house person is always the one who gets screwed, rarely the director. If I had blown it, it would have been I, not Peter, who would have vanished. Peter had a theatre rather than a news background. This was equally true of Christopher Fitz-Simon, another young director occasionally assigned to the newsroom in those days. Their addition to the newsroom tended to give the place an altogether more glamorous air than it might otherwise have had.

For the first two years of the new television service, I remained a radio announcer/newsreader, moonlighting as television newsreader and news presenter. All that was to change when towards the end of 1963, the head of news appointed three of us (Charles Mitchel, David Timlin and myself) as full-time radio and television newsreaders. That represented a significant consolidation of my position within the network.

However, the head of news, Pearse Kelly, was none too pleased when I told him that before taking up the new position, I wanted to attend a month-long seminar in January 1964 in Salzburg; the topic was mass communications. The event was organized by the Salzburg Seminar in American Studies, a body set up in the postwar years to show off what was best in American culture, research and politics. The star academic name at the seminar was the psychologist Percy Tannenbaum, co-author with Charles E. Osgood and George J. Suci of *The Measurement of Meaning* (1959).

There were also two leading American journalists who gave lectures, Walter Goodman and Peter Bart, who both wrote on media matters for the *New York Times*. Peter Bart would later become vice-president in charge of production at Paramount Pictures and, later still, editor of *Variety*. The major talking-point at the seminar was the assassination and funeral of John Fitzgerald Kennedy which had occurred just two months before, particularly the dignity shown at the funeral by his widow Jacqueline. The topic tended to eclipse discussion of almost everything else. At that stage I had begun to take an interest in American affairs and in media analysis.

One of Tannenbaum's key maxims about media influence was that television, like other media, tends to reinforce whatever beliefs the viewers already have, rather than to change them. That idea is something of a commonplace now, but it was a novelty fifty years ago. Little did we realize in 1964 that forty to fifty years later, the U.S. television news environment would be become so polarized that the tendency of media to reinforce existing attitudes would intensify beyond recognition. The traditional news networks of ABC, CBS and NBC, whatever biases existed among their respective editorial staffs, made a serious effort at impartiality. Cable news channels like Fox and MSNBC are openly partisan. I have no data to indicate the inroads the cable channels have made on national opinion. Some argue that they cancel out one another.

In December 1965, a few months after I had completed my studies at UCD, Gerry Murray, a current affairs television producer, offered me a job presenting *The Course of Irish History*. It would be a 21-part series and would begin in January. The consulting editors were the historians Professors Theo Moody of Trinity College and F. X. Martin of UCD. The lectures were later published in book form by Mercier Press.

It seems extraordinary to me now that RTÉ would have chosen a professional broadcaster (a television newsreader) rather than a historian to front the series. After all, that great historian A. J. P. Taylor had by this stage dazzled British audiences with his lectures. But television was new to Ireland and the feeling at that stage was that only television professionals could handle the medium. Looking back, I think the producers should have asked each historian to present his particular lecture, but at the time I was delighted to get such an opportunity at that early stage of my career.

Each historian sent me their script beforehand. Having studied it carefully, I then visited each, discussed the script, and then, before leaving, read it to them to ensure they were happy with how I was interpreting their material. I had to make sure they were happy that I would convey their meaning as intended. It was a presentation/narration role, rather than a journalistic one, but one for which my broadcasting experience of newsreading had appropriately prepared me. Unfortunately, none of the historians lived in Tokyo, Moscow or even Berlin. The farthest I got was Cambridge to see Kathleen Hughes, an expert in early Irish Christian history; she was then at Clare College.

I was far less interested in Irish history or indeed European history then than I am now. As I get older I'm reading much more history than I did in my early years. As I write, I have the happiest memories of spending this past summer at the Widener in Harvard browsing in the medieval history stacks. I have a particular interest in historical sociology. I remember during *The Course of Irish History* series, Theo Moody, co-founder with Robin Dudley Edwards of modern Irish historiography, quizzed me one evening over dinner in his house about my intellectual interests. I told him I had just completed a degree in philosophy and logic, and had studied economics before that. Was I interested in history? I replied that at that point I was less interested in say the Irish famine than in the wider question of what patterns there were to famines generally. 'You're interested in historical sociology,' he said with commendable precision.

In later decades I would become more interested in trying to understand the *methods* that historians deploy in their work. R. G. Collingwood's *The Idea of History* (1946) was very helpful in providing a map of the terrain. In that book he indicates his approval of Lord Acton's famous injunction to historians to study problems not periods. Collingwood points out that scissors-and-paste historians study *periods* in the hope that something will emerge from all the data they collect; however, scientific historians study *problems*, and do so by first formulating a question before collecting the relevant data. In effect, Collingwood is saying to historians that before they begin to collect evidence, they need to do some thinking: it's a help to know what you're looking for.

The pattern may not have altered all that much in the intervening decades, but my recollection of the 1960s is that Dublin had an unusually high quota of interesting visiting speakers. John Bowman, later to blossom into a distinguished current affairs broadcaster and historian, who wrote a landmark book about de Valera and the Ulster question (1982), was then editor of two radio programmes called *Who's News* and *Topic*. John invited me to contribute interviews to both programmes. We shared an interest in architecture and planning, which was reflected in the choice of guests. These included Nicklaus Pevsner, the architectural historian, his student Reyner Banham, author of *Theory and Design in the first Machine Age* (1960) and Lewis Mumford, a leading authority on cities and urban planning. I was kept abreast of developments in architecture by my friend Fergal MacCabe, a highly informed architect, who later moved on to town planning.

Among the historians I met in the sixties were Arnold Toynbee and a great academic foe of his, Hugh Trevor-Roper (later, Lord Dacre). My encounter with Trevor-Roper in 1966 never quite got off the ground because in our preliminary chat I cited a book by the writer Ved Mehta that was anything but sympathetic to Trevor-Roper. Mehta was an Indian writer who authored *The Fly and the Fly Bottle* (1962), a series of portraits of Oxford philosophers and historians. The essays in the book had originally appeared in the *New Yorker*.

My recollection is that either in the Trevor-Roper profile or in the A. J. P. Taylor piece, Mehta had suggested that Trevor-Roper had used government influence to outmanoeuvre Taylor for the post of the Regius Chair of History at Oxford in 1957. My mention of the offending article caused Trevor-Roper to erupt in a manner that would rattle any inexperienced interviewer. 'I am absolutely furious with you', he said. 'Do you realize that I resigned from my London club because the writer of that article had been accepted as a member.'

Not merely had I pressed one of this distinguished don's sensitive buttons, I figured from his reaction that I had disturbed whatever neural nucleus held in place his entire psychological architecture. In Adam Sisman's splendid biography of Trevor-Roper (2010), he details the offending Ved Mehta article. What I had forgotten in the intervening forty-four years was that Mehta in his original article said he found Trevor-Roper cold and haughty, but had found Taylor 'beguiling'. Sisman says that Trevor-Roper believed he had been cast as 'the villain of the piece'.

The only other exchanges I recall from that encounter in 1966 are Trevor-Roper's outright dismissal of Arnold Toynbee's work, and his response to my raising the matter of John Sparrow's criticism in *The Observer* of Trevor-Roper's own 'conspiratorial' take on the Kennedy assassination. 'Sparrow', said Trevor-Roper, 'doesn't count'. Trevor-Roper's views had surfaced in a preface he had written for Mark Lane's *Rush to Judgement* (1966), which challenged the findings of the Warren Commission. Whether it was the combination of Mehta, Toynbee and Sparrow that did it, I know not, but it became clear that the great man had decided not to proceed with our recording. The location was Alexandra College, an elite girls school, then situated on Earlsfort Terrace in Dublin. Trevor-Roper had been invited to give a lecture there on 'The Revolt of the Netherlands in European History'. The headmistress of the day was completely bewildered, as I bundled up my newly bought Uher recording machine and walked out into the late September sunshine. A valuable lesson in those early days: no interview, no fee. Come to think of it, in a lifetime of broadcasting, nothing comparable has happened since.

I naturally took a more than average interest in this historian's subsequent career, and would be lying if I didn't admit to a feeling of acute *schadenfreude* when it became known that he had been duped by the forged Hitler diaries. Furthermore, in later years I found his anti-Catholic prejudice, as evidenced in, say, his *Letters from Oxford* (2006) to Bernard Berenson, quite offensive, even for someone as critical of the Catholic Church as I am. Bearing those letters in mind, I smiled when I learned in Sisman's biography about Trevor-Roper's 'creative' adaptation of sociologist Max Weber's celebrated theory about the rise of capitalism. Trevor-Roper transformed Weber's question as to why capitalism was created in *Protestant* countries in the sixteenth century into what he considered a more interesting question, namely 'why was capitalism *not* created in *Catholic* countries'. Reading that reminded me of historian John Vincent's brilliant one-liner: 'the sociologists provide the concepts; the historians get the peerages'.

Biographer Adam Sisman, while acutely aware of Trevor-Roper's failings, also draws attention to his good points: he could be very kind to students, regardless of their academic performance. In similar vein, Sisman quotes a letter from the Irish historian Desmond Williams to Herbert Butterfield, which is considerate in tone: 'I suspect his [Trevor-Roper's] tongue is more unkind than his behaviour, except where an extraordinary sensitive vanity is affected.'

Those interviews in the mid-sixties weren't all devoted to architecture and history. Quite a few were conducted with writers, musicians, movie directors and theatre guests. Edith Evans, the actor, Jonathan Miller, the director, and playwrights Tom Murphy and Paul Vincent Carroll were among those who featured. Among musicians were the cellist Mstislav Rostropovich and the pianist Julius Katchen.

The Edith Evans interview, which took place in her suite in Dublin's Gresham Hotel in 1965, was typical of that era in that it was a case of the interviewer travelling to visit the famous guest, rather than the guest coming to the studio. She was in Dublin to play Lady Gregory in a film about Seán O'Casey called *Young Cassidy*. Ms Evans, of course, was renowned at the time for having made the part of Wilde's Lady Bracknell her own. It was widely agreed that no one could deliver the famous 'A handbag?' line quite like Dame Edith. Who but she could prolong a single syllable across a myriad of octaves. When I raised that very matter, she engaged in a bout of mock horror with me. She startled a late arriving waiter with the line: 'I have a good mind to put you across my knee and spank you.' She was then seventy-eight; I was thirty-one.

To the best of my recollection, my meeting with Paul Vincent Carroll took place in a vacant radio studio. To that extent, it was atypical. He wrote *Shadow and Substance*, a play that, apart from its local success, ran on Broadway. At its centre is a cultivated Roman Catholic canon who has been educated on the European continent. The canon is now ministering in a rural Irish parish and trying to come to terms with a clerical culture less beholden to the life of the mind than he would like. One of the canon's more memorable lines is: 'I refuse to argue, because to argue is to assume equality.' The play is rarely performed nowadays.

In 1967, Jonathan Miller was directing Robert Lowell's *Benito Cereno* (a dramatization of Herman Melville's novella) at the Mermaid Theatre in London; he had already directed it at Yale University. Miller and I met at the Mermaid during a rehearsal break. However, what we spoke about was not that particular production but about his interest in Marshall McLuhan, at that time one of the most-talked about communications gurus in the world. Essentially, McLuhan claimed that new technologies altered the way we perceive the world, sometimes in a reductive way that seemed to be claiming that changing consciousness was *solely* a function of new technologies. Miller made it clear to me that even though he was planning to write a book about McLuhan, he was more interested in communications theory in general than he was in McLuhan, about whose theories he had serious reservations. Quite by accident recently, I picked up from my shelves a copy of Frank Kermode's *The Uses of Error* (1990). It contains an excellent essay about McLuhan, in which Kermode recalls the disagreement between the Canadian and Jonathan Miller. In fact, it was Kermode who commissioned Miller's book about McLuhan, which appeared in 1971. It was part of the highly successful 'Fontana Modern Masters' paperback series. It seems McLuhan was more stung by Miller's criticism than by anyone else's.

Kermode points out that Miller made explicit the Catholic component in McLuhan's thought and the manner in which McLuhan's appropriation of Catholicism undermined his claim of disinterestedness. Kermode, in an admirably even-handed fashion, acknowledges the merits of Miller's critique but also believes that McLuhan's line about consciousness ultimately being partly a function of changing technologies has been vindicated with the years. I believe Kermode was right in that assessment.

The interviews I recorded in the early and mid-1960s were part of my broadcasting apprenticeship. It was work I sought out and welcomed because it did not come within my remit as a radio and television newsreader. Whereas the interviews I did from the late 1960s onwards were recorded in a studio setting or in an acoustically suitable location, earlier work was always done on location, invariably in hotel bedrooms, conference rooms or private sitting rooms.

It would have been the primitive L2 recording machine that served my purposes in recording a piece with the playwright Tom Murphy, who even at that early stage had already achieved renown in the wake of an acclaimed East End of London production of *Whistle in the Dark*. I met the playwright through my close friend Tom Naughton. That was in March 1967, at the

Queen's Elm pub in Fulham. My first impression of Tom Murphy is one that hasn't changed in the intervening years. The x-ray alertness of the man to his immediate environment, and particularly to his interlocutors, was palpable from the beginning.

On the following night, Tom's wife at the time, Mary Hipsley, cooked an Italian meal for us at the Murphy home in Barnes. Then the next afternoon, I recorded a piece with Tom in which, among other things, he said that an Irishman has three mothers: his birth mother, the Virgin Mary and his country. Even though he's a superb interviewee (Tom Murphy and David Hare are probably the best playwrights I have seen or heard in interview), Tom for a number of years had ambivalent feelings about talking to interviewers.

In 1966 I heard Rostropovich play the Dvorak Cello Concerto at the Gaiety Theatre in Dublin. Afterwards, I spoke to him through an interpreter, whose name was Phillips. Since I had no reason to make a point of remembering the interpreter's name almost fifty years ago, the fact that I can recall it proves that there is a category of memory that functions independently of motivation or mnemonic prompting. Working through an interpreter is not ideal, but it was better than nothing. Anyway, I was still at the stage of being more concerned about my questions to the great man than with establishing a rapport. It takes a while to realize that rapport is everything.

Even in the mid-1960s, Julius Katchen had a legendary reputation as a pianist. I recall putting to him a question that would surface in later interviews I did with performers: how relevant was the personal culture of the performer to the interpretation of the work in hand. For Katchen, it was crucially relevant. After a gap of many years, I remember the way in which that prompt brought him alive: despite my championing of rapport in the previous paragraph, sometimes specific questions *do* matter.

Chapter 10

NEWSREADING CAN BE BORING

NEWSREADING WAS MY FIRST JOB IN Irish television. I devoted the best part of a decade to it until I quit in 1972 to do further study. It is one of the few low-risk jobs for broadcasters in television. Unless you lose control and suddenly begin to tell the viewers what you think, you are perceived sympathetically. The job carries no risks comparable to those, say, of a talk-show host, who may end up with an uncontrollable guest or, worse, an incoherent one. On that score, it never ceases to amaze me how little television or indeed radio guests realize the power they have in a live show.

In my time in the newsroom, because I tended to get bored with the nightly routine of news, I longed for something to go wrong. Then you could show your initiative, such as answering the desk phone with, 'I told you not to call me at the office'. My favourite fantasy line was: 'And that's the end of the news. Any questions?' When I left the newsroom after a decade, the first thing that struck me was how quickly we forget the long stretches of dull patches in news. We tend to think of it as one sequence of highs, but it isn't. From my time, the items that stand out are the assassination of President Kennedy, the death of Marilyn Monroe, the Aberfan disaster in Wales, and the assassinations of Martin Luther King and Bobby Kennedy. Bloody

Sunday in Derry in January 1972 was the last major story in my period as newsreader.

Charles Mitchel was RTÉ's very first television newsreader and accordingly always occupied a special position in the hearts of Irish viewers. He had for most of his life been an actor with the Gate and Longford theatre companies. He had been to Clongowes, an elite Jesuit boarding school, which had briefly housed James Joyce. He studied forestry at Trinity College Dublin but, to my knowledge, never pursued the subject further. Charles took the matter of correspondence with viewers and listeners much more scrupulously than either David Timlin or myself. In that regard he was the most professional of us, but David was the most meticulous preparer of a script. I became notorious among newsroom colleagues for leaving my scripts in make-up, mainly because I tended to get engrossed in conversations in the make-up room.

David Timlin and I liked nothing better than rearranging our duty roster so that we would be free to spend the evening drinking together. Our friendship revolved quite a bit around alcohol. We did most of our drinking in the nearby Merrion Inn or in Gleesons of Booterstown Avenue. David had worked in the *Irish Press* and moved into broadcasting via sound effects in the drama department. He had been a child actor and came from a family with long associations with the Dublin Grand Opera Society. He was wonderful company, full of good stories, an excellent mimic and, most important of all, a good listener. How well he told the one about the photographer covering a women's day out in north Yorkshire. As the photographer fiddled with his readings before taking a picture of the group, a woman was heard to say, 'What's he going to do, Mabel?' 'I don't know, Lucy, I presume he's trying to focus.' 'What, *all* of us?'

I was David's best man at his wedding in 1968, an occasion graced by a number of cabinet ministers, including Charlie Haughey. David's sister was married to Haughey's election agent, the solicitor Pat O'Connor. To my surprise, when I visited Haughey at his home in 2001 to discuss a radio programme, the first thing he referred to was my friendship with David Timlin.

What intrigues me from this vantage-point is how important those regular drinking sessions with David were to me then. Perhaps it was the sense of release from the high-tension job of nightly newsreading. These days, and indeed, for many decades now I have no interest whatever in sessions of that kind. I will take a glass of wine with a meal or a bottle of beer on a hot day, but that's it. When David Timlin got married, our nights on the town faded. I myself got seriously involved that year with Maireóg Golden. However, I continued a life of regular boozing, until early 1970, when I gave up alcohol. In fact, I abstained altogether for sixteen years. The days of wine and roses were truly over. I often recall what Pat Moynihan, a colourful U.S senator said after the death of JFK: 'We may laugh again, but we'll never be young again.'

It was in Groomes Hotel in Parnell Square, Dublin in April 1968, that I first met Maireóg Golden, then twenty-one. A daughter of Abbey Theatre actors Geoffrey Golden and Máire Ní Dhomhnaill, she herself had no interest in pursuing a career in the theatre. In fact, she seemed to be less interested in a job of any kind than in pursuing her three great interests: dogs, sketching and astronomy. Her originality of mind was palpable. The night we met I was chatting to the actor Donal McCann by the stairs outside the spacious back room in Groomes, opposite Dublin's Gate Theatre. Maireóg emerged from that room as if preparing to go home. I was instantly attracted. Off and on, we spent five years together that shaped us both in different ways.

Those were the nights of Dubonnet and soda
Of Mozart concertos, the young Leonard Cohen
O'Toole and McCann at the Abbey in Godot
Op Art shows at Hendriks, a weekend in Rome
The phone calls, the taxis, Mount Merrion Avenue
Shopping at Straneys, Sion Hill was next door
I got news of her death on my way to Stillorgan
Not far from the place that we used to call home.

Maireóg and I parted in early 1973, when she was twenty-five and I was thirty-eight. We had broken up before, but then mended our fences. This time we broke up for good. She died in August 2008, just forty years after we first met. She was only sixty-one. Her drawing of an Egyptian goddess on a wall of our Dublin flat is long gone by now but no more erasable from my mind than Maireóg herself.

The RTÉ newsroom, like newsrooms everywhere, had its share of heavy drinkers, but it wasn't an exceptionally boozy place, even by the relaxed standards of the time. Charlie Ward, who was chief sub on the radio desk, enjoyed approaching any one of us newscasters in the Merrion Inn and asking, 'Are you reading for me tonight, son? As we became well-known through television, this gave him quite a kick. Charlie had a wide range of knowledge, though at times he could overreach himself. I once asked him whom he would choose to design a new house for him. 'As long as it was designed by Courvoisier, I'd be quite happy.'

Another stereotype about newsrooms is their indifference to cultural matters, their lack of interest in ideas. Our newsroom didn't disappoint on that score. The view that anything that makes more than minimal demands on human intelligence is described in newsrooms throughout the world as 'waffle' is probably overstating the matter, but there is some element of truth in it. Newsrooms see not only arts departments as 'other' but even current affairs divisions. This has to do with years and years of conversations at the chief-sub's desk in which an ethos of 'nothing but the bare facts' is assiduously nurtured.

There were some remarkably cultivated journalists there in my time. Seán Cantwell, chief-sub on the television desk, spoke fluent Russian and had a deep knowledge of Soviet affairs. Seán Purcell, also on the television desk, was particularly well read in modern fiction and poetry. Norman Walker, on the radio desk, spoke fluent German and had a deep interest in classical music. I relied on Norman to get me new records at a good price through a contact he had in the trade. His thriftiness was legendary: it was rumoured he had flown to America on RTÉ meal vouchers. Eddie Liston had studied Middle Eastern languages, and Joe Doyle ancient classics. One of the most colourful characters of all was Ultan McElligott who once told me that he had gone to Edinburgh to read metaphysics under John Ellis McTaggart, 'but when I got there, the bloody fellow was dead.' Kevin O'Kelly, who specialized in religion and outer space affairs (travelling to the moon and so on) was known as 'urbi in orbit'. Kevin, who was one of the most gifted journalists around, gradually gravitated away from news to feature programme-making. In 1972 he was imprisoned for contempt of the Special Criminal Court for refusing to disclose details of the location of an interview he had conducted with the IRA chief of staff.

Though confined mainly to reading bulletins, I occasionally accompanied reporters on location. I once went with Ultan to the Hugh Lane Gallery in Parnell Square to a reception for the lord mayors of Ireland. The occasion was the publication of a book about regional affairs by the sociologist Jeremiah Newman, then president of Maynooth College and later bishop of Limerick. The idea was that Ultan would interview the author for a spot on that night's television news. What the news editor hadn't allowed for was Ultan's 'partiality to the drop'. As the afternoon progressed and Ultan shifted a drink from every passing tray (there must have been at least twenty waiters), he abandoned the author interview and instead decided to invite every passing waiter on stage for a public interview. As an appreciative crowd gathered around, Ultan really warmed to the task of interviewing those waiters hired to ply the assembled mayors of Ireland with strong drink.

Those waiters were now becoming stars in their own right. 'What is your name?' Ultan asked of some youthful hired hand. Ultan was by now getting pissed at an alarmingly rapid rate. The din in the Hugh Lane gallery was rising. 'I see,' said Ultan after he had asked the waiter his name. 'Mulcahy ... No, McGinty. Sorry, McClafferty. My goodness, nomenclature in this country can be so problematic.' The television news that night did not carry an interview about that new book on regional planning.

When I was presenting *The Course of Irish History* television series in the first half of 1966, I continued reading the evening news. That was reasonable enough, but one week I made the mistake of doing the television news on the evening of a full day spent in studio recording the history programme. Those day-long sessions on Fridays were gruelling because of rehearsals in addition to the final recording. One particular Friday after a day in the studio, I read the 6.00 pm news and then retired to the Merrion Inn for a beer and a sandwich.

Exhaustion began to set in. I thought a gin and tonic would help revive me. But a few minutes into the later evening bulletin, it began to have the opposite effect. I got through the bulletin, and few if any seemed to notice anything different. If they did, they may well simply have said, 'Andy looks a bit tired tonight.' No one in the news room commented. A family member thought my eyes looked odd. That was it, but it was a close call.

In 1967 I was invited by the head of news, Jim McGuinness, to present *Féach*, a new current affairs programme in the Irish language. He did so not because of my proficiency in the Irish language, but as part of a general policy at the time to make use of well-known news broadcasters to front programmes in the Irish language. The editor was John Ross, at heart a features man who revealed his true 'non-current affairs' colours during a week of the Watts riots in Los Angeles in 1968. Asked if we planned to feature the riots on our programme, John replied that we had covered the riots the previous week, indifferent to the fact that that particular outbreak had occurred in some part of Africa.

John hired George Hodnett, without whom no late night review in those days would be complete, to write a signature tune. The impossible brief that 'Hoddy' was given was that the signature tune should combine a feel for native values with a sense of the 'now', a sort of 'Faith of our Fathers' meets The Rolling Stones. Among the items I recall: the opening of the Peacock Theatre in Dublin and an interview with Máirtín Ó Cadhain, one of the greatest writers in the Irish language. What I particularly remember about Ó Cadhain was a session with him afterwards in the Montrose Hotel, a favourite RTÉ watering hole in those days. Breandán Ó hEithir, one of the leading television journalists of the period, also joined us. Both writers indulged my school-level command of the Irish language. That was quite a privileged occasion for me.

Joe Conneally and John Williams joined the team to relieve John Ross of the tedium of keeping up with current events. I had a soft spot for John Ross because he was the very first editor to commission radio interviews from me when I began that line of work in early 1962. Moreover, he was the first person to show me how to use the old L2 recording machine. John had the kind of grace and civility that would become much scarcer in Irish broadcasting. He was a great lover of women and connoisseur of the sensuous life.

In November 1967, I went to Moscow in the company of my close friend Tom Naughton, on the occasion of the fiftieth anniversary of the Russian Revolution. Tom had trained as an accountant and was then managing director of a liquor whole-sale business in Tuam, County Galway. We had known each other for a decade ever since first sharing 'digs' in Ballsbridge. This would be our second trip abroad together. The first trip to Munich also included the late Tony Phelan of the Bank of Ireland, but we disagreed so vehemently among ourselves that we vowed never to repeat the exercise. Yet here we were, Tom and I about to travel together again. There was a significant difference, though, on this occasion: this trip had been organized for us by Progressive Tours, a factor likely to eliminate personal disagreements about matters like, say, how long we should spend in Leningrad. As tourists neither of us had any trouble getting a visa. However, at that same time, my colleague Seán Duignan, one of the newsroom's star television reporters, couldn't get a working visa.

Knowing that I was definitely going to make it to Moscow, I suggested to Jim McGuinness that I avail of my tourist status to hire a crew in Moscow. I could then top and tail a piece saying 'Here in Red Square' etc. for the *Féach* programme. Jim opposed the idea, perhaps because he was uncomfortable with the mildly 'illicit' nature of deploying someone not equipped with a work visa, or maybe because I had asked for a fee. On the eve of my departure for Moscow, I found myself in the Irish Club in Eaton Square in London. There too was Seán Duignan ('Diggy') waiting to learn whether the Russian embassy in London would give him a visa. There was quite a buzz in the bar that November evening with various people preparing to head for foreign soil, be it New York, Moscow or Cairo. There was a group of well-known Irish artists there, among them the portrait painter Tom Ryan and the pianist Charles Lynch. I turned to Charles and asked him what his plans were. 'I'm going on tour'. Where does the tour begin? I asked. I was thinking it had to be Leipzig or Prague. 'I open in Ballinrobe', he said. I thought straightaway of the poet Patrick Kavanagh, whose faith in his local townlands of Ballyrush and Gortin was revived by the realization that it was from a local row that Homer made *The Iliad*.

On that trip to Moscow, Tom Naughton's passport designation was 'company director', normally a respectable passport description, but in that environment you couldn't be sure. I reckon the closest brush Tom had had with radical thought was reading the book reviews in the *New Statesman*. We were joined on the flight by a middle-aged American poet and a London trade union official. There was also a doctor and his wife from Liverpool. The American poet asked Tom and me if we were writers. The poet's categories of the human species were straightforward: you were either a writer or you weren't. For the duration of the flight the Irish duo played its favourite game of being neutral to everybody: you find out first the way the other fellow thinks, and then you can't go wrong.

This was the fiftieth anniversary of the Russian Revolution. We learned that up to sixty per cent of people on the streets of Moscow were from the provinces. Many of them stood in Gorki Street, gazing up at illuminated portraits of their leaders. Their dress was American-Depression style. Our hotel in Gorki Street was quite close to the Kremlin and Red Square. This was heady stuff. There we were, nodding knowingly in the foyer to delegates from Ethiopia and Peru. The joke, of course, was that neither Tom nor I were known to have notable leftward leanings, let alone communist ones. Our main interest was in observing the unfolding spectacle.

We made a quick trip to Leningrad before returning to Moscow for the formal celebrations. Leningrad I had thought of beforehand as an amber, autumnal city. I was right but the light was dull and murky. Not unexpectedly, a trip to the Hermitage was arranged for us. I still treasure a catalogue I bought there for the rouble equivalent of six pounds. There was a first performance of an opera set to Sholokov's *Quietly Flows the Don* at the Kirov Theatre. We had champagne and caviar during the intervals. The denizens of Leningrad not only did not erase the symbols of Czarist rule, they restored many of them.

At a certain point on the trip, the members of the group began to wonder who each tourist was. We began to speculate whether our fellow tourists were indeed genuine tourists or perhaps were travelling under cover of some kind. Remember, this was 1967, at the height of the Cold War. That middle-aged woman could be CIA? Did you see the way she reacted to such and such? The speculation ran riot when the two Irishmen were absent for a night and a day. The explanation was simple but a British journalist in the group was on the point of cabling London. It was the eve of and day of the major Moscow celebrations. What happened was that an Indian air pilot had invited Tom and me to a party at his hotel. The party lasted much longer than parties usually do. Then because of traffic and security regulations on the day of the celebrations, we were unable to join our party until late in the evening.

Parades are pretty much the same everywhere: visiting provincial delegations, brass bands, a strident public address system. I was surprised to hear 'decadent' Strauss waltzes on the PA system in the evening. By day, Red Square looked like any big market town; at dusk it was something else. The National Hotel, situated on the corner of Gorki Street and Marx Square, was the locale for our evening meal and subsequent revelry on the great day. At the hotel we met Tim Pat Coogan, then editor of the *Irish Press*. As the Russians rubbed their noses against the ground-floor windows, one of our number, a Surrey-born Russophile, insisted on joining the locals outside: he felt guilty about enjoying good food inside. The American poet and I were later conducted to the Writers Union.

Anthony Haden-Guest, the British writer, was in our group. There were rumours some years ago that Haden-Guest was a model for the drink-sodden British journalist in Tom Wolfe's *A*

Bonfire of the Vanities (1987), but I gather Wolfe insists that the prototype was someone else. At any rate, Haden-Guest wrote pieces in those days à la Wolfe's New Journalism. In recent years he has focused on New York's visual arts scene. He's both a collector and a critic. That particular interest goes way back: when Tom Naughton and I and called to see him in his King's Road pad in 1968, I spotted a copy of Harold Rosenberg's *The Anxious Object* (1964), a voguish book of the time. That same day Haden-Guest introduced us to his neighbour, Richard Neville, the founder of *Oz* magazine. When we were shown around the Kremlin, the guide remarked that the eighteenth-century French painter François Boucher had been commissioned to paint the doors of royal coaches. That prompted Haden-Guest to reply that that was rather like asking Picasso to paint a refrigerator.

I did not visit Moscow again until November 2005. On that occasion, the historian Judith Devlin, an expert in nineteenth-century Russian history, had recommended me as a speaker at a conference there about national memory. It was a gathering of Irish and Russian historians and journalists organized by the Irish Embassy in Moscow. Apart from the stimulus of encountering a wide variety of Russian intellectuals, it was an opportunity to meet up with old friends like historians Dermot Keogh of UCC, Vincent Comerford of NUI Maynooth and Paul Gillespie of *The Irish Times*.

One is always slow to infer national characteristics on the basis of limited data, but that never stops us. There was a palpable difference in the comparative presentation styles of the two countries at that seminar in 2005. The Russians weren't as yet all that partial to the notion of dialogue. Here was a culture not comfortable with the practice of questioning. It is not that Irish contributors did not deliver lectures as such, but we were much more attuned to the idea of being challenged. Another way of expressing this is to say that the Russians on that occasion not merely went on a bit, but gave the impression that they did not welcome interruptions.

I dare say many of us who in 1967 attended the fiftieth anniversary of the Russian Revolution assumed that there would be a hundredth anniversary of it in 2017. Few would have predicted the collapse of the Soviet system in a little over twenty years. The country to which I returned in 2005 had of course changed but not beyond recognition. I felt freer there than I did thirty-eight years before, but was still wary: despite the thawing of relations between Russia and western countries, one still had a sense of being watched.

Chapter 11

WHAT GREAT TALK SHOW HOSTS HAVE IN COMMON

SHORTLY AFTER I RETURNED FROM MY trip to Moscow I met the then leader of the Irish Communist Party, Mick O'Riordan, in an RTÉ television studio. He was being interviewed about a housing issue in the city of Dublin. When I told him I had been to Moscow, he said it was a pity he didn't know I was going there: he could have arranged for me to meet 'some of the lads'. That drew a smile to my lips: it was as if he were talking about members of a poker group. The remark indicated to me that he had assumed that my decision to travel to Moscow for the fiftieth anniversary of the Revolution was a gesture of solidarity on my part, and not an act of sheer curiosity, which it was.

In those days, I was beginning slowly to develop a genuine political awareness, thanks mainly to a group of politically radical theologians who came to speak to a post-Vatican II discussion group in Dublin. I have written earlier about these priest-theologians, who were British and attached to the Dominican monastery of Blackfriars in Oxford. The main speakers were Herbert McCabe and Laurence Bright. McCabe was a theologian who had one of the finest philosophical minds I have ever come across.

In so far as there was a visible political left in the television centre in the late 1960s, it revolved mainly around Eoghan Harris, a newly minted producer/director, and Jack Dowling, a much more senior producer/director. Harris was a clever, fast-talking history graduate of University College Cork, who electrified many a gathering with the occasional impromptu address. Since those days, Eoghan has gone through a number of well-publicized political *bouleversements*, but in the 1960s he was an unadulterated Marxist of the old school. None of your newfangled Althusserian guff; just his Master's Voice unadorned. As a result, I believed for years that Marx himself must have spoken with a Cork accent. It was Eoghan who in his play *Souper Sullivan* gave us what is one of my favourite lines in modern Irish drama: 'The Irish are a very Christian people: they always ask, "who is my neighbour and what is he doing now?"'

Jack Dowling, an ex-army officer and born philosopher, could be categorized as 'old left'. As could Jim Fitzgerald, a theatre director then working in television; James Plunkett, television director and author of *Strumpet City* (1969); and former BBC producer Chloë Gibson, then head of drama at RTÉ. I perceived Lelia Doolan and Bob Quinn as 'individualist' left. Seán Ó Mordha, a young director who subsequently won international acclaim for documentaries about Joyce and Beckett, was not as overtly political as the others, but would have shared their growing concern that commercial pressures would ultimately undermine the making of high-quality programming.

Having listened to what the visiting Dominican theologians had to say, I was beginning to find great merit in socialism, and could see the inescapable links between it and Christianity, but my politics were far from fully formed. At best, they were of the armchair variety: I never felt the need to join a political grouping or party. I was, however, increasingly alive to the congruence of political views between the visiting theologians and sections of the producer corps in the television centre.

Jack Dowling had the intellectual vigour of a young graduate student. Whether he was discussing Merleau-Ponty in the Merrion Inn or Marx in the television centre, Jack became so animated, your attention couldn't but be held. Moreover, he was willing to suspend all conventional beliefs in the interest of keeping a discussion in play. I remember saying to him one day, 'Jack, if Marshall McLuhan is right, then metaphysics is dead.' 'Exactly,' said Jack. He probably didn't believe a word of that; he was simply encouraging me to continue. When Jack died in 1977, the politician and historian Conor Cruise O'Brien paid him a most perceptive tribute. Among the things O'Brien said were that Jack had a way of looking at you that was particularly difficult to decode: you were unsure whether he regarded what you had just uttered as a profound insight or as utter rubbish. That observation was spot on.

Lelia Doolan typified the intellectual restlessness that characterised sections of the network in the late 1960s. Equipped with a degree in modern languages from UCD, she had studied Brechtian theatre with the Berliner Ensemble, and was deeply interested in ideas. Actor, director, producer, thinker and programme executive, Lelia made a key editorial contribution as founder and editor of the *Seven Days* current affairs programme. A year after she had quit RTÉ in the late 1960s because of concern over the network's undue reliance on advertising, I met Lelia at an international philosophy conference on phenomenology at Trinity College, Dublin. 'I think I am getting the hang of the difference between metaphor and analogy,' she confided on that occasion. It was, I suppose, a change from a life precoccupied with shooting schedules and programme budgets. Lelia later became artistic director of the Abbey Theatre, qualified as an anthropologist and continued film-making. She was a very rare breed, even among the unusual mix that a newly emerging television station attracted. Pat McInerney, a Dominican priest, had studied theology at the Saulchoir in

Paris, and then trained as a television producer at CBS in New York.

When Lelia Doolan, Jack Dowling and Bob Quinn resigned from RTÉ in 1969 because of their unease with the increasingly commercial ethos that was beginning to infiltrate the network, they wrote a book with the wonderful title *Sit Down and Be Counted* (1969). The late sixties was a heady period in Irish television, marked by turbulent meetings in the canteen which were in tune with the world-wide student unrest of the period. It was an exciting time for someone like myself who was drawn to the discussion of ideas, but in my case there it ended. At that point, I had all the timidity and caution of your average public servant. There was no way that I would have sacrificed my job in the way that Lelia, Bob and Jack did.

Some months before the resignations, Eoghan Harris, then closely associated with the three producers, asked me to chair a meeting at Liberty Hall, the Irish trade union centre, with the stated objective of setting up a new organization for producers. All I remember of that first meeting was that Jack Dowling had said to us that the only principle that should govern the inauguration of the producers' union was that there should be no principles. Jack was having one of his Nietzschean moments.

A few weeks earlier I had attended a meeting of network staff at the Gresham Hotel, which was addressed by Raymond Williams, then Professor of English Literature at Cambridge and a prominent radical scholar. His thinking was very much in accord with the ideas of the dissident producers. Looking back on it now, it is clear that Lelia, Jack and Bob were quick off the mark in striking an early blow for the values of public service broadcasting in a battle that would eventually be won hands down by commercial interests.

The problem for producers in a system with dual funding like that of RTÉ (that is, with money from government *and* from commercial advertising) is that if up to half of the revenue comes from advertising, then advertisers have a major influence on programme content. Advertisers are interested essentially in high ratings. To keep them happy, programme-makers are obliged to concentrate on material that appeals to the lowest common denominator. The extent to which programme schedules are compromised by having to marginalize the kind of material that attracts smaller audiences has increased gradually over the years. In the late 1960s that trend was beginning to make itself manifest; it now defines the character not just of commercial television but of public television as well.

In the autumn of 1968, RTÉ's radio hours were extended. This meant more work opportunities for broadcasters. Donncha Ó Dúlaing, newly appointed head of radio features, asked me to edit and present a weekly arts programme called *Focus*. What was really new for me at that point, and quite significant, was the element of personal editorial involvement. Up to that point I had contributed interviews to programmes edited by others; now I was getting an opportunity to help decide on overall content. I was taken aback when a psychiatrist friend, Dr. Eimear Philbin Bowman, congratulated me on this new development, adding that now I could have all my friends on air, but, in truth, I never thought like that: my main concern was that we get the best person for each task.

Donncha Ó Dúlaing was an enterprising radio executive, whose real heart was in on-air presentation. He is easily the most underestimated radio interviewer in the business. Donncha has a unique way of getting people to talk. I was so fascinated by an interview he did with Frank Patterson about the tenor's experience of working with John Huston on the filming of the Joyce story 'The Dead' that I made a point of asking Donncha how he had brought Patterson to such a level of animated engagement. He probably didn't know himself. I suspect it had something to do with Donncha's own level of engagement.

One of the most embarrassing moments attached to the first season of the arts programme *Focus* in 1968, was a meeting that producer Diarmuid Peavoy and I had with Terence de Vere White, novelist, historian and literary editor of *The Irish Times*. We had hoped to commission him to do reviews for *Focus*. The meeting was careering to a climax after we had all shared our various literary enthusiasms and felt we could work well together. Suddenly Terence asked what used to be called the $64,000 question: what's the fee per review? Terence was a seasoned professional, which meant that the idea of proposing to him that exposure on the airwaves was a compensatory factor would not be a runner. I can't remember how much we offered him, but it became clear that it was less than half of what he had in mind. To borrow from Browning's poem about the last duchess: 'Then all smiles stopped together'. Remember, both Diarmuid and I were then new to the world of programme-making; at that stage my broadcasting experience had been confined to radio and television presentation. So this was an unfamiliar terrain for us both. We left the Pearl Bar in Dublin duly chastened.

The programme style of *Focus* was a compound of direct reviews of a play, book or film, and one-on-one interviews. The straight review has tended to fall out of fashion, but there is a lot to be said for a scripted piece by a perceptive reviewer. I recall a review by Sean O'Faolain of a book about the short story. That we selected one of the world's leading practitioners of the form suggests that we aimed high, and we did, despite our rebuff at the hands of the literary editor of *The Irish Times*. A subsequent literary editor of *The Irish Times*, a then unknown John Banville, came into studio in 1970 to talk to me about his first published book, *Long Lankin*. A mere fifteen years later, the managing director of Secker and Warburg would assure me that Banville was Nobel Prize-winning material.

Dominic O'Riordan, who loved to say, 'Like Aristotle, I don't have a degree in philosophy', was one of our best reviewers, when he turned up. He was particularly good on the anthropology of north Kerry in his discussion of John B. Keane's play *The Field*. That great Beckett interpreter Jack McGowran was the subject of one of our interviews, as was the painter Norah McGuinness. It was during the McGuinness interview that I had my first broadcasting 'peak' experience, this one a humbling one: the realization that once I had got Norah going, there was no further need for me in studio.

A review of a film about Woodstock was the first indication that the programme was moving towards the inclusion of discussion items. Woodstock was a three-day music festival held in 1969 in New York state. It has become a much-remembered moment in the history of Rock and Roll. A 1970 documentary film based on the event had won an Academy award. This was an opportunity for *Focus* to discuss the ideas that were animating the American counterculture. Other items that took a discussion format were Tom Murphy's play *Morning After Optimism*, with Seán MacRéamoinn characteristically insisting on the distinction between optimism and hope.

The Abbey drew some stellar power in those days. Colin Blakely starred in *Morning After Optimism*; Peter O' Toole and Donal McCann in Hugh Hunt's production of *Waiting for Godot*; and Ray McAnally played Macbeth. Peter O'Toole turned up again at the Gaiety Theatre in 1969 with Siobhan McKenna, Jack McGowran and Jim Norton in *Juno and the Paycock*. I was a regular theatre-goer anyway, but arts coverage meant that I saw more than I usually would.

Kenneth Tynan, the illustrious theatre critic, was a writer whose first book I discovered while working in the Bank of Ireland in Listowel, County Kerry in the mid-1950s. I was already full of admiration for his reviews in *The Observer*, but it was only when I borrowed *He That Plays the King* (1950) from the local library that I became fully aware of how unique a critic he was. He was scarcely down from Oxford when he wrote it.

The book was an eye-opener for a twenty-year-old bank clerk in rural Ireland.

Tynan doesn't have many contemporary equivalents, though John Lahr's name springs to mind, as does A. A. Gill's, television critic of the *Sunday Times*. One of the earliest Tynan reviews I remember, began: 'This is the worst production of Shakespeare I have ever seen; I say that, I, who have seen the full Wolfit company not once but many times'. His elucidation of the difference between Olivier's romantic and Gielgud's classical style of acting will still be read with profit in a few hundred years. Tynan was as much aficionado as critic. Still, his hero worship never got in the way of the slighting put-down. He had the temerity in his early twenties to savage Orson Welles's *Othello*, even though Welles had written the preface to *He That Plays the King* (1950). It was a surprise when Tynan abandoned theatre criticism to become literary manager of The National Theatre, at the invitation of Sir Laurence Olivier. The consensus at the time was that it was an astute move by Olivier to silence Tynan the critic. Tynan loved to relate that one of the first manuscripts sent to him at the National was set in a period 2000 years before the birth of Christ, and that the second act took place two weeks later.

Tynan came to Dublin in the late autumn of 1968 as co-producer of *Soldiers,* a play by Rolf Hochhuth about Churchill. We arranged to meet at a pub beside the Olympia Theatre about an hour before rehearsal time. It is not uncommon to be disappointed when you meet your heroes. It may have been that rehearsals for the Churchill play weren't going all that smoothly, but Tynan had an air of taciturn cautiousness about him. He seemed all pallor and shiftiness that evening. Subsequent diaries and memoirs in the intervening years have portrayed Tynan as something of a dedicated voluptuary, but that autumn evening in 1968 the man I and my girlfriend Maireóg Golden met had the air of a wan ascetic.

At that stage, Tynan had become better known for his pro-files of performing artistes than for his reviewing. I recall fine pieces about Miles Davis's *duende* and Eric Morecambe's patter ('Would you like a pork pie, or would you like to die naturally?'). The most recent profile I had read was of that doyen of all talk show hosts, Johnny Carson, about whom Tynan had written a long piece for *The Observer*. What was it that made Carson so unique, I asked him, expecting from Tynan a masterful analy-sis of one of the twentieth-century's television greats. The best Tynan could do that evening was to say that Carson could think on his feet faster than anybody else. I recently came across a piece by Peter Conrad which says Tynan's profile of Carson is nothing but puffery. That judgement would chime with Tynan's seeming lack of interesting things to say about Carson on the night we met. I don't agree though that all his profiles lacked in-sight: those of Miles Davis and Eric Morecambe certainly don't.

As to what made Carson (and a handful of other talk show hosts) so great, there is a school of thought which speaks of an inverse correlation between an individual's capacity to success-fully master a television talk show and their capacity to enjoy social gatherings. The suggestion here is that the best talk show hosts are those who are least comfortable in ordinary social situations. Dick Cavett is on record as saying that Carson was always the shyest man in the room; he tended to huddle in a corner with his side-kick Ed MacMahon. The argument here is that these star hosts use the talk show as a substitute for ordi-nary social interaction. The very energy that does not get free rein in private explodes on to our television screens. This is an idea with immense intuitive appeal. I first heard it floated fifty years ago by the American psychologist Percy Tannenbaum.

Gay Byrne, a master of the talk show trade, while he is clear-ly not ill-at-ease in ordinary social situations, does not seem to revel in them. What is certain is that he is never more himself than when on the box. Before and after is a different matter.

The novelist Jilly Cooper used a striking image when speaking to me about Gay in the mid-1980s. She had guested on *The Late Late Show* the night before. She said that Gay had entered her dressing room like 'a surgeon on the night before an operation'.

I recall meeting Gay one night in the early 1980s at a party at the American ambassador's residence in Dublin's Phoenix Park. It was given by the then ambassador William Shannon and his wife Liz. Eamonn Andrews, who was still presenting *This is Your Life* on British television, was also one of the guests. To my surprise, Gay acted as compere for the entertainment segment of the evening. I was intrigued to see a professional broadcaster in this role on his night off, until I heard someone speculate that perhaps that was his way of avoiding social interaction. It was an interesting explanation.

I have spoken already of my interest in Kenneth Tynan's work, an interest shared by the late Donal McCann, and indeed many other actors. Donal came to my flat on Mount Merrion Avenue, Blackrock, one night in the late 1960s after a few drinks in Groomes Hotel. The poet Eavan Boland, who had joined us in Groomes, also came along. There was the customary chat about current plays and books. Then it moved on to a more general discussion about the the role of art in life. McCann was more listener than talker on those occasions. When someone spoke of art as 'ordered symbolic orgasm', Eavan's response indicated that we all had had too much to drink.

We listened to some music before breaking up for the night. On his way out, Donal borrowed a copy of *Curtains* (1961) by Kenneth Tynan. Nothing unusual in that. What was unusual was that a month or so later he returned it to me at the television studios. He had the reputation of being a bit of a hell raiser, finally ratified when he and Peter O'Toole teamed up on and off stage in *Godot* at the Abbey Theatre in 1969 in a production directed by Hugh Hunt. That returning of the book, though, bespoke a quality of discipline as well, presumably of a piece with the kind of discipline that made him one of the great Irish actors of the twentieth century.

I bought my first painting in 1965 at the Dawson Gallery in Dublin. It was an Austrian landscape by Brian Bourke and it cost me fifty pounds. Leo Smith, the owner of the gallery, was one of the most skilled dealers I've ever watched. One of his favourite ploys was to try to whet a client's appetite for a particular painting by deliberately putting them off. One afternoon in my presence, a well-heeled estate agent expressed interest in a painting from a current exhibition. Leo's immediate response was to say, 'You don't really want that painting', whereupon the intending purchaser became even keener to buy it. I am not suggesting that line of Leo Smith's is a surefire ploy, but it certainly worked on that occasion. The art of selling has always fascinated me. A master of the trade once told me that the secret was to let the potential buyer believe that he or she was controlling the transaction.

Apart from Brian Bourke's Austrian oil landscape, I also bought one of his drawings. Brian was then mounting his first exhibition. I bought a few pictures and some sculpture over the next few years, but ceased doing so in 1972, following my decision to cut my workload significantly. I had purchased lithographs by Vasarely, Appel and Ballagh at the Hendriks Gallery, a Kane lithograph (purchased directly from Michael Kane himself), two pieces of sculpture by Gerda Fromel at the Dawson, and a sculpture by John Behan at the Project Gallery.

In the late sixties, I first met the art critic and artist Brian O'Doherty, who had returned to Dublin from New York to give a public lecture. A few years later in 1972 he changed his name to Patrick Ireland and pledged to retain that name until the British army withdrew from Northern Ireland and all citizens were given their civil rights. Following the Belfast Agreement in 1998 he dropped the assumed name. The act of name change was presented as a piece of 'performance' art, and therefore as an artist's imaginative response to the Northern Ireland conflict. It also ran the risk of being interpreted as a piece of sixties' drawing room Che-Guevaraism.

Born in County Roscommon, O'Doherty trained as a doctor and emigrated to the U.S. in the 1950s, where he gravitated to art criticism. When I first met him, he had written for the *New York Times*, broadcast for NBC, and was editing the periodical *Art in America*. In those pre-internet days, I felt privileged to be getting the inside track on the New York art scene, which had by then supplanted Paris as the centre of the art world. Abstract expressionism, which, thanks to the polemical talents of critic Clement Greenberg, had dominated postwar art in America, was now giving way to competing strands. Brian was highly articulate and generous with his knowledge. He was also a modest fellow: it was only much later that I learned of his friendship with major artists like Mark Rothko, Marcel Duchamp and Edward Hopper. Both Duchamp and Hopper had dedicated art works to him. I recently saw a French documentary about Hopper to which O'Doherty and Wim Wenders were the most insightful contributors. Brian O'Doherty was a friend of the composer and painter Morton Feldman. One of the prevailing orthodoxies of the time associated with minimalists like Feldman was that an art work shouldn't shout at you, merely whisper. O'Doherty had also known Jack B. Yeats, who consented that the younger man should do a portrait of him. Brian subsequently donated the drawing to the National Gallery of Ireland.

On the occasion of Brian's visit to Dublin in 1969, we went to the Shelbourne Hotel, where he indicated a preference for a hamburger at the bar rather than a formal lunch. The more informal choice suggested that after life in Manhattan, he was finding Dublin in those days on the formal, buttoned-up side. He asked me if people smoked pot in Dublin. No, I told him, they just got legless via other means. Still, it was an innocent city even in the late sixties. The impression Brian gave of New

York was one of treacherous quicksands, where everybody anxiously wondered what the next major development would be. It was not yet the big bucks scene it would become. I heard a New York dealer say in interview not too long ago that the narrative of western art was now solely about money. No kidding. He said that when Jasper Johns, on whose behalf he acted, had first earned a million dollars for a picture, Johns said, 'That's it; it's now about money.' Not that he was complaining. The 1960s art world that Brian O'Doherty sketched so comprehensively was, as yet, comparatively free of that. Abstract expressionism had by then given way to pop art, minimalism, and conceptualism, which three movements were now slugging it out for temporary supremacy.

Arthur Danto in *After the End of Art* (1997) argues eloquently, if not altogether convincingly, that pop was the most significant of the new art movements in the 1960s because of the kind of philosophical questions it raised about the nature of art itself. On that very point, I recall that O'Doherty was then in hock to the idea that art was not really about life: it was about itself, self-referential. As for Danto's claim that the questions pop art raised about the nature of art were more significant than those raised by conceptualism, I am not convinced. Danto talks a good game, though. As does Brian O'Doherty, who was a breath of fresh air in 1960s' Dublin; full of ideas and a really gifted talker. The city at that point still had something of the insularity of the early post-war years.

In New York, aspiring artists, according to Brian, were beginning to talk for the first time, not of being a painter or sculptor, but of 'making art.' Conceptual art, in particular, shifted the emphasis to the artist as thinker rather than doer; designer rather than craftsman. Brian O'Doherty and his wife, the art historian Barbara Novak, once invited Marcel Duchamp, the founding father of conceptual art, to their New York apartment for dinner. O'Doherty's own contribution to conceptual art that evening was making a piece that consisted of measuring Duchamp's heartbeat and taking a photograph of it.

As for conceptual art, which is essentially about the privileging of ideas over execution, I have never been fully engaged by it, deeply interested though I am in ideas. It is as if an architect's blueprint for a building takes precedence over the construction of the building itself. Oddly enough, when you see the retrospectives of giant architects like Frank Lloyd Wright or Mies van der Rohe, what always strikes you is the number of their projects that were never built: all you see are the blueprints. As of 2010, of twenty airports designed by Norman Foster, only four were built. To complicate matters, there is also today a category of architecture called *conceptual* architecture.

O'Doherty in those days radiated a 'prescriptive' attitude towards art, meaning that he sounded impatient with art that did not conform to what was then acceptable to the small coterie to which he belonged in New York. He seemed to be a lover and champion of 'the new', which at the time amounted to an amalgam of conceptualism and minimalism: it is the idea that matters; and when you're at it, remember less is more. Not merely was the School of Paris deemed dead; so too was abstract expressionism. I have always been fascinated by how persistent, through so many fields, the idea of the normative, of the prescriptive, of the idea of the one true faith, is. The assault on modernism was meant to rid us of it, but it didn't.

The only reference Brian made to the commercial side of the art world was to ask me if it were true that Sir Basil Goulding, then one of Ireland's leading art patrons, had sold off all his Irish art. Today, almost fifty years on, a corresponding conversation would probably discuss nothing but sales prices. It wasn't until well into the 1970s that I became alert to the market aspect of the Irish art world. For example, it became known that when Terence de Vere White sold his art collection in 1978, it realized

£100,000. While not a fortune even in those days, it was a considerable sum, particularly when one bears in mind that he had bought the work for sheer pleasure, and not for investment.

I didn't see Brian O'Doherty again until the late summer of 1976, when I had dinner with him and Barbara at their upper West Side apartment. Among their guests were Stuart Schulberg, then producer of NBC's *Today Show,* and his wife, and the writer Richard Grenier and his wife. Also present was my companion Michaela O'Brien, whom I first met at Trinity College, Dublin in 1974/75 and who was then a graduate student at the University of Georgia. There was less talk on that occasion about the visual arts in New York, though Brian did make a slighting reference to Tom Wolfe's *The Painted Word* (1975), which had come out the year before. The gist of his remark was that painters, critics and dealers in New York dismissed Wolfe as an interloper. Most of the chat that August evening was about film, arts administration, and the implications of a possible upcoming Jimmy Carter Presidential victory for the life of cultural institutions in America. Brian later worked as an administrator for the National Endowment for the Arts. He also wrote an influential essay for *Artforum* at that time that would eventually surface as the nucleus of his book *Inside the White Cube: The Ideology of the Gallery Space* (1976). It is a study of the manner in which architectural space affects the art shown in it and, how, in turn, the art shown affects the architectural space. As a measure of how well *Inside the White Cube* has weathered the years, the architect and designer Edwin Heathcote, writing in the *Financial Times* in 2011, argued that nothing written on the topic in the intervening thirty-five years had come close to the penetrating nature of O'Doherty's book. My overall impression of Brian is that for all his many-sidedness as artist, novelist, curator, administrator, he is primarily a gifted writer about art.

I moved from Mount Merrion Avenue in Blackrock in early 1970 to Wilton Place, close to the canal off Baggot Street.

This was near my first accommodation in the area, a good old-fashioned 'digs' in Percy Place. The cultural high altar of this district was Parsons Bookshop on Baggot Street Bridge, run by the Misses King and O'Flaherty. They had ministered to a galaxy of writers from Patrick Kavanagh to Brendan Behan to Liam O'Flaherty, Frank O'Connor and John Montague. The painter Michael Kane lived in Waterloo Road; the broadcaster and historian John Bowman in Pembroke Lane. The historian Frank D'Arcy used to refer jokingly to Parsons as one of the last bastions of western civilization.

The Economic and Social Research Institute, ESRI, was nearby, as was the Irish Tourist Board. The staff at these institutions (plus many at UCD) were regular patrons of Parsons, as were those architects and senior civil servants who worked in the area. Parsons was always renowned for its comprehensive section on architecture. This unusual bookshop relied heavily on recommendations from all these nearby erudite sources.

One of the founders of the ESRI and also of the Central Statistics Office, the statistician Roy Geary, lived in the same block of flats as I did. When I told him once that I was thinking of embarking on a piece of academic research at Trinity, he told me he had just one piece of advice: keep it as confined as you can. I hadn't the heart to tell him what an unwieldy project I had in mind. However, Roy Geary was a dedicated research scientist; I was no more than a well-read critical reviewer, reaping the benefits of the hard-earned, front-line research of others.

Also living in that same block was the novelist Liam O'Flaherty, who had achieved international fame with the filming of *The Informer.* He lived in the apartment overhead. I could hear the reverberations of the whiskey bottles he dropped down the shute that connected our apartments. Why had he left Paris, I once asked him. Answer: towards the end of his stay, he could find no one to talk to. O'Flaherty grew up on the Aran Islands, on an island off an island. He lived in Paris for years, but never really warmed to the place. In Dublin he could ramble into one of a myriad pubs and talk as much of the day away as he wanted to. When Liam spoke about his Paris days, he occasionally spoke about the less overtly literary aspect of life there. He told me once that James Joyce one night bit off part of a man's ear. Not the kind of detail that gets into, say, *Raritan* or *The Partisan Review*.

One night after a television discussion circa 1971 that I had conducted with the writer Ulick O'Connor and other guests, Ulick and I adjourned to the now demolished Royal Hibernian Hotel in Dawson Street. Ulick was riding high at the time on the strength of his biography of Brendan Behan. Towards the end of the evening, Liam O'Flaherty came into the bar. I introduced Ulick to O'Flaherty along the following lines: 'You know Ulick O'Connor, don't you, Liam?' There was quite a long pause. Ulick looked down at his feet and shifted uneasily. Eventually O'Flaherty spoke: 'Are you the man who wrote that awful book about Brendan Behan, while his widow, Beatrice, was still alive?' At that split second, I wasn't sure what Ulick would do. Surprisingly, he looked down at his feet again, and smiled. It seemed that, as far as Ulick was concerned, recognition by the older writer was what mattered; the accompanying criticism didn't bother him.

The television programme series that Ulick O'Connor featured on that memorable evening was a discussion programme called *If It's on Your Mind, Say It*. It consisted of a small panel of contributors with a studio audience of university students. The series never really got off the ground, though it did feature some outstanding student speakers. One of the emerging student stars was a clever young history student, Adrian Hardiman, later to become a justice of the Irish Supreme Court and a noted historian. I also remember the charming Sheila Lawlor, who wrote a book about Churchill and the war, and is now a Cambridge history don; she married the medievalist John Marenbon. The young Hardiman displayed his quick-wittedness from the beginning. When I remarked in conversation after the programme that our schooling can't have been too bad, if it left us with reasonably open minds, he responded: 'Oh, they left you with that illusion, did they?' Adrian Hardiman died unexpectedly in March 2016 at the height of his powers.

I began to make programmes for the Music Department in RTÉ radio at the invitation mainly of Jane Carty, a senior producer there. These tended to consist of one-on-one interviews with singers and other musicians. Among the singers were the soprano Rita Streich of the Vienna State Opera, British contralto Janet Baker, the French baritone Gerard Souzay, and the British bass-baritone John Shirley-Quirke. I had always had a deep interest in singing, and particularly in voice production, though, apart from Rita Streich, most of these conversations would have focused on matters of interpretation rather than of voice. Among the instrumentalists I spoke to were the cellist Paul Tortelier, the pianist Stephen Bishop, the flautist James Galway, then with the Berlin Philarmonic, and the pianist Charles Lynch.

Jane Carty also invited me to compile a radio documentary in 1972 to commemorate the tenth anniversary of the death in Mannheim, Germany, of the Irish tenor Dermot Troy. The U.K. Mario Lanza competition of 1952 was what brought Troy to prominence. A student of the baritone Michael O'Higgins, Troy sounded notably unlike the traditional Irish tenor: the timbre reminded you more of Richard Tauber or of the Canadian tenor Léopold Simoneau. Listening recently to some recordings of Dermot Troy singing Lehar, it was clear that he had a natural aptitude for Viennese light opera. He went to Mannheim Opera House shortly after his success in the Lanza competition, and died prematurely in 1962.

At the request of the composer John Kinsella, then a radio producer with RTÉ, I recorded a documentary about the first Dublin Contemporary Music Festival held in January 1969.

Peadar Keogh, who was on the news desk in the television newsroom, told me that he couldn't make head or tail of it. The fact that Peadar *heard* it meant that, at least, it was broadcast at a decent hour. Declan Lynch, witty television critic and columnist with the *Sunday Independent*, once said that most of my radio interviews were broadcast at an hour when only axe murderers were listening. The reason Peadar Keogh may have found that documentary hard-going was that it focused on the idea of meaning in music, a thorny enough subject, but one that really interested me, and still does. *The Music Instinct* (2010) by Philip Ball makes a good stab at answering that question. What had caught my attention in 1969 was Deryck Cooke's book *The Language of Music* (1959), in which he argued that particular note combinations and harmonies had specific emotional referents. It is a thesis as hotly contested then as it is today, though few will deny that there are broad correspondences, such as major and minor keys indicating happiness and sadness.

The philosopher Suzanne Langer has argued that music, rather than representing specific emotions felt by the composer, represents 'the forms of feeling', that is to say, music captures the ambiguities and tensions of actual feelings in some kind of *analogous* way. I am not sure I fully understand that. Yes, I can rephrase her formulation, but as to understanding her point, I am not sure. At any rate, what the programme represented for me was an opportunity to pursue my own interests within the framework of a broadcasting career in a manner which news-reading did not.

In the summer of 1971 I went to Harley Street to talk to Alfred Alexander, author of *Operanatomy*. Alexander was a surgeon and music buff. Though I was heavily influenced by Herbert-Caesari's *The Voice of the Mind* (1951), in its scepticism about an anatomical approach to voice production, I looked forward to talking to Alexander. He turned out to be a charmer, but did not offer much enlightenment beyond generalizations about the kind of voices that different countries produced. I can't remember off-hand how the Turks or the Albanians did on that score, but the English rarely seem to produce the kind of tenor voice I like. Apart from Heddle Nash, I can't think of another. The late Robert Tear was a highly intelligent singer but lacked the kind of open, Italianate quality of Heddle Nash. A recent glance at Alexander's book reminded me that I had forgotten how ambitious a book it was. It is described as an introduction to the art of the conductor, instrumentalist, composer, and producer. And, for good measure, he throws in 'score-reading'.

For the centenary of Beethoven's birth in 1970, John Kinsella suggested that I talk to Peter Heyworth, music critic of *The Observer*, to Neville Cardus, the retired music critic of the old *Manchester Guardian*, and to Martin Cooper, music critic of the *Daily Telegraph*. Peter Heyworth had read modern languages at Balliol and was working on a biography of Otto Klemperer. He had a well-appointed, book-laden and sunny flat in Hampstead, complete with upright piano. He was eager to talk about Klemperer, whom he characterized essentially as a master of structure, a conductor whose primary concern was to discover and assert the governing architecture of a piece of music.

Neville Cardus lived in comfortable but light-starved accommodation, tucked away behind a red-brick exterior in north London. For some odd reason, he had a gas-fire turned up on that summer's day. One of Neville Cardus' trademarks was that he wrote about cricket as well as music. He wrote with remarkable authority given his lack of conventional schooling and formal musical training. The quality of his prose made up for any gaps of that kind. He became something of a legend in Manchester and then in London. He was eighty-two when I met him. The purpose of the visit was to talk about the Beethoven centenary. It was well known that, although he hadn't much time for Karajan otherwise, Cardus admired his early 1960s' recording of the Beethoven symphonies.

Martin Cooper had just published a book about Beethoven's last decade (1970). As with Heyworth, Cooper enjoyed markedly light-filled, living quarters in London. We conducted our business on the terrace. He was in noticeably good form that day because he had heard that very morning that a daughter of his had got a First in Russian at London University. He himself had studied at Oxford and Vienna. Odd as it may seem, none of the Beethoven centenary interviews were broadcast because that particular commemorative programme was never made.

At Eastertime in 1969, the Religious Programmes department in RTÉ television gave me a most interesting assignment. Dom Hélder Câmara, the cardinal archbishop of Recife in Brazil, was due to visit Britain. I went to Manchester to talk to him. Given the way television staffing has shrunk in the intervening years, it is astonishing to recall the number of people involved in the making of that half-hour programme. First, we had a programme meeting attended by at least six personnel, including the head of religious programmes and the network's religious adviser. Then four or five of us travelled to Manchester for the interview. We called to see the cardinal the night before, and then recorded the interview with him the following day in the BBC studios. Dom Hélder Câmara was the closest I have ever met to a living saint. To this day I remember his gentleness. Whatever the polar opposite of non-threatening is, he embodied it. What made those qualities all the more striking was his reputation for standing up to the military dictatorship in Brazil. From 1970 on, that dictatorship prevented him from speaking in public. This was the man who famously said: 'If I feed the poor they call me a saint; if I ask why they have no food, they call me a communist.' He was no more than five feet tall and at the time I spoke to him was as renowned as the footballer Pelé in his native Brazil. As for his gentleness, I have never witnessed anything like it. No wonder it is said that a hired assassin simply couldn't do him in; the would-be killer walked away.

One thing I remember about religious programmes in which I was involved in the late 1960s and early 1970s, before the Northern Ireland conflict intensified, was the regularity with which the question of the morality of violence came up, that is to say, violence in South America or Africa or elsewhere. It was noticeable that some of us had no problem justifying violence elsewhere, but when it erupted on our doorstep, we began to see this strategy in a different light. I am not at this point making a judgement about the rights and wrongs of individual cases (perhaps, violence *was* justified in some cases). What I am drawing attention to is the ease with which we can recommend a course of action that we would refrain from doing were we ourselves more directly affected.

Chapter 12

THE CULT OF BERNARD LONERGAN

NOT LONG AFTER I HAD COMPLETED studies in philosophy and logic at University College Dublin in 1965, I decided to attend lectures and seminars at the Milltown Park Jesuit Centre on the writings of the philosopher and theologian Bernard Lonergan. How I heard about those lectures I cannot remember, but that I attended them is no surprise, given that I had had an interest in Lonergan since buying his seminal book *Insight* (1957) in the late 1950s at Parsons on Baggot Street bridge. Lonergan's initial appeal for me had to do with the importance he attached to the pure, disinterested desire to know, which he captured in a striking metaphor: the Eros of the mind. That primordial drive manifests itself in our propensity to ask questions. Lonergan also draws our attention to the different kinds of bias that can undermine the flowering of that native intellectual desire. His ideas dovetailed with my reading of John Henry Newman around 1952, though I hadn't heard of Lonergan at that point, let alone had an awareness of how much Newman had influenced him.

This Canadian Jesuit interests me for two reasons: his influence on my own thinking; and the fact that he became the object of a cult at Milltown Park in the late 1960s and early 1970s. By that I mean that he came to be seen as the fount of all truth, as the group's main intellectual lodestar. At first, I was as caught up in this hero worship as the next person, but I gradually moved to a position of acknowledging Lonergan's major intellectual contribution without making him the sole or pivotal reference point of my thinking.

Anyone who reads the introduction to *Insight* is likely to be intrigued, if not captivated, by the following claim: 'Thoroughly understand what it is to understand and not only will you understand the broad lines of all there is to be understood but also you will possess a fixed base, an invariant pattern, opening upon all further patterns of understanding.' How, the reader asks himself, can an understanding of understanding, an insight into the nature of insight, guarantee eventual understanding of all there is to be understood. That is alluring stuff for any curious young person to read. The chapters that follow that invitation make for difficult but rewarding reading. I was lucky to hear lectures on *Insight* in the late 1960s by Philip McShane and Conn O'Donovan, who at that time were members of the Jesuit order and who knew the book really well. McShane is today among the foremost interpreters of Lonergan worldwide.

What interests me, quite apart from Lonergan's own powerful ideas, is the fact that he also provides a window on to an educational/psychological phenomenon that is of interest in itself. Other recent examples of thinkers who have generated loyal intellectual discipleship are Heidegger and Wittgenstein, and more recently an illustrious cluster of French thinkers which includes Foucault, Lacan, Derrida and Levinas. The more acceptable face of discipleship occurs at the point at which we can describe someone as being under the *influence* of a particular thinker; the less acceptable face involves the surrender of intellectual autonomy.

In the case of all the aforementioned thinkers, it is their ideas that ultimately matter, but the sociology of their contemporary influence is an alluring spectator sport. In that respect, Bernard Lonergan, a formidable thinker, has attracted a devoted and discerning international following, with research centres in Boston, Toronto and Dublin. If what I heard in Boston over thirty years ago is true, namely, that Lonergan was miffed by the attention paid by students to Heidegger – it proves that not merely is he a formidable thinker, he is also reassuringly human. In the early years of the new century, I wondered about Lonergan's current standing in Dublin among young Jesuits, a group who had lionized him forty years before. 'What are young Jesuits reading today?' I asked my good friend the philosopher and mathematician Bill Mathews, a member of the Jesuit order himself, and author of *Lonergan's Quest* (2005). 'There *are* no young Jesuits today,' was Bill's reply.

Lonergan was born in Buckingham, Quebec, of Irish and British extraction, and lived from 1904 until 1984. His two most influential books are *Insight* (1957) and *Method in Theology* (1972). He also wrote numerous essays on topics in logic, religion, the philosophy of history, the philosophy of science, the nature of culture, and education. A many-sided thinker, he himself characterized his main scholarly objective as one of bringing Catholic thought 'up to the level of the times', or as 'putting history into theology'.

The British philosopher Anthony Kenny, formerly Master of Balliol, and quondam student of Lonergan at the Gregorian in Rome, once said that, although he was sure that Wittgenstein was a genius, he wasn't as sure about Lonergan. That Kenny compared the two thinkers at all in that context is itself revealing, but the remark also captures something of the uncertainty of Lonergan's stature as a philosopher. However, I learned from philosopher Michael Dummett in 1982 that his erstwhile Oxford colleague Elizabeth Anscombe considered Lonergan to be the greatest Catholic philosopher/theologian since Aquinas.

Readers of Lonergan will have known him for many years solely as a philosopher and a theologian, but in recent years they will have become increasingly aware of him also as an economist. That he had done theoretical work in economics came as quite a surprise to many readers; to some it was incredible. They learned that in the 1940s he produced two manuscripts in macroeconomic theory, which he then shelved owing to a lack of interest in them by economists. He returned to these manuscripts towards the end of his life, and there is little evidence that the reception was any better.

The main exponent of Lonergan's ideas in Dublin in the late 1960s was Philip McShane, at that time a Jesuit priest who had taught maths and physics at UCD, and was completing a doctorate at Oxford in the philosophy of science. He co-authored *Towards Self-Meaning* (1969) with Garrett Barden, a former Jesuit seminarian who later became a professor of philosophy at University College Cork. Both authors were Lonergan enthusiasts, but Barden seemed more alert to Lonergan's cult-generating potential and its dangers. At least, that is how I interpreted a contribution by him at a conference in Dublin in 1971 to mark the publication of *Method in Theology*. On that occasion, Barden articulated convincingly the threat to intellectual autonomy that Lonergan represented. He said the problem for him personally in that regard was the fact that Lonergan had devised an analysis of the act of knowing (a cognitional theory) that sounded so right, one wished one had come up with it oneself. And yet Barden was aware of a certain tension in himself between embracing these ideas and maintaining a sense of his own intellectual independence. The loss of such independence is what characterizes the flowering of a cult: allowing someone else to do our thinking for us.

What helped turn Lonergan into a guru was the emphasis he placed on self-scrutiny as the proper context for reading *Insight*. In other words, he insisted that it was not enough simply to learn *about* the foundational components (experiencing, understanding, judging) of the act of knowing; the reader was invited to appropriate personally the procedures involved. The challenge was to identify accurately within one's own experience the set of cognitive operations that Lonergan had specified as constituting the act of knowing. Self-scrutiny in philosophy, however, is a double-edged sword: it can be highly productive or else it can turn the student into the kind of anxious apprentice who becomes much more concerned about whether he has got the master's point than with thinking for himself.

That distinction between the two kinds of understanding just referred to – the one based on simply knowing *about* something, and the other based on personal experience of it – will be familiar in rudimentary form to readers of John Henry Newman. The distinction is described by him as that between *notional* and *real* apprehension. It is the difference between the schoolboy's understanding of '*dulce et decorum est pro patria mori*' ('It is sweet and glorious to die for one's country') and the manner in which a soldier at war understands it. Later on I learned that Lonergan viewed the scrutiny of one's own *intellectual* operations as analogous and, indeed, complementary to the examination of one's *emotional* life. In other words, one can usefully locate his ideas about intellectual self-appropriation within the context of adult psychological development. I found that appealing.

In a radio programme I chaired in 1984 on the occasion of Lonergan's death, Garrett Barden said that, for him, Lonergan's main contribution was in the field of *cognitional theory*, that is, in attempting to provide foundations for human knowledge. For others, it is his *epistemology* that is central, namely his contribution to the great Kantian problem of how minds know the world (Bill Mathews); or his ideas about *method* and the dynamics of scholarly collaboration (Phil McShane); or his concept of *emergent probability*, the integration of the results of classical and statistical investigations into a single world view (Kenneth R. Melchin); or finally, his *theory of history* (Fred Crowe).

What is reasonably clear is that whatever disagreement exists about Lonergan's *ultimate* contribution, there has to be agreement that all those destinations presuppose the importance of his cognitional theory. To that degree, Barden is right. We hardly need reminding that Lonergan's efforts to provide foundations for the act of knowing run against the contemporary tide. In recent decades, Richard Rorty captured perfectly the widespread tendency to regard the search for such foundations as a fruitless exercise. Rorty and others argue that we simply have to get on *without* foundations. Lonergan believed that such foundations *do* exist and that they reside in cognitional theory. By this, he means that these foundations reside not in a set of *propositions* from which other propositions can be logically deduced, but in the *data of consciousness*: the foundations reside in *cognitive operations*.

That last point is pivotal for Lonergan: establishing foundations for the act of knowing has to do not with *propositions* (with content) but with cognitive *operations*. The key cognitive operations here consist of asking questions, formulating tentative answers, and making judgments about the truth of those hunches. Furthermore, he argued that this three-fold process of experiencing, understanding and judging provided reliable foundations, because that very process was itself unrevisable: you cannot revise that foundational process without employing the same three-fold pattern of cognitive operations. There are readers who regard that schema as too formal in character: they wonder what Lonergan is saying beyond making a claim that knowing is just a matter of asking and answering questions. I think that is enough to be getting on with. I was reminded of the value of Lonergan's approach recently when a young German historian told me that his colleagues were so bewitched by mere data collection, few of them knew what a question was.

The very title of Lonergan's first major work, *Insight*, tends to peg him as someone primarily concerned with understanding the nature of understanding itself, but there is good reason to believe that that particular project was a means to an end, namely the transformation of the social order. The transformation of theology, eventuating in *Method in Theology*, can be seen as part of that project, but only as part. My net impression after re-readings of even so theoretically focused a book as *Insight* is that Lonergan's fundamental drive is towards transformation of the world, towards action of some kind. That is the ultimate context in which his work has to be seen. Admittedly, his vision of 'cosmopolis', as outlined in *Insight,* refers more to a transformed state of consciousness and collaborative intellectual endeavour than to a desirable set of institutions, but what he appears to be saying is that a revolution in consciousness is a precondition of institutional change.

Even though Lonergan and Marx differ as to where the ultimate explanation of social change resides, and also differ as to the importance of the role of individual conversion in bringing about social change, each geared his thinking towards social transformation. In other words, Lonergan appears to agree with Marx that the purpose of philosophy is to change the world as much as to understand it, even if they differed in their remedies. What Marx actually said, of course, is that the purpose of philosophy is to change the world, *rather* than to interpret it, but one suspects that he was being rhetorical. Marx would surely have known that understanding was a precondition of the kind of appropriate action that brings about social change. I suppose the ultimate difference between the two as *social* thinkers is that Marx is more of a determinist in the matter of material economic/technological conditions; Lonergan leaves more space for the role of the transforming human subject. That said, it should be added that interpreters of Marx differ as to the precise weight he assigned to human agency in the matter of social change.

Lonergan's theoretical work in economics is further evidence that the context in which to see all his work is transformative action. We know that he was stirred to do theoretical work in economics with a view to improving economic conditions. On the other hand, he was impatient with well-intentioned people, including liberation theologians who hadn't worked hard enough at the preliminary task of understanding economics. Fred Crowe, in an essay in *Appropriating the Lonergan Idea* (1989) on the thinker's relationship with liberation theologians, is surprisingly defensive in trying to clear Lonergan of charges of not being sufficiently concerned about the plight of the less well off. No one who reads either *Insight* or *Method in Theology* could doubt Lonergan's interest in transforming the social order.

As I have already indicated, by the late 1960s Bernard Lonergan had achieved guru status at the Milltown Jesuit Centre in Dublin and further afield on the strength of his cognitional theory. It is a measure of how gripped I myself was by Lonergan fever that around 1970 I sought the assistance of Phil McShane to help me with a talk I had been invited to give by St Peter's Catholic seminary in Wexford. He prepped me with a brief summary of Lonergan's ideas from Lonergan's soon-to-be-published *Method in Theology*. I blush at the thought of what my eventual talk must have sounded like, and certainly can't blame Phil for it. Twenty-five years later, the novelist Colm Tóibín told me at a party in playwright Tom Murphy's house that he was a young student at St Peter's in Wexford when I spoke at the college on that occasion. What he remembered was being addressed by a prominent newscaster of the day. Mercifully, Colm remembered nothing of the content. Either that, or he was too kind to say.

When a thinker is elevated to the status of key repository of the truth, as happened with Lonergan, one possible corrective to such one-sidedness is to remember that what matters in philosophy and theology, as in the physical sciences, is the *problem,* not the individual philosopher or scientist. In other words, if we keep in focus the notion that it is the problem that is central (as in the sciences) the less likely the philosophical community or theological community will be to consider the contribution of any one thinker as definitive. In that regard, it strikes me that Whitehead's famous remark that the history of philosophy is a series of footnotes to Plato puts Whitehead firmly in the wrong camp, in that he is implicitly placing the individual thinker ahead of the problem.

Lonergan has been written off as well as idolized. The renowned theologian Hans Küng, who was a student of Lonergan in Rome in the early 1950s, dismisses him in his memoir *My Struggle for Freedom* (2003) as someone from whom he did not learn a lot. Küng says of his former theology teacher: 'He leans towards philosophy and bores us with his dry traditional lectures on Christology. In vain he tries to convince me in personal conversation that Thomas Aquinas anticipated Einstein's theory of relativity.'

The distinguished Irish theologian James P. Mackey, in an early evaluation of Lonergan's work, saw little merit in *Method in Theology* beyond a brazen dressing up of old scholastic certainties in new cognitional clothes. Somewhere in between the adulators and the dismissers, is the assessment of the Oxford philosopher Anthony Kenny, who in claiming that he is unsure as to whether Lonergan warrants being called a 'genius', conveys to us, nonetheless, how highly he thinks of him.

Like Hans Küng, Kenny had been a student of Lonergan's in Rome during the 1950s. I have raised the matter of his former teacher with Kenny in a number of conversations over the last twenty-five years. In the second of these, I developed a related point that has always fascinated me about the author of *Insight*: namely, the fact that Lonergan says in that book that it was in 'stretching up to the mind of Aquinas' that his own intellectual development really lay. That last piece of information invites us to reflect on the precise role that grappling with someone else's ideas plays in an individual's development. There is something counter-intuitive, though, in the idea that a *genius* is someone who owes his own intellectual development to wrestling with the thought of another. Counter-intuitive, but not necessarily wrong. Lonergan has always foregrounded not just his debt to Aquinas, but the precise nature of that indebtedness: it was in trying to understand Aquinas that his own intellectual growth lay.

That Lonergan chose Aquinas in the first place is explained by the fact that he was a young Jesuit in the first half of the twentieth century trying to bring Catholicism up to-date, trying, as he once said, to introduce history into Catholic theology. In a word, he was attempting to do in the twentieth century what Aquinas had done in the thirteenth. All Lonergan's attempts to provide philosophical foundations have to be seen in the context of that ecclesial project. On the other hand, the fact that that ecclesial project propelled his inquiry does not mean that his cognitional theory does not have validity, regardless of what initially drove that inquiry.

I found Lonergan to be particularly helpful in his elaboration of the legitimate role of belief in coming to rational conclusions. In other words, if we assume that we cannot check everything, there are times when the most rational course of action is to accept certain things on trust. We do it all the time. In that respect, Lonergan's thinking reflects that of John Henry Newman. But, more than that, Lonergan underlines the likely relevance of a scholar's mind-set in the context of solving scholarly disagreements. Let me clarify.

Some years ago, I came across *A Life of Bishop John A.T. Robinson* (1988) by Eric James. Bishop Robinson was a New Testament scholar and author of the controversial book *Honest to God* (1963). James made the point that Robinson rarely worked with primary sources. He would master the secondary literature that surrounded a particular problem until he got a firm sense of the contours of the debate. Then, if at that point he encountered a conflict of evidence, he would either look at the relevant primary sources or talk to the relevant experts. If he was capable of assessing the primary sources himself, then presumably he would make a judgment on that basis. If, however, someone working with secondary sources is not capable of assessing the primary sources involved, then one option for such a person is to talk to the relevant experts in the primary sources, who may well disagree.

But how are we to choose between disagreeing experts? Lonergan is helpful in this matter. Fred Crowe reminds us in *Appropriating the Lonergan Idea* (1989) that, at moments of disagreement between experts, Lonergan's position is that one should choose between them on the basis of their mind-set, and, particularly, their degree of openness and their fairness. In a word, you base your choice on their respective records; you choose the *person* who is more open and more fair.

Another notion of Lonergan's that made a deep impact on me was his idea that the concrete is the locus of intelligibility. When I said that one day to my broadcasting colleague Joe Duffy, one of the wittiest people I know, he replied: 'Roadstone should put that on the side of their trucks.' What Lonergan meant was that it is only through images that we understand things. Hence the power of examples. There is a certain irony here in that the received view of philosophy is that it is essentially a very abstract activity. Lonergan insists that without the deployment of concrete images, understanding does not occur. What can happen in such an instance is that we repeat the words involved, without having really got the point.

Furthermore, Lonergan's acute awareness of the role of what he calls 'general bias' in economic, social, political and cultural decline, is powerfully articulated. By 'general bias,' he is referring, among other things, to short-term thinking, the curse of our age. The disease has affected the contemporary corporate world to a marked degree, where short-term thinking has undermined any kind of long-term planning. One notable recent exception was the late Steve Jobs, co-founder of Apple. Jobs was notoriously indifferent to the short-term implications for the company's share price of the kind of technological and investment decisions that bore long-term fruit. Lonergan was deeply aware of the lack of synchronization between economic and political cycles as a factor that contributed to the worship of the short-term.

As to the educational implications of my own experience of the Lonergan sessions in Dublin forty years ago, this is what they are. From the point of view of the formation of a student, the most important aspect of presenting the ideas of an individual thinker is that this thinker be seen as part of a larger philosophical, theological or scientific conversation. The mediator, in presenting the ideas of any one thinker should ensure that the students never lose sight of the fact that the problem itself is larger than the thinker. If I may amend Lord Acton slightly, we should study problems not people. The problem is bigger than the individual thinker; physics is bigger than even Einstein. Without a strong sense of this context, the individual thinker, rather than the problem(s) he or she is addressing may become central. This can lead to a universe in which everything is seen through the eyes of that individual thinker. I saw that happen with Lonergan. Where a thinker cannot be integrated into a larger conversation, the student ends up trying to navigate two separate universes. In the context of physics, that would be like treating the ideas of Einstein or Bohr, of Heisenberg or Schrödinger as if they constituted a world separate from the ideas of other physicists.

Chapter 13

A RESEARCH PROJECT IN PSYCHOLOGY

BY THE EARLY 1970S, I HAD BECOME a very busy broadcaster. This involved a full-time roster as a radio and television newscaster, and also as a presenter of programmes about the arts and about religion. I was getting hints here and there that I should slow down. For some time I myself had really felt a need to cut my workload in order to engage in intellectual pursuits I found more fulfilling. Then eventually in 1972 I made what for me was an important decision: I left my job as a radio and television news anchor to create the necessary space for further study. My decision wasn't as foolhardy as it sounds, in that although my income was suddenly reduced, I was still earning enough from feature programmes in radio to sustain myself.

One option to which I gave serious consideration when I left the newsroom was the study of ancient classics. I had always regretted not having been in a position to study classics at university immediately after boarding school, where Latin and Greek had been my favourite subjects. My current qualification in commerce was fine and practical; better still was my grounding in philosophy and logic, but I really coveted a good formation in classics, because it encompassed history, literature and philosophy.

My reading since school had made me more alert to the foundational nature of the ancient Greek world. Besides, the professor of Greek at Trinity, W.B. Stanford, sparked my interest by telling me that the poet Eavan Boland had taken courses in Greek thought and literature to get a sense of the world before Christianity. I should add that another poet, John Montague told me much later on (circa 1998) that Samuel Beckett once wondered aloud to him what he might have done had he known Greek. Richard Ellmann in his biography of Joyce (1959) informs us that Joyce, too, didn't have Greek. Beckett may well have been mocking the late Victorian romanticization of all things Greek which would have lingered on into his student days in the 1920s. Maybe not. To my knowledge, not many of my journalist colleagues in Dublin had Greek, apart from the columnist Con Houlihan and in earlier days, Alec Newman, editor of *The Irish Times* in the 1950s.

When I told the late Val Rice, who was then professor of education at Trinity, that I was toying with the idea of studying ancient classics, he suggested that his own department's newly instituted two-year graduate degree would be a more practical option. He pointed out that were I ever to leave broadcasting, this qualification would furnish me with expertise of a kind that would allow me to work, say, as a consultant in education. At that juncture in the early 1970s, I hadn't ruled out the possibility of a life abroad, probably in America. So, it seemed to make good sense to increase my employment options.

Moreover, here was an opportunity to reflect at leisure and in a systematic manner on an interest of mine that had begun with my early reading of John Henry Newman. In the matter of studying the more institutional aspects of education, both nationally and comparatively, this venture would mean access to the expertise of one of the country's leading authorities in the field, Professor Séamus Ó Buachalla. So, I took Val Rice's advice, but as I began to write term papers on various aspects of education from the psychological to the sociological to the philosophical, I could feel the pull towards even further study. My interest was shifting at that point to psychology, in particular towards an examination of ideas about adult psychological development. I noted that three subjects that interested me then were all preoccupied with personal transformation: education, religion and psychotherapy.

Feeding into that interest was the widespread influence at that time of the American counterculture, with its emphasis on notions of personal psychological growth. Humanistic psychology, associated with Abraham Maslow, Carl Rogers, Rollo May and others, was all the rage at the time. Norman Brown, author of *Life Against Death* (1959), a psychoanalytical reading of history, was also an influential figure. I recall first reading Brown's book in 1972 on the Portuguese island of Madeira, and having read it again recently, I am not surprised that Lionel Trilling rated it the best interpretation of Freud that he knew. Brown distances himself from Freud on a number of issues: for example, he doesn't agree with Freud that the 'primal crime' (in which the sons kill the father) cited in *Totem and Taboo* (1913) is a historical fact but is rather an infantile fantasy. He is, however, captivated by the material, corporeal rootedness of Freud's thinking, and for that reason has much less time for Jung and even Fromm.

Of all those figures who flourished in the 1960s and 1970s, Maslow was the one who influenced me most, if only because his theory of motivation, which distinguished between *deficiency* needs (for shelter, food, belonging and so on) and *growth* needs (for self-development), had an initial intuitive appeal. Moreover, Maslow laid great stress on self-actualization as a desirable state. This was a highly admirable goal provided it was anchored to a framework of social obligation and responsibility. Any doubts I had that Maslow was too unrealistic about what humans were capable of by way of psychological growth were later dispelled when I read *The Journals of A.H. Maslow* (1979). Moreover, any doubts I had that he saw nothing but good in people were also put to rest: Maslow, though always open to the possibility of humans attaining a high degree of creative fulfilment, was also deeply aware of our destructiveness. In fact, the journals revealed the flawed side of Maslow himself.

When I discussed my growing interest in psychology with Derek Forrest of Trinity's psychology department, he suggested I enrol for a doctorate with him. Professor Forrest impressed by his own lack of need to impress: he spoke about his interest in Freud, Francis Galton and in hypnosis, but also about the number of subjects he knew nothing about, including the then fashionable 'personal construct theory', associated with George Kelly.

The research proposal I submitted to the department was atypical in that it was more conceptual than empirical: my main interest was in clarifying the *meaning* of a key term, namely that of psychological growth. The more customary approach for anyone less preoccupied than I was with exploring the meaning of the term would have been to settle more expeditiously for a particular working definition of the concept and then conduct whatever empirical tests (statistical or experimental) were appropriate to answering the research question that interested them. This might, for example, mean asking, 'what are the conditions that facilitate or impede psychological growth (as so defined) in a specified context?' That last approach had less appeal for me because my background in philosophy had alerted me to the fact that different definitions of psychological growth were likely to carry competing philosophical presuppositions. In other words, such definitions would carry different understandings of what was meant by the human good: people differ as to what kind of psychological, developmental goals they consider to be desirable. So, there was ultimately no escaping a discussion of *values* in any attempt to conceptualize psychological growth.

My dissertation would be inescapably conceptual in character and also unavoidably philosophical, at least partly so.

On the other hand, since this was a project being conducted in a psychology department, I was obliged to flesh out that conceptual debate with whatever empirical data were available. The primary data of my research were the theoretical contributions of others. But, in addition to analysing and coordinating those theoretical contributions, I had to assess the level of evidential support, if any, that girded them. This meant that I had to locate and assess any relevant empirical studies that purported to support the claims being made.

In the autumn of 1977, I decided to spend more time in the Berkeley library at Trinity, where I was assigned a carrel. The historian and former diplomat Dr Conor Cruise O'Brien, who had just lost his seat in the Dáil, was at a neighbouring carrel researching a book. The following year I landed an RTÉ radio assignment which, though extremely attractive, caused significant disruption. *Inside Europe* involved regular travel to European capitals. When the series ended in the autumn of 1979 with a visit to Helsinki, I decided it was time to begin writing up my research.

After a period of intensive reading of books, journal articles and doctoral dissertations, I had concluded that the two overarching features of what is variously called optimal functioning, positive mental health or psychological growth were 'integration' and 'flexibility'. The most personally rewarding part of this doctoral research project lay in analyzing the second of those variables, namely the meaning of the term 'flexibility'. My proposed context for flexibility was cognitive: it was seen in the context of a willingness to revise one's beliefs.

I eventually found it useful to distinguish between two fundamentally different kinds of belief: the substantive and the procedural varieties. An example of the first would be the kind that people hold in the fields, for instance, of politics, morality, or religion. When we talk about revising our beliefs, that is the kind of belief we usually have in mind. It is a quite straightforward matter. It is only when we migrate to what I am characterizing as 'procedural' beliefs that matters get more tricky. An example of a 'procedural' belief would be a belief that expressed one's attitude to the desirability or not of revising whatever 'substantive' beliefs one held. People differ widely in the matter of their attitude to a revision of their beliefs. Let's look at some examples.

At one extreme, some people believe none of their beliefs should be subject to revision; at the other extreme are those who believe that *all* their beliefs should be subject to revision. This is further complicated by the fact that one can distinguish in that last group between (a) those who believe all beliefs should be subject to revision, *except* the belief that all beliefs should be subject to revision, and (b) those who believe that even that last belief should be open to question. Working through the ins and outs of 'procedural' beliefs was for me the most rewarding part of the research. I realized that I was having the time of my life with a problem dear to my heart.

That 1970s' interest of mine in what was at the time called 'humanistic psychology' which fed into my decision to pursue a particular research topic, may look quite dated now, little more than a passing fashion spawned by the youth culture currents of the 1960s. I was certainly susceptible to intellectual fads. Yet, shorn of its sixties' counterculture trappings, the idea of human development is of perennial interest to me. It dovetailed with a developing interest of mine in the study of religion, particularly in the role of personal experience in theological reflection.

It seems to me now that the real lacuna in my understanding of adult psychological growth at that time was my failure to attend adequately to the wider historical and social contexts in which such concerns might have been set. What was missing at that point was the deployment of a wider socio-political lens. That enlarged lens really came into focus for me only in the early 1980s when I began to study social theory at Harvard University. Before such study, I certainly had a *crude* awareness of social and political contexts, but mostly I saw the world in terms of the individual and of personal development.

Also missing was a strong sense of the relevance of a historical context to understanding ideas about human adult development. Jean Paul Pittion, a friend in Trinity's French department and a seventeenth-century specialist, was a big help in alerting me to that. Because psychology is such a relatively new discipline (dating from the end of the nineteenth century), there is a tendency to overlook its historical dimension. Furthermore, we shouldn't forget that concepts of human development actually predate the arrival of scientific psychology.

In due course I came to see the need for *two* interacting axes in any serious attempt to understand the evolution of human functioning: a historical axis and a theoretical one. The first would mean a greater sensitivity to the unfolding and periodization of human history, since the Greeks (at least); the second, was the deployment of the kind of analytic framework that might help identify those forces that account for social change.

All those considerations arose after I had finished my research. Most projects in the psychology department at Trinity in those days were direct empirical studies, either statistical or experimental in character. Mine was one of the few projects that had a conceptual and partly philosophical focus. It was also one of the few that did not come under the rubric of behaviourism, a theoretical orientation that was enjoying a particularly favourable innings in the department in the 1970s.

Even cognitive psychology, let alone humanistic psychology, was not in vogue then at Trinity. Animal studies were fashionable, and 'operant conditioning' was one of the buzz terms of the day. There were notably open-minded 'behaviourists' like John Masterson, later executive producer of RTÉ's *The Late*

Late Show, and theoretically inclined psychologists like Sheila Greene, who later ascended to the heights of college administration. Ken Heskin had done valuable work on the psychological dynamics of the conflict in Northern Ireland.

Given the popularity of behaviourism at the time, I was surprised at the cordial reception given me when I presented a 'work in progress'. It may have been that I was so far off the prevailing radar that nobody bothered. Yet Dr. Ray Fuller did push me quite hard as to whether I envisaged psychological growth as a concept that had cross-cultural validity. Moreover, I may be overestimating the extent to which a behaviourist/operant conditioning ethos prevailed at the time.

After a few years at Trinity, I had abandoned the notion of going abroad to work in America, though it would resurface later when I took a sabbatical. I really did not envisage myself working as a psychologist, either in industry, education, or medicine. More and more, I saw myself as a broadcast journalist furthering his own education. I began to read widely in various aspects of religion, from theology to the philosophy, psychology and sociology of religion. This dovetailed with my work at that time for religious programmes, which consisted mainly of one-on-one interviews with a range of thinkers, including the philosophers James Cameron and Leszek Kolakowski, the theologian Hans Küng, the publisher Frank Sheed, the novelist David Lodge, and the journalist Marghanita Laski. I also began to study French and German. This led to further courses at the Sorbonne in 1975 and at Passau in Bavaria in 1977.

Meeting an American student, Michaela O'Brien, at Trinity College in late 1974 was a chance happening that enriched my life in many ways. She was born in Tampa, Florida and had studied English literature at the University of Georgia. At first she mistook me for Brendan Kennelly, who was her professor in whatever graduate course in Anglo-Irish studies she was pursuing. Michaela was exceptionally bright, with a highly developed sense of humour. Recalling her now puts me in mind of some of the running gags we enjoyed, like 'an evening *without* John Betjeman' or 'it all depends on what you mean by *mean*.' She spoke eloquently about the importance of constantly combining philosophy with poetry. Otherwise, one never transcended knowledge of a conceptual kind, no matter how broad the range of interests one had. In her view, I had neglected poetry for philosophy and psychology.

In theory, I was on her side, but old habits die hard. It was not unusual for me to try to hold my corner in this kind of debate by arguing that the discursive level was ultimately primary, because it was only at the discursive level itself that one could debate the limitations of the conceptual. Still, I knew she was right. Even Aquinas, master of the conceptual, had affirmed the role of non-conceptual knowledge, what he called *scientia per conaturalitatem*: put crisply, my knowledge of you cannot be reduced to propositions about you.

Michaela was both a poet and a perceptive critic. Her idea of a gift invariably consisted of the collected works of a particular poet, one of the first of these being D. H. Lawrence. She was very helpful in the matter of clarifying my thoughts about my research topic. She encouraged me to write essays about culture and religion, which unfortunately I failed to do, because of other commitments.

Rather than attempting to curtail my book-buying habits, which were becoming more and more wayward, Michaela approved of this habit. Holidays in New York and Atlanta were occasions of memorable splurges. She had a healthy disregard for books about books, though there were exceptions such as Northrop Frye's study of Blake, *Fearful Symmetry* (1947) and Harold Bloom's *The Anxiety of Influence* (1973). Whereas I approached Catholicism/Christianity through the lens of theology and history, she showed me the rewards of deploying a literary lens, that of poetry in particular. Another member of the broad O'Brien clan, the writer Conor Cruise O'Brien, said to me once that if anyone ever cracks the mystery of God, it won't be a theologian. Though sceptical by nature, Michaela had a deep respect for the category of mystery. Yet mystery does not rule out rational inquiry.

In the summer of 1975 I stayed at the Cité Universitaire in Paris and took courses at the Sorbonne to brush up my French. This was the first time I saw the work of the Austrian painter Friedensreich Hundertwasser at the Musée d'Art Moderne. I recall the painter Anne Madden telling me a decade later that she disliked his work intensely, but I found its self-conscious primitiveness engrossing at the time, though I can now see its derivative sub-Schiele character. The small black catalogue, shaped like a Roman missal, cost five pounds, which seemed a lot in those days.

Breakfasts at the Cité Universitaire might mean the company of a Marxist anthropologist from Tunisia or a well-read American music critic. One lunchtime I was drinking a café crème on a café terrace near the Sorbonne. A man walked by with such elegance of gait that he well nigh stopped the traffic. I watched him 'glide' from one end of the sidewalk to the other. An hour later I saw him ascend the podium where hundreds of us had assembled to hear his lecture. It was the great Serge Lifar. As recently as 1975 it was still possible to see on the streets of Paris a protégé and lover of Diaghilev, a friend of Cocteau, Picasso and Prokofiev, and one of the leading dancers and choreographers of the century. He was then seventy years of age.

What struck me most about the Sorbonne was the emphasis on education as transmission. Admittedly, my main interest was simply to get exposure to the French language. Still, my recent study of education had alerted me to the fact that an emphasis on transmission indicated a conservative philosophy of education; an emphasis on critical assessment, meant a more liberal one. The American pragmatist John Dewey was the high-priest of discovery-based learning with its emphasis on active engagement by the student. In those years, I was deeply critical of the stress on transmission, with its concomitant downplaying of student-based discovery. Nowadays, I am more receptive to the central role that transmission plays. Traditions of all kinds can die without it. Even in the mid-1970s I was swayed by the arguments of my classmate Dan Murphy, since deceased, who was an expert in literary criticism before concentrating on educational theory. He saw the perils of absolutizing the critical response of the student, and the need for a measure of authority.

My main memory of walking to Trinity from Baggot Street in 1972/73 was the fear of car bombs. The Northern Ireland conflict was spilling over into the Republic. Indeed, one day in May 1974 I got a lift into Trinity, where I discovered that the city had been hit by two huge car bombs, one of them in South Leinster Street beside Trinity's railings.

The most painful memory of all from those years is that of the death of my close friend, Tom Naughton, who lost his life in a car accident outside Galway in February 1973. At the time of his death, Tom had been managing director of a liquor company, John Egan & Sons, in Tuam, County Galway for over a decade. He had married a very attractive local girl, Frances Hardiman, in 1969. Tom was only thirty seven when he crashed in a BMW he had just bought. A successful businessman, he had the mind of a scholar and the sensitivity of an artist. As I have already indicated in a previous chapter, we were the closest of friends over a period of sixteen years. About a year or so before his death, he had phoned me to ask me to recommend a physician to him. He was experiencing certain symptoms at the time that might turn out to be innocuous, he said, but that could also lead to his being told to put his affairs in order. As a result of that phone call, when I was told that he was dead, my first response was to ask if his death had been sudden. In other words, I presumed that Tom had accurately surmised that he might have had a fatal ailment. In fact, it was an accident: he had lost control of a newly bought car.

Tom was contemplating a career in politics when we lost him. On that score, I recall his irritation with the actual title of Bernard Crick's *In Defence of Politics* (1962). He had called to my flat one night in Mount Merrion Avenue and when he caught sight of Crick's book, commented witheringly but passionately: 'as if politics needed defending'. It was only in later decades that I developed a level of interest in politics comparable to Tom's. It is remarkable that, despite that lack of synchronization in so important a domain, we were such good friends.

At the funeral in Tuam, Tom Murphy the playwright spoke to me of 'the awful fucking finality of death'. He said he began to resent the fact that day that the mountains around us would outlast us all. A measure of the day's grief was that the usually irrepressible Vincent Caffrey was lost for words. Fergal MacCabe and P. J. Grealish were equally silent. A mere six years before in London, Tom Naughton had introduced me to Tom Murphy at the Queen's Elm in Fulham. They themselves had first met in Tuam in the late 1950s. In his play *The White House* the writer drew on his friend's obsessive interest in JFK. On that cold February day in 1973 we buried not just Tom Naughton but his constant reminder to us of the Kennedy era. We also said farewell to those close harmony songs that always surfaced at the same late hour. Just one more time: 'All in the April evening, April airs were abroad...'

In early 1975, producer Colm Ó Briain, later director of the Arts Council, and later still head of the National College of Art and Design, asked me to front a television arts programme with the radical chic title *Over the Barricades*. The opening montage featured the music of Monteverdi and Robert Ballagh's painting, 'After Delacroix'. The invitation to join the programme team came about through the generosity of fellow broadcaster Tom

McGurk, who informed me that this particular series was soon coming on stream, and that I should indicate my availability.

Shortly afterwards, Ó Briain left to run the Arts Council; he was replaced by Ted Dolan, another highly cultivated producer/director. The most memorable programme I did with Ted consisted of a comprehensive interview with Francis Stuart about his novel *Black List, Section H* (1971). On that same programme, Tony Cronin, a staunch admirer of Stuart (and later, a biographer of Beckett and of Brian O'Nolan) presented a tribute to the novelist. Stuart has had to endure much contumely about his broadcast work for the Nazis. Not an easy one to defend, but I don't think Francis had a destructive bone in his body. I'm prepared to accept that he misguidedly saw Hitler in the early days as a kind of Samson who would replace the existing order with a better one. Stuart certainly got it wrong: he was hoping for an improved new order.

Black List, Section H is an autobiographically-based piece of fiction that essentially asks how one can fruitfully expand individual consciousness. For the protagonist, there were two main ways of achieving that: first, identification with that segment of society which suffered most; and secondly, adopting a contrarian position to the prevailing consensus in religion, politics and culture. The poet Pearse Hutchinson wrote a detailed review of that particular programme for *The Irish Times*, as did critic Tom O'Dea for *The Irish Press*. The attentive nature of that coverage was gratifying, given the amount of work Ted Dolan and I had put into the programme. For Stuart it was a rare appearance on Irish television. I am always intrigued to see Graham Greene trotted out regularly as one of the great *religious* novelists of the twentieth century. He certainly operated nimbly at the level of moral conflict and psychological guilt, but lacked that feel for the cavernous terrain of the mystical, so evident in Stuart's work.

A young television director, John McColgan, joined *Over the Barricades* towards the end of its run. Eventually a theatre producer and director of international distinction (he co-devised the global runaway success *Riverdance* with his wife Moya Doherty, and became chairman of the Abbey Theatre), McColgan's interest in theatre manifested itself from the beginning. We spent the Easter weekend of 1975 at Liberty Hall, the Irish Transport and General Workers' Union's headquarters, where John Arden and his wife, Margaretta D'Arcy, were mounting *The Non-Stop Connolly Show.* This was an attempt to present the 1916 socialist revolutionary James Connolly in a show-biz context. Agit-prop meets the Ziegfeld Follies. As you can imagine, the shadow of Bertolt Brecht hung uneasily over the piece.

Arden, the author of *Sergeant Musgrave's Dance,* had moved to Ireland shortly before that, and seemed at that particular stage of his life to be undergoing a crisis of some kind. McColgan and I spent a lot of time with him in a nearby hostelry, most of it trying to find a suitable opportunity to interview a playwright who, though perfectly sober, seemed on the verge of nervous collapse. John Arden was a highly talented man and the gentlest of souls.

Chapter 14

Beckett at Seventy; George Steiner at Trinity

I N THE SPRING OF 1976, AN RTÉ SERIES of six hour-long radio programmes about Samuel Beckett, on the occasion of his seventieth birthday, proved to be a very rewarding assignment. The idea was proposed by Kieran Sheedy, who produced the series and also recorded some valuable interviews for it. We structured it in such a way that the first three programmes were biographical in character; the second three focused on Beckett's work. After the earlier programmes were broadcast, Eavan Boland commented favourably to me on the lack of critical jargon. 'Wait till she hears what's to come' was Sheedy's response. In fact, the critical contributions were models of lucidity.

The great man himself did not give broadcast or print interviews. The best we could have done was to arrange a meeting, but Beckett was in London overseeing a production at the Royal Court during the week I visited Paris to meet those who knew him well. These included his publisher Jérôme Lindon, his old Trinity friend Con Leventhal, and Maria Jolas, a Paris friend, whose husband, Eugene, had edited *Transition*. One of the most valuable interviews was recorded for us in London by Terry Kelleher with Geoffrey Thompson, a psychiatrist and close friend of the writer during his London days. John Calder, his London publisher, was also an important contributor.

When I read a piece recently by the playwright Conor McPherson to the effect that John Osborne disapproved strongly of the manner in which Beckett was deified, it was something I could recognize. In fairness, the writers and critics I spoke to in 1976 were not groupies: they were interested in other authors as well. But there were devotees around who regarded Beckett as beyond critical reproach. On that score, the playwright Tom Murphy was a breath of fresh air. When I said to him once that I had myself come round to the view that Beckett's plays could not match the novels, I remember him saying, 'You were a bit slow on that one.'

In recent years, it has occurred to me that Harold Pinter was more successful than Beckett in bringing comparable existential concerns to effective theatrical fruition. I am not saying Pinter was as deep into the well as the Dubliner, nor as good with language, but he converted, at least, *similar* existential concerns much more effectively into theatrical form than Beckett. In that theatrical regard, Pinter is to Beckett as say Synge is to Yeats. Furthermore, in the matter of the celebrated Joyce/Beckett polarity, which says that the one put everything in, while the other left everything out, give me the spendthrift plenitude of Joyce every time. I acknowledge the paeans of praise for Beckett the parer, but my preference in this matter is for the Royal University/UCD man.

Among the Irish commentators on the programme, Denis Donoghue, John Banville, Brendan Kennelly, Tom Murphy and Tony Cronin were particularly good. Donoghue's central point was that, for Beckett, reality couldn't match the opulence of language. Cronin spoke eloquently about the relevance of the question, 'what does it mean to have something to say?'

I spoke to Frank Kermode in Cambridge and George Steiner in Geneva about large questions such as whether Beckett was ending an era or beginning a new one. Not a great question really, because it invites all and sundry to say 'a bit of both.'

Steiner, surprisingly, likened him to Wilde. We also got hold of Beckett specialists like John Fletcher and James Knowlson, who later wrote a biography of Beckett. The visits to Kermode at Easter 1976 and George Steiner in Geneva in May carried an added pleasure in that they extended the range of conversation beyond the Beckett series. After the recording, Kermode and I were joined by an American academic whose main interest was aesthetics. The three-way discussion became more animated than I expected as we each sounded off on current preoccupations.

At that time my academic research interests were focused on openness of mind and the idea of continually revising whatever positions one held. I had become particularly interested in whether or not the laws of logic were revisable. Instead of returning to London as planned, I spent the evening in Cambridge because Kermode invited me to dinner at King's. I was seated between Tony Tanner, who also worked with Kermode in the English department, and Norman Pittenger, a well-known Anglican theologian. Tanner had been a product of the Cambridge of I. A. Richards and F. R. Leavis, which placed English literature at the nerve centre of a humane education. He was one of the first British academics to take a serious interest in American literature. Not long after, he took up an appointment at Johns Hopkins University, but became so disenchanted that within months he successfully reapplied for his old job at Cambridge.

Pittenger was born in America and educated at Princeton. He was one of the leading exponents of process theology, which was quite fashionable in the mid-seventies. It consisted of applying the thought of the British philosopher A. N. Whitehead to a theological context. God is thought of not so much in terms of substance as in terms of process. Pittenger's main moral interest was defending the legitimacy of homosexual relations. He seemed to be in the right college given King's noted tolerance of Bloomsbury mores. That May evening we discussed recent revelations about Paul Tillich's sexual peccadilloes, but mostly we talked about Tillich's claim that Catholicism without Protestantism was demonic, and equally so, Protestantism without Catholicism. The first is too authoritarian; the second could do with more authority.

George Steiner was then professor of comparative literature at Geneva, and also held a post in Cambridge. We thought of him for the Beckett series as one of those oft-quoted diagnosticians of contemporary culture, who would always provide good copy. He and I met in a vacant classroom at the University of Geneva in late May 1976. His opening greeting was, 'You work for Conor'. This took me slightly aback, given the purpose of the visit. He was referring to Conor Cruise O'Brien, who as Minister for Posts and Telegraphs in the Irish government, had responsibility for the affairs of the national network, RTÉ. Steiner and O'Brien had both taught at NYU in the 1960s.

He asked me what I thought of Conor with the air of a man who was simply offering a routine preliminary inquiry, prior to the main business of letting me know what *he* thought. Steiner's assessment of O'Brien was complimentary. The only criticism pertained to the Irishman's stubbornness in argument over seemingly inconsequential matters. The main point of commendation was that Conor had 'a big book in him'. He was right about O'Brien, though he hadn't yet written that big book about Edmund Burke. Steiner felt that literary critics like Kermode and Donoghue were spending far too much of their valuable time going to conferences. In the same breath, he told me he had turned down a mammoth BBC television series based on his book *After Babel* (1975). I should add that Christopher J. Knight has lumped together not just Kermode and Donoghue but also Steiner in his book *Uncommon Readers* (2003). No surprise there, because whatever their differences, what they all have in common is a clear commitment to engaging a wider public in literary debate.

Well-known for his disapproval of the insularity of British intellectual life, Steiner was on form that day in Geneva. Heidegger had just died. Steiner reminded me that *Le Monde* on that occasion carried the simple headline 'Heidegger est Mort'. That would have been unthinkable in Britain, and not just because of the German philosopher's involvement with Nazism. Steiner said that, unlike London, in bookstores in Paris he always found something interesting. Yet he maintained a sense of proportion about this. I recall a review he wrote a decade later for *The Times Literary Supplement* of *Noise* (1977), a book by the French politician Jacques Attali, about 'the political economy of music'. What British politician, Steiner asked (with the possible exception of Ted Heath), could produce a book of this kind; yet, what London publishing house would have allowed through so many typographical errors.

There's a postscript to the Steiner/O'Brien story. Three years later my friend Peggy O'Brien, then teaching in the English department at Trinity College Dublin, and now at the University of Massachusetts at Amherst, invited me to hear a Steiner lecture at Trinity. The lecture was a not altogether unexpected diatribe against the fashionable French critics of the day, a group he called 'Byzantine terrorists'. This group of deconstructionist thinkers, typified by Derrida and de Man, held sway in Paris and New Haven. For these critics, the text, in Steiner's view was just a *pretext* for their own fitful excursions. None of them had as much as created a single literary character. Afterwards we all adjourned for a post-lecture discussion in the common room.

It was for the most part a polite affair, but at the very end Tommy Murtagh of the French department, stirred things up by asking Steiner where he stood politically. The great man shuffled slightly before responding, in the manner of someone who over the years has had this kind of questioner for breakfast, whether in Toronto or Tokyo. Those familiar with his work could see the avowal of elitism coming, with its implicit interrogation of political notions of equality. 'As I see it,' he intoned in that most distinctive of resonant tenor voices, 'we crawled out of a primordial slime x million years ago, and in the course of history men of genius have emerged in music, mathematics, philosophy and literature. As for the rest of us, well.... But, don't worry. The rest of us have one consolation. In the Library of Congress in Washington are stored the telephone directories of every city in the world. So, don't worry, my friend, you'll survive.' Tommy Murtagh for an instant looked vanquished, but then delivered a knock-out blow: 'I'm ex-directory, Professor Steiner.'

The following morning I happened to be visiting Conor Cruise O'Brien at his home in Howth. 'Met an old colleague of yours last night', I said. 'Who's that?' he asked. 'George Steiner'. 'What did George have to say?' Not much, I said. 'That's George, all right.' Given Steiner's earlier tribute to O'Brien, that response seemed a tad ungracious, but then George could dish it out too.

I was in Howth to record a radio programme about O'Brien's revised views of religious feelings in the wake of a car accident that his wife, Máire Mhac an tSaoi, a leading poet in the Irish language, had recently had. He told me that the fact that people were praying for his wife moved him not to the point of abandoning his life-long agnosticism, but of transporting him to what he considered an even more radical form of agnosticism, namely the realization that what *he* thought about the world made not a whit of difference to the world. He expressed his view of the limitations of theology that morning by telling the story of a young child at a religious examination. The bishop asked him what the Trinity meant. The boy offered a hesitant and unclear answer. 'I don't understand,' said the bishop. 'You're not supposed to,' said the child; 'it's a mystery.'

A notable omission from the list of contributors to the Beckett radio series in 1976 was the poet John Montague, who has written the best pieces I have read about meetings with the man himself in Paris, while avoiding the laughable 'me and

Sam' idiom often deployed by people who scarcely knew Beckett. Montague's report in his memoir *Company: A Chosen Life* (2001) of a conversation between Beckett, Joan Mitchell, the American Abstract Expressionist, and Montague himself is extremely illuminating: as recollections go, it is an absolute gem. That piece made a strong impression on me for two reasons. First of all, Mitchell did not seem in any way intimidated by Beckett; she treated as an equal a writer who was much more accustomed to deference from other artists. Secondly, Montague was writing about perhaps the only Abstract Expressionist whose work I really admire, ever since seeing a show of hers some years ago at the old Whitney Gallery in New York.

Seamus Heaney, too, was a notable absentee from our Beckett series. It seems strange now, but in 1976 Heaney was perceived mainly as a Northern poet, and was not part of the regular circle of artists called on as cultural commentators in the Republic. The Nobel Prize was twenty years away. It is often forgotten that while Harvard offered him a job around 1980, none of the leading universities in the Republic did.

Paul Muldoon was likewise perceived essentially as a Northern poet and had achieved nothing like the international eminence he was subsequently to attain. Neither did another Northern poet, Derek Mahon, feature, though he impressed with an account in *The Observer* some years ago of a meeting with the great man in Paris. That account ended with Mahon saying: 'I should add that for all his cordiality he did not invite me back to the famous flat, backing on to the Santé prison yard.'

In the summer of 1975 I got to know the poet Brian Coffey, a realy close friend of Beckett. Both men befriended Peggy Guggenheim, but Beckett had a more intimate relationship with her. Coffey had written a doctorate at the Institut Catholique in Paris on the concept of order in Aquinas. I first met him at the home of lecturer and literary critic Maurice Harmon and later with Jim Mays, an expert on Coleridge, who also wrote perceptively about Coffey. Coffey told a story about having met Beckett recently in London and he thought it significant that when out walking together, Beckett stopped suddenly, pointed to a bird that had just landed and said excitedly, 'Look, look'. Coffey's story has to be seen in the context of how Beckett was generally regarded at the time, namely that of someone with a very dark view of the world. What Coffey implied was that there was now some indication that Sam was changing. It seems a trivial enough example, yet Coffey set great store by it.

That reference to the way in which Beckett was perceived in the early 1970s reminds us that Beckett is no more immune than other writers to changing fashions either in the theatre or in the academy. Opinions also fluctuate as to the main influences that shaped his writing. On that score, it is striking that missing from all the commentaries in the series I made about Beckett was any reference to his wartime experiences. Since then the view has gained ground that these experiences were critical to much of his work. On a more general note, what I personally had difficulty with was the coexistence in Beckett of a laissez-faire attitude to textual interpretation (whether by the performer or the reader) and a finicky controlling one in the matter of stage directions. If an actor asked him what a particular passage meant, he would shrug, whereas in the matter of stage directions he insisted that things be done his way. I suppose that apparent conflict can be resolved by saying that Beckett is asking us first to respect precise stage directions in order that some specific intentions of his can be realized, but that once those limitations that he has imposed are respected, the reader/actor is free to make what he or she wants of the text.

Chapter 15

SEAMUS HEANEY EN ROUTE
TO THE BBC

ARLY IN 1977, I GOT AN UNEXPECTED phone call from a
BBC television producer in Belfast. Robin Wylie, who had
heard my work on an RTÉ Sunday afternoon radio programme
Lookaround, was sounding out my interest in presenting a television series of interviews with the widows of Irish writers. The
writers concerned were Frank O'Connor, Seán O'Casey, Walter
Macken, Louis MacNeice and Patrick Kavanagh. We had hoped
to talk to Evelyn Nolan, the widow of Flann O'Brien, but when
I phoned her, she declined, saying, 'I was just a writer's house-
keeper; I have nothing to say.'

That unexpected phone call from Robin Wylie in 1977
would lead to a very fruitful professional relationship over the
next decade. That wasn't the first overture I had received from
the BBC (I had already presented occasional arts programmes
for Brian Barfield on radio and Gerry McCrudden on television)
but it was to prove to be the most productive. The interviews
with the widows of writers led to a series of conversations with
writers, scholars and artists that continued for a decade.

In addition to that studio-bound series, Robin and I also
made three hour-long television documentaries in the early
1980s for BBC2. These documentaries consisted of profiles of
the playwright Seán O'Casey, the tenor John McCormack and

Harry Ferguson, inventor of the tractor. Another documentary profile, that of the County Down classical scholar E. R. Dodds, did not enjoy the wider UK network exposure of the O'Casey, McCormack and Ferguson programmes, but it was particularly rewarding to make. Dodds, author of *The Greeks and the Irrational* (1951), was one of the great classical Greek scholars of the twentieth century. It was especially gratifying that he was captured on film for us by a highly gifted lighting cameraman Rex Maidment.

Wylie, who died too young in 2011, was a delight to work with. An art school graduate, he was a fine painter. That offers a key to the kind of television producer he was, someone more alert to images than television producers usually are. A corollary of that was that he tended to delegate editorial choices to me in the matter of selecting guests more often than would customarily be the case. Thankfully, Robin had the kind of quiet self-confidence that allowed me a relatively free hand. The BBC in Belfast was a highly creative broadcasting centre at the time: the poet Paul Muldoon was both a radio and television producer there; likewise David Hammond. Judith Elliott, who commissioned me to make several arts documentaries for radio, gave some of her best years to the BBC.

The first interview in the television series with the widows of writers was with Harriet Sheehy, widow of Frank O'Connor. The pair had first met at Harvard, where Harriet was a student and Frank was teaching. They then moved to Dublin. She told me that she had once threatened to leave him. Frank looked her squarely in the eye, and said: 'By all means go, but if you do, don't come back.' There is something quite chilling about that.

Eileen O'Casey was then in her late seventies and still looking really good. She must have been a stunning-looking actor in her day. It was no surprise to discover that Harold Macmillan, the former British prime minister, fell in love with her.

Macmillan was O'Casey's publisher. Eileen was not as intellectually inclined as Harriet Sheehy, but she had a rich fund of stories.

Hedley MacNeice spoke about Louis's intense dislike of dining with senior BBC personnel: it drove him to drink, if indeed he needed provocation. Hedley was an artist in her own right, as an interpreter of Schoenberg's music for voice. In 1977, the year of the recording with her, she was running a restaurant in Kinsale.

In her recollections about her husband, the playwright and novelist Walter Macken, Peggy Macken displayed the kind of personal warmth that audiences loved. My memories of Katherine Kavanagh relate more to the post-programme conversation. She had picked up on Patrick's high regard for critic John Jordan and poet Tony Cronin, though she herself seemed a tad afraid of Cronin.

That series with the widows led to a series called *Lifetimes*, which consisted of conversations with writers, artists and scholars. Among the guests were poet Seamus Heaney, literary critics Seamus Deane and Denis Donoghue, the architectural historian Maurice Craig, Theo Moody, co-founder of modern Irish historiography in the 1930s with Robin Dudley Edwards, novelists Maeve Binchy and Julia O'Faoláin, playwrights Hugh Leonard and Denis Johnston, Charles Monteith the publisher, Robert Elegant an American writer, politician Seán MacBride, writer Ulick O'Connor, actor Niall Toibín, poet Brendan Kennelly, the tenor Josef Locke and the contralto Heather Harper. As I look at that list now, it is very light on women, which doesn't reflect creditably on either Robin or myself, but most of the blame lies with me.

It is worth recalling that those years of weekend return taxi journeys from Dublin to Belfast occurred at what used to be called 'the height of the Troubles'. I never experienced any problems, though I was edgy enough returning late at night from Belfast with Katherine Kavanagh, when she began to sing 'Kevin Barry' at a British checkpoint. What I had not known at the time is that she was a relative of Kevin Barry.

The only worrying incident during that series occurred on the morning after a rugby international in Dublin. Seán MacBride and I were with a relatively inexperienced driver who took us through a loyalist area as we made our way to the BBC in Belfast. MacBride was a political luminary at both national and international levels. He had been awarded the Nobel (1974) and the Lenin (1977) Peace Prizes and was a founder member of Amnesty International. And, of prime significance on that Sunday morning in a loyalist area of Belfast, he had been (briefly) chief of staff of the IRA in the 1930s.

Suddenly a police car waved down our taxi. The driver was asked for his driving licence. He tendered his passport instead. If I recall it right, in that context a driving licence was a more important badge of identity than a passport. The police asked our driver to step out of the car. I noticed that MacBride was becoming quite nervous. 'What are they doing?' he asked me. 'They're just asking him a few questions', I said. 'No they're not', he said. 'They're taking him away.'

At that point, I began to feel uneasy myself. After all, MacBride was a former senior IRA man, and here we were in 'enemy' territory. All sides must have known that someone as distinguished as MacBride was on his way to Belfast. The uneasy moment passed. It was not an ambush, just a regular police check-up. During the interview itself a few hours later, McBride appeared even more nervous when I pressed him about his military past. *Lifetimes* interviews were not confrontational, yet I felt I had to ask him about that segment of his life. Most of the conversation dealt with his recent Nobel and Lenin peace prizes and his mother, the patriot Maud Gonne, immortalized by Yeats. I was always intrigued by the similarity between the kind of nervousness MacBride displayed when our car was stopped and the unease he showed in studio when asked about his subversive past. On the way home we discussed Conor Cruise O'Brien, an old foe of his, and at that time a leading critic of militant nationalism. 'Did you ever do Conor a favour?' he asked. 'No,' I replied. 'Well don't, because he won't forgive you.'

Seamus Heaney was another guest in that series. By the late 1970s he was already a poetic star in the making but not yet the global superstar he later became, particularly in the wake of winning the Nobel Prize in 1995. I first met Seamus in the mid-1970s when we were both guests at the wedding of Richard Ryan, then a young diplomat and published poet, and later Ireland's permanent representative at the United Nations. The much-attested-to kindness of both Seamus and his wife Marie was evident immediately: they drove me to the Abbey Theatre right after the reception so that I could catch a performance of Lorca's *Blood Wedding*.

Heaney had moved in 1976 from his first south of Ireland home in County Wicklow to Sandymount Strand, not far from where I bought a house in 1979. Around that time, he and Marie had put their home at the disposal of the BBC so that I could record a television interview with Seán O'Faoláin about his latest publication. I met the Heaneys again in 1983 at Harvard where Seamus was teaching, Marie was visiting, and I myself was on sabbatical.

During that sabbatical year in Cambridge, Massachusetts, I had lunch with Heaney and Anne Bernays, an American novelist, whose father Edward, a nephew of Sigmund Freud, is widely regarded as the founder of public relations. Anne and I had both been attending a series of seminars in the philosophy of psychiatry conducted by the philosopher Robert Nozick, a longtime friend of hers. Anne, who had just met Seamus in Cambridge, arranged a lunch for him, herself and myself at a restaurant in Harvard Square.

We had decided to meet after one of Nozick's seminars, which at the end of April 1983 was held outdoors in the environs of Emerson Hall, the headquarters of Harvard's philosophy department. Anne and I left early because of the planned lunch. Seamus was sitting on the ledge outside Emerson Hall waiting for us. He was wearing a grey suit, light blue shirt, and held a rain coat in his hand. He told us that as he watched Nozick, he said to himself, 'I'd say that guy is charming them, whoever he is.' The poet didn't seem particularly pushed about either the pedigree of the seminar-convenor or his topic. It was essentially as a fellow teacher that he related to Nozick: for Seamus it was an opportunity to watch a colleague at work. He thought at first that this leading American philosopher was a psychiatrist, perhaps because he was presiding over a series of seminars on the philosophy of psychiatry.

On our way to lunch, we talked about a recent *New York Times* profile of the poet. Seamus remarked that there was an awful lot of 'bogs' in it, in a manner that indicated he thought the profile writer had perhaps gone overboard on it. I remarked on how good I thought the *Crane Bag* interview was that he had done with Seamus Deane. He replied that Deane was an unnerving person to be interviewed by; they had shared too much of the same past. I got the impression from Anne that, as an American writer, she quite enjoyed observing how two Irishmen abroad behaved: what they spoke about and didn't speak about.

We walked from Harvard Yard to Mass. Ave. to the restaurant Potato One, Potato Two, now no longer there. The waitress recognized Heaney and gushed over him. Greek salad for Anne and myself; oysters for Heaney. There was chat about his colleague Derek Walcott, the abortion referendum in Ireland, and something of teaching at Harvard (Seamus regarded it as a holiday). He was worried about being a public figure: it could obscure the work. 'What tends to happen is that people just want the whiff of you; they don't care about the work. The persona can become more powerful than anything you could write.' He referred to the BBC television interview we had done in 1978. He didn't want to do it. 'That was having it both ways', he said. He doubted even if his teaching was good for his writing.

I spoke about having recently heard Jonathan Culler and Joseph Margolis at Northeastern University talk about aspects of literary theory, and wondered how the two writers with me felt about that kind of discourse. Anne had her doubts, and Seamus partly agreed, but said he wished, all the same, he could say what structuralism was all about in four simple sentences. In that same vein, he spoke to me admiringly on another occasion about the critical writings of Oxford academic Valentine Cunningham. We tend to forget what a brilliant critic Heaney was himself. Francis Stuart once told me he rated the criticism above the poetry. That's pushing matters, but it does highlight the quality of Heaney as an analytical critic. That work is probably best described like that of Helen Vendler, Christopher Ricks and Harold Bloom as firmly belonging to a belle-lettrist tradition, but Heaney himelf was always alert to more subversive critical stirrings from Paris and elsewhere.

When I recorded a television interview with Heaney in 1978, the BBC provided a car and driver for the journey from Dublin to Belfast. The trip itself proved as rewarding as I had expected. Here was a poet who viewed art as partly a search for wisdom, and it showed not only in his poetry but also in his conversation. We spoke about Bryan Magee's television series with philosophers, then being broadcast on the BBC. Seamus was much taken with a line by reviewer Denis Potter in the *Sunday Times* that morning to the effect that philosophers are 'the butlers of the intellectual world': they sniffily adjudicate on the offerings of practitioners in other disciplines.

He spoke that autumn morning of a friend in Scandinavia who had 'a dolorous Arctic sensibility'. Seamus was a good storyteller and a good audience too. I had recently gleaned a story from an essay the Australian poet Peter Porter, had written for *Encounter*. Porter went to a party where he met and was enchanted by one of the leading opera singers of the day. To impress her, he ransacked his brain for whatever clever thoughts he could muster about the arts of opera and singing. He thought he was making great progress until suddenly she stopped him in his tracks. 'Listen,' she said, 'I just came here to get laid.'

Heaney responded with a better story. The actor Cyril Cusack had invited him to the Abbey during the run of a play in which Cyril was starring, possibly *The Play of Hadrian VII* by Peter Luke, but he couldn't be sure. The young poet had been instructed to come backstage on whatever night he was in, which Heaney duly did. When he arrived in the actor's dressing room, Cusack introduced him to a quartet of the actor's admirers. It was in the making of such introductions that the actor could really score a bull's eye: it was a godsend opportunity to make a point. When he came to Heaney, Cusack said: 'And this is the poet Seamus' ... [hesitation] ... Murphy.' In telling that story, Seamus said to me: 'I'd like to think it was deliberate.' I once tried to get the great actress Siobhan McKenna to open up on Cusack's reputed naughtiness, but without any success. The prevailing lore in Raidió Éireann was that during a particular recording, Siobhan had one of those heart-stopping moments with a line like, 'Oh my god, he is truly dead,' at which point Cyril piped up almost inaudibly, 'What did you say?'

In a radio interview with the actor I once 'bravely' tried to broach the subject. Cusack, who had been taught by Dominican priests, said that for him his professional life was guided by *veritas* in all things. When he denied ever violating that principle, I protested that I wasn't suggesting that he ever did, but was asking him to tell us what a violation of that principle might consist of in the context of a theatrical performance. How would we recognize such a violation? But he was way ahead of me, far too fleet-footed for the likes of me. He said he had no idea.

Niall Tóibín, another fine Irish actor, told me once that one man who had Cusack's measure was Richard Burton. He says that when the pair worked together, Burton, fully aware of Cyril's trick of underplaying, of coming 'in under' the other actors, began to come in under Cyril. Apparently, that's what the old actor-managers did: instead of dominating the cast by overplaying, they came in *under* the other actors. Burton and Cusack first worked together in *The Spy Who Came in from the Cold*. I watched the movie recently on television: Tóibín was spot on.

Mind you, I doubt if that great actor-manager Donald Wolfit ever underplayed, whatever the circumstances. The best example I saw of underplaying in the last two decades was Richard Harris's performance in Pirandello's *Henry IV* at the Wyndham Theatre in London. His opening cat-like entrance in stockinged feet took everybody by surprise. A mad king underplaying? Come on.

The first of the television documentaries that Robin Wylie and I made for BBC2 was a profile of Seán O'Casey. Enter his widow Eileen once more, and Harold Macmillan. Robin and I went to Birch Grove in Sussex in late 1979 to talk to Macmillan on his home turf. I have met charmers in my time, but the former prime minister took the biscuit. 'I feel I *should* know you,' he said to me, 'but I don't watch the box much nowadays.' Here was a man who knew how to minister to media egos. When we were recording, Thatcher's first Tory Party conference as leader was in progress in Brighton. Robin Wylie asked Macmillan how he thought she was doing at the conference. 'What's the weather like in London?' was all we heard in reply.

Cusack surfaced again in the O'Casey documentary for the BBC, as one of the great O'Casey interpreters. Not long before we spoke, he had toured America with the Abbey company as Fluther in *The Plough and the Stars*. He had also recently starred in Bill Bryden's production of the play at the National Theatre in London. We went to talk to him at his home in Hatch Street, Dublin. The television crew were taken aback when he asked them to return in ten minutes. He said they had arrived too early.

I noticed that Cusack didn't quite allow himself to be interviewed: like many actors, he was happier with a prepared script, which he was intent on delivering, regardless of what I asked him. He could surprise you with his comments about playwrights. He told me on that occasion that at the personal level he found Tom Murphy 'too sure'; he preferred Hugh Leonard's sense of wounded vulnerability. Cusack seemed to be implying that there was an artistic downside to personal confidence. At moments like that, you sensed the kind of perceptiveness that made him a great actor. The writer Mary Lavin also made a remark to me about the feeling of sureness and strength she got from Murphy in his handshake. Interesting, though, that suggestion from Cusack that personal sureness may have an artistic downside. Or was that just a case of romanticizing vulnerability.

A trip to New York meant recording a piece with the great critic Eric Bentley, author of *In Search of Theatre* (1953). Then on to Rhode Island to talk to David Krause, editor of the O'Casey letters. Peter Foges, the BBC's man in New York, was particularly helpful in getting us to Rhode Island despite a bad oil spill on the highway. Much of the critical analysis was a matter of discussing how much of a nationalist the playwright was, and how much of a socialist. I wince now at the reductive character of this, but that was due mainly to my own critical biases at the time.

We featured certain top flight academic critics like Seamus Deane and Katharine Worth. After his great trilogy in the 1920s, *Shadow of a Gunman, Juno and the Paycock*, and *The Plough and the Stars*, audiences and critics alike wanted O'Casey to go on repeating himself. Everyone was impatient with his desire to break new ground. Only in recent years is *The Silver Tassie* getting recognition. Mind you, he perpetrated some real turkeys, like *Purple Dust*. And Kenneth Tynan was far too kind in his review of *The Bishop's Bonfire*, which had its premiere in Dublin in 1954: 'O'Casey was never a great thinker; he is no longer a great craftsman; but he still can sing.'

Ulick O'Connor's appearance on *Lifetimes* was a very enjoyable affair, though he was up to his usual tricks, looking for that extra bit of attention. Styrofoam coffee cups were not acceptable. Ulick is an all-round man of letters – poet, playwright, biographer and translator – who has also worked occasionally as a journalist. I have known him since we spoke around 1970 about his fine biography of Brendan Behan. You can't but like a man who in one particular volume of his diaries quotes the actress and theatre director Shelah Richards, as saying (and I am adding my own gloss here) that there are *two* Ulick O'Connors, the posh-voiced saloniste who can quote Schlegel and Rilke, and the docker-like Dubliner, who enthuses about boxing. Shelah was on the button. You're never sure which persona or voice Ulick is going to deploy. We're not talking fakery here, but sheer imaginative richness of personality.

Brendan Kennelly is a poet and former Trinity professor who, through television appearances on *The Late Late Show*, has become a household name in Ireland. He so charmed the *Lifetimes* production team in Belfast that they offered him work not just as a guest but as a presenter. He must be one of the greatest Irish talkers since Wilde or Shaw. We have known each other since Trinity in the late 1950s. Brendan was always wary of my interest in literary criticism, let alone literary theory, and even warned me off Leavis, neither of us knowing at the time that with the arrival of the French deconstructionists and their American disciples, Leavis would be consigned by the fashionistas to the belle-lettrist dust-heap. On the morning we recorded our programme, I had just returned from the Kennedy Library in Boston. I spoke about JFK's rhetoric and asked the question whether the rhetoric still worked even if you were cynical about it as you listened. Brendan had no doubt but that it worked, re-gardless. That was what was meant, he said, by 'the power of the word' in the Christian gospels. 'In the beginning was the Word', and all that. That day he gave me a present of a small green-covered notebook, and encouraged me to write. I didn't take up journal-writing for a further two years, but that planted a seed. One of the first lines I inscribed was about 'gossamer fidelities'.

Brendan loved teaching and is a born encourager of others. The poems and conversation testify to a subtle awareness of the contradictions in himself, especially the uneasy coexistence of 'outsider' rebel role and Trinity insider; of unbridled wordsmith and dutiful committee man. I have just been looking at some of his poems in the recent *Harvard Collection of Irish Poetry*. My impression is that his poetry was underestimated for years mainly because of his gifts as a talk-show guest.

Niall Tóibín was still basking in the glory of his Brendan Behan show on Broadway in the early 1970s, when I recorded a *Lifetimes* with him in 1979. I had known Niall since his days in the Raidió Éireann repertory company. He was notorious for quickness of temper. I asked him in that interview if he ever lost his temper on purpose. 'There is no other way to lose it,' he replied.

He told a story about an Irish-American who feted him in a nearby pub every night during the run of *Behan* on Broadway. The first Monday night after the show closed, Niall went into the pub as usual. His regular patron ignored him. I consider Niall the best teller of a story I have ever heard. I can still hear his deadly accurate lisping impersonation of the theatre direc-tor Frank Dermody. The actor Chris Curran approached Der-mody after rehearsal to ask him what the scene just rehearsed meant. 'Aw, for fuck's sake, Chris, let the *critics* tell us what it means.' Dermody always pronounced 'ah' as 'aw'.

After the O'Casey documentary in 1980, the next one I made for BBC was a profile of John McCormack in 1984. Oddly enough, Tony Barry of RTÉ approached me at the same time to make a programme about McCormack for RTÉ. However, I had already agreed to make one for the BBC with Robin Wylie; there was no question of doing the two. In the end, there was an interesting difference of emphasis in the two documentaries. RTÉ, with Senator David Norris fronting the programme, travelled to Italy but ignored America. We ignored Italy and travelled to America. I am convinced the BBC decision was the correct one. McCormack trained in Italy, but achieved his main success in America. The important feature of McCormack's life was that he abandoned opera for the concert platform: it was in America that he gave most of his recitals. Apart from that editorial difference of emphasis between the two networks, there was a difference in presenter-presentation styles: there was no way my subdued into-camera pieces could match David Norris's bravura style; I envied the bold éclat of his television presentation.

The BBC programme drew extensively for its preliminary research on the work of Gordon Ledbetter, the Dublin writer and music critic. Ledbetter knows everything there is to be known about McCormack, and has a deep knowledge of the evolution of the art of singing in the last few hundred years. We also spoke to Desmond Shawe-Taylor and to Henry Pleasants. Shawe-Taylor had been music critic with the *Sunday Times* and loved the recordings of the early McCormack. Pleasants was one of the few world authorities on the art and history of singing. After recording our interview, we chatted about singing for hours in his piano-furnished flat close to Victoria station in London.

We recorded material in New York and Chicago. I remember the Irish-born tenor Hubert Valentine; he had had close connections with the subject of our programme, but was more inclined to talk about his own career. In Chicago we spoke to the music critic Paul Hume, born in 1916 and very familiar with the details of McCormack's American career. Hume's main claim to fame was that in 1950 he was the recipient of a most abusive letter from President Harry Truman because of a poor review Hume had given to Truman's soprano daughter in the *Washington Post*. Truman told him that if they ever met, Hume would 'need a new nose, a lot of beefsteak for black eyes, and perhaps a supporter below'.

We had been promised an interview by Placido Domingo's management, but it never materialized. Robin Wylie was bitterly disappointed. I told him later, much to his amusement, about the famous encounter, reported in the magazine section of the *Daily Telegraph* between Domingo and former British Prime Minister Ted Heath, somewhere in the north of England. Heath was brought backstage after a performance to meet the great tenor. 'Mr. Heath, this is Placido Domingo'. 'No, you're not', said Heath. 'Yes, I am', said Domingo. 'No, you're not' 'Yes, I am'. Heath persisted: 'He'd never sing in a place like this. Oh, of course, he'd *say* he would. But he wouldn't actually turn up'. Domingo got madder and madder, but Heath wouldn't relent.

By the time I began making programmes for BBC in 1977, I was doing research in psychology at Trinity. In fact, I began that project in 1975. My *idées fixes* at the time pertained to the ⸺rtance of autonomy and openness of mind. The reason I ⸺ested in personal autonomy was that I was begin- ⸺that my particular kind of religious upbringing ⸺my capacity for independence of thought. The ⸺you come to believe that one particular ⸺on of the truth, all that remains for you ⸺urce thinks on various matters, be it ⸺nce or business. So the kind of ques- ⸺will occur within that framework: ⸺tion the framework itself.

⸺dividuals question the belief frame- ⸺prominent in my mind when I read ⸺*e Best and the Brightest* (1972) in the ⸺ase of the word 'brightest' in the title, the question I then turned to was what it really meant to be 'intelligent' in this context. Furthermore, I wondered what the connection was between being intelligent and being inclined to question inherited frameworks.

President Kennedy had surrounded himself with some of the best and the brightest, who worked extremely well within a given framework, but who seemingly never queried the framework itself. The question was: if these men were so intelligent how did they get into the irreversible quagmire that was Vietnam? Take Robert McNamara, the Secretary of Defence. He was reputedly a human computer who could process raw data, spit out numerous options and the implications of each course of action, all in a matter of minutes. Yet he accepted the political/military framework within which he was quite happy to operate. He was essentially confining himself to questions of a means/ends character, such as calculating how many warheads were needed within what space of time to achieve such and such an objective.

My question was: what does that example tell us about what it means to be intelligent. Does the refusal to question an inherited framework indicate a lack of intelligence or something else. First of all, I think we can say that if the individual is not *aware* of the governing framework within which he is working, that indicates a failure of intelligence. However, if we assume that he *is* aware of the framework, the refusal to question it may mean that he is either lacking in intellectual independence, or it may indicate a political decision to accept a system of which the individual personally disapproves. The first course of action involves obedience to the system from a loyal servant who is aware of the governing system; the second involves pretending to go along with the system with a view to securing a personal advantage. Neither of those two examples demonstrates lack of intelligence, though a case could be made for saying that lack of intellectual independence is much closer to a failure of intelligence than is the political decision to live with a framework of which one disapproves.

In effect, where intelligence manifests itself is the capacity to (a) see the framework, and (b) see the implications of operating within that system. To return to my opening question: it is clear that someone who (a) doesn't notice the governing framework, and (b) the contradictions between existing policy and what would prevail in a different system is less than intelligent. So the term 'the best and the brightest' has to be seen in that light. It is reasonable to assume that those Kennedy advisers who went along with the invasion of North Vietnam were not unintelligent, but they failed either because of unquestioning loyalty to Kennedy, or in the sense that they secretly disapproved of the policy but for political reasons went along with it.

This was a period when I began to reflect on three interrelated concepts: intelligence, creativity and wisdom. It became increasingly clear that intelligence had to do with the power to see relationships, to see connections. But that skill in itself, could flourish without curiosity. Curiosity manifests itself in the activity of questioning. One can conceive of someone skilled at perceiving connections in data of all kinds but who is not given to asking questions. Eavan Boland asked me one day, 'why do you ask so many questions?' What she was hinting at was that since the asking of questions presupposed that there were answers, perhaps in many instances there were no answers, and so questioning was a waste of time.

Wisdom appears to presuppose some measure of both intelligence and creativity. If we take the second component, creativity, as exemplified by the impulse to question, then wisdom might well relate (apropos Eavan Boland's query) to the capacity to realize which questions merit pursuing and which don't. Worth *pursuing*, mind you, not just asking, because all questions are surely worth *asking*. It seems to me that the capacity to identify one's needs is a measure of wisdom; and an even greater index would be the capacity to adjudicate between competing needs. The ultimate measure of wisdom, presumably, is the capacity to integrate the satisfaction of those needs in the service of others. For some spiritual writers, God is to be found where your deepest self is; for others, it is in the service of others. This is a horses-for-courses question. We don't expect the mystic to turn up at the barricades; but the kind of prayerful wisdom he achieves may well be what energises the activist.

In 1975 the combined sciences departments in Trinity organized weekly seminars in the history and philosophy of science. Whether or not the so-called human sciences or social sciences are sciences at all is still debated. What is certain is that there is a hierarchy at work here, with physics at the top of the pyramid. A. J. Ayer, in an unguarded moment in his memoir, reveals that Einstein remarked to someone that he thought highly of Ayer's intelligence. It is clear that, for Ayer, physicists were at the top of the disciplinary tree. It doesn't seemed to have dawned on him that he might have been a better philosopher or logician than the great physicist was.

Michael Dummett, an expert on Frege, speaks in the manner of a physicist when he argues that until we get the philosophy of language right, we cannot construct a philosophical system: the constituent building blocks at the level of language, like the constituent components in physics, are foundational. And, of course, for W. V. O. Quine, philosophy is continuous with the physical sciences. A few years after those philosophy of science seminars, I had the privilege of meeting Ayer, Dummett and Quine. Ayer spoke to me in London about a particular volume of his memoirs. 'Is there any philosopher of genius about today?' I asked. 'Not since Wittgenstein.' 'What about Quine?' 'Definitely in the front rank, but not a genius.'

I have strayed lovingly from those mid-70s' Trinity seminars on the history and philosophy of science. Those weekly get-togethers organised by the science departments were days of heated encounters between the Kuhn and the Popper protagonists. Thomas Kuhn's *The Structure of Scientific Revolutions* was published in 1962, but didn't begin to enjoy popularity in the academic community until the 1970s. In crude terms, he was seen as the relativist to Karl Popper's more absolutist line. Kuhn was interested in the kind of major shifts that occurred whenever an entire theoretical perspective had to be jettisoned; Popper had a more piecemeal approach, where the emphasis was on regular revision of what was, in effect, a more *continuous* theoretical orientation. One stressed discontinuity; the other continuity.

To describe the overturning of an existing theoretical perspective, Kuhn introduced the notion of 'paradigm shift'. This has become one of the most promiscuously deployed terms in contemporary critical discourse: it is used in a myriad contexts, from astrophysics to ballroom dancing. The main competing voice to Kuhn at that time in the philosophy of science, that of Karl Popper, became identified with the concept of falsifiability, which was for him the ultimate criterion in determining whether a theory was scientific or not. He used it to give short shrift to Marxism and psychoanalysis.

One thing I realized early on was that it was all too easy to sound off on the philosophy of science without having engaged in the actual practices one was philosophizing about. While psychology was not a so-called *hard* science, it did have a rigour appropriate to its subject matter. Not that with the conceptual focus of my own research interests, I could claim great kinship with the *harder* experimental and statistical dimensions of the discipline. Nonetheless, while I wasn't conducting an empirical investigation myself, I was at least learning how to assess the value of whatever existing empirical studies were relevant to my own research inquiry and so get a sense of the governing methods of the discipline. It was a useful perspective for a broadcast journalist to acquire.

Chapter 16

A Sunday Morning in Rome
with Gore Vidal

IT NEVER CEASES TO AMAZE ME THAT I haven't made more headway with European languages, given that I appear to have a particular aptitude for them, probably because of my solid school background in Latin and Greek. Like many another, when Ireland joined the European Union or European Economic Community (as it was then called) in 1973, I enrolled at the Alliance Française. I subsequently took courses for a summer at the Sorbonne, but never pursued the matter with comparable zeal. Likewise with German, which involved courses in Dublin and Passau, Bavaria, but without any rigorous follow-up.

In 1977 I began to take classes in German at the Goethe Institute in Dublin. I wasn't starting from scratch because I had already studied German at Trinity as part of a Commerce degree. That particular Goethe Institute class was a very small one (five participants at the most) consisting of, among others, Joan FitzGerald, the wife of the then Irish Foreign Minister, Dr. Garret FitzGerald. Also participating was Richard Kearney, the philosopher, who is now a professor at Boston College, but was still a graduate student at the time.

I hired a private tutor before I spent a month in 1977 at the Goethe Institute in Passau. With the help of the tutor, I tried an experiment that worked to a limited degree. I first analyzed my own conversational patterns in English to see what kind of expressions I used more than others. Then I had the tutor translate these expressions into German. I discovered that I tended to focus on connectives like 'that depends on what you mean by' or 'in other words'. The problem was that by mastering certain connecting phrases, I gave the impression of being more fluent than I actually was.

One of the things I learned on that occasion is that it is a myth to think that by simply living in a country you pick up the language. You don't; you have to work at it. I met people who had been working in Germany for years but whose German was still quite poor. I also learned that the capacity to speak a foreign language, to read it, and to listen, are quite distinct skills. It was not uncommon to discover someone who had taken a degree in German literature but who was incapable of stringing together a few sentences.

Later that year I got an opportunity to practise my German again, when Dick Warner, at that time an RTÉ radio producer, suggested I go to Écône in Switzerland to record a programme about the dissident Catholic archbishop Marcel Lefebvre, who had been expelled from the Church because of his rejection of Vatican II reforms. When I arrived in Écône, I was told that Lefebvre was 'out of town'. However, I did speak to others, including some American clerical students, happy to fly the Lefebvre flag in objecting to liturgical and other reforms.

Since 1977, the Vatican line on the Lefebvrists has softened, especially with the reinstatement by Pope Benedict of the Latin Mass, but at that time, in the era of Paul VI, the Lefebvre camp were outcasts. I recall the precision with which the church historian Monsignor Paddy Corish of Maynooth insisted that Lefebvre had a *defective* notion of tradition, not an inadequate one. After all, an *inadequate* understanding of tradition could mean that though the understanding wasn't adequate, he was still on the right track; a *defective* understanding meant that he was definitely on the wrong track. As the theologian Yves Congar pointed out, Lefebvre had an understanding of tradition as something fixed. That view of tradition as a living thing that changed was the *official* church view, not just that of a liberal theologian like Congar.

In 1977 I recorded a number of interviews in Oxford on religious themes. The best laugh I got was after a long conversation with a Carmelite contemplative, Father Matthew McGettrick, on Boar's Hill outside the city. He had been holding forth on the intractable imponderables of the mystical life, a life beyond time and space, when suddenly he asked: 'Do I get paid for this, by the way?' That my interviewee on that occasion should make a query of that kind was perfectly in accord with Herbert Fingarette's assessment of mystics in his book *The Self in Transformation* (1963), where he says that mystics are highly integrated people. When you think about it, why, in principle, shouldn't mystics be as alert to a post-dated cheque as to a post-inspiration state of consciousness.

Peter Hebblethwaite, an expert on Vatican affairs, with whom I had planned to record a programme in Oxford on that occasion, recommended that I talk to Leszek Kolakowski, the Polish philosopher, then at All Souls. Kolakowski was at that time in the middle of his magnum opus, *Main Currents of Marxism*. My only knowledge of him was as the author of a book a few years earlier on Husserl, not an obvious runner even for a radio programme not inhospitable to ideas. His trilogy on Marxism was in progress. In it he argued that Stalinism was not a freak outcome of Marxism but an inevitable one. Kolakowski was becoming increasingly interested in the role of Christianity in Western thought. In fact, Hebblethwaite had told me that there was a rumour in Oxford that Kolakowski was about to convert to Rome. I have only the haziest recollection of our conversation, but I do recall that he knocked any idea of an imminent conversion straight on the head.

Hebblethwaite, a former Jesuit, was already a budding Vaticanologist. He would later produce two well received papal biographies, one of John XXIII (1984), the other of Paul VI. At Oxford in 1977, he was teaching French at Wadham. That came about because one day shortly after he had left the Jesuits, he ran into his old tutor on High Street, who offered him a job. Peter was clever and the unkind said he knew it. He was a classic Catholic liberal in that he fully backed the reforms of the Second Vatican Council. He was appalled by the Vatican decision to haul theologians like Schillebeeckx and Küng before the Holy Office for suspected heresy,and he vigorously disapproved of the emerging pontificate of John Paul II from 1978 onwards. In a BBC studio in London, I recorded a head-on clash between him and Paul Johnson on the merits of that same pontificate. Neither contributor was a blushing violet. It was Christopher Hitchens who famously said that we have to be tough not just on Paul Johnson but on the causes espoused by Paul Johnson.

I have mentioned Hebblethwaite's brilliance, but he also had inexplicable insecurities. When his book on Pope John XXIII came out in 1984, I said to him in Rome that I wished I'd written it. Peter responded quite sharply to that: had I been approached but refused? Or did I mean I wished I could have written it? The second was an hypothesis more congruent with his self-esteem; the first he found unsettling. In fact, I meant the second. I was saying that I wished I'd had the *ability* to write it: I didn't have Peter's skills to do a job of that kind. A trivial but interesting glance into the workings of the mind of a man who was undoubtedly the most gifted English-language, Vatican affairs commentator in the twentieth century.

Peter told me his biography of Pope John XXIII sparked congratulatory letters from Cardinals Hume and Suenens. The theologian Hans Küng had also written approvingly to him but his publishers were unsure as to the wisdom of using any of Küng's laudatory words as a testimonial because of his controversial standing. A delightful footnote was told to me by Hebblethwaite himself: Cardinal Casaroli, who was Vatican Secretary of State, gave him a classic non-committal reply: 'Dear Mr Hebblethwaite, I have received and read your biography of Pope John XXIII, With Best Wishes...' Apparently, Casaroli read it with the cover off, on a visit somewhere with Pope John Paul II.

Because I had built up a connection with the Goethe Institute in Dublin, I was invited in November 1978 to a seminar in Munich for '*kulturjournalisten*'. Germany, notoriously, has had great difficulty getting the matter of national identity right: it tends to be either too rigid or too flabby. For example, at that particular time the German Foreign Office was worried that Germany had been going through too 'flabby' a phase, in which it had been dancing to the American tune for far too long. Now was the time for more national assertiveness. That was the context of this seminar for European journalists who reported on cultural matters and ideas.

I do not recall any of the speakers, apart from the novelist Martin Walser. I recorded interviews with a couple of film directors, including the highly controversial Hans Jürgen Syberberg, whose film on Hitler I had just seen at the Pagode in Paris. He was accused of trivializing Hitler by using a puppet device, of turning Hitler into an object of mystery, when in fact what was at issue was unspeakable moral evil. Syberberg was polite and low key and not interested in creating sparks of any kind. There was another German film showing at the time, which was in tune with Hannah Arendt's 'banality of evil' thesis: the idea that most of the Nazi perpetrators were no more than middle management carrying out orders without paying much attention to the implication of what they were doing. The film's director was Theodor Kotulla.

Since the days of Ludwig Erhardt's economic miracle in the mid-1960s, Germany has managed to sustain an image of itself

246

as the paymaster of Europe. I remember Michael Casey, an economist friend, saying to me in the 1970s that a country like Ireland could always rely on Germany to bail it out. Since that time Germany has not merely continued to improve its economic standing but has become the dominant political force in the EU. Despite its disenchantment with Greek profligacy from 2010 onwards, Germany still gives the impression of accepting that it is always going to be the continent's paymaster.

An interesting aspect of German identity resides in its relationship with Britain, as explored say in E. M Forster's *Howards End* (1910). On the British side there has been a tendency to downplay the German component of British identity. Emblematic of that (as Goethe's biographer Nicholas Boyle has reminded us) is the manner in which British philosophy, in the person of Bertrand Russell, deserted Hegel for mathematical logic at the end of the nineteenth century.

The November seminar in Munich tied in with a radio series I was doing for RTÉ called *Inside Europe,* and some consultancy work I did for UNESCO in Hamburg in 1978. So in the late 1970s I got to see more of continental Europe than usual. This allowed me, among other things, an opportunity to catch up on the continent's opera productions and to visit La Hune bookstore in Paris. Up to then, I rarely saw more than what was on offer at Covent Garden and the English National Opera. The first operatic production I saw in Germany was *A Masked Ball* in 1962. In Munich in 1977 there was a fine production of *The Magic Flute* and in Nürnberg a Lehar operetta. In Vienna I saw Verdi's *The Force of Destiny.*

As far as opera is concerned, I really like good voices. So I'm a bit impatient with, say, Jonathan Miller's routine dismissal of Covent Garden as 'a concert in frocks'. The fact is, I like good imaginative productions too, and am particularly won over by arresting design. I am often less sensitive to what the conductor is doing. I recall a production of *The Magic Flute* at Covent

Garden in the early nineties, after which I ran into the poet and Blake scholar Kathleen Raine. I was full of chat about the staging and about the bass, Robert Lloyd, when suddenly she made it clear that what she was most concerned with was Colin Davis's musical take on the opera.

As to voices, no voice gives more pleasure than a good bass. In the autumn of 1978, I first heard the Bulgarian bass Nicolai Ghiaurov at the Paris opera in *The Force of Destiny*. I had never heard a voice like it, with such a smooth legato line. Tom Walsh, founder of the Wexford Opera Festival, was in agreement, but said the first time he heard Kurt Moll at Bayreuth was a comparable moment. In May 1979, I was visiting Vienna to record material for *Inside Europe*, when I heard Ghiaurov again in *Boris Godunov*. It was not easy to get tickets, but Richard Burke, a European Commissioner then visiting the city, was a big help. Glorious singing from Ghiaurov, but it was a conventional enough production. When the following morning, I spoke to Jonathan Miller about a production of *King Lear* he was doing in Vienna, I really had no answer when he asked me about the production of *Boris Godunov*. 'Awful, was it?' he asked. I suspected that Ghiaurov's singing would mean less to Miller than it did to me. Ghiaurov's smooth legato would not have compensated for an indifferent production. On the other hand, it does take a really imaginative production to compensate for poor singing. That said, I *did* see a stunning but vocally indifferent production of *Macbeth* at the ENO in the 1990s with the soprano in the opening scene climbing on a rock's edge. It was a production by David Pountney, who is now the artistic director of Welsh National Opera.

Also in Vienna in May 1979, apart from the Vienna State Opera productions and Miller's *King Lear*, were the Irish actress Siobhan McKenna who was doing a one-woman show, and the French actor Jean Louis Barrault, who was also giving solo performances. Siobhan was playing in the English Theatre. What I

The poet Eavan Boland asked me why I
asked so many questions

Herbert McCabe, an English Dominican
theologian and Marxist

Bernard Lonergan, a twentieth century Aquinas

Brian O'Doherty, a brilliant Irish art critic, based in New York

Derek Forrest, Professor of Psychology at Trinity and thesis supervisor

Michaela O'Brien was an American graduate student at Trinity, 1974/75

Architects De Blacam and Meagher designed a space for my books

Michael Campion, dedicated producer of *Dialogue* from 1978 to 2002

Aidan Mathews, stylist supreme
and broadcasting colleague

John Moriarty, philosopher and mystic
who enchanted listeners

With Marian Finucane in a shot for the RTÉ Guide, 1981

Poet Dennis O'Driscoll who first suggested I write a memoir

Thanks to persistent encouragement from Irene Goodman, I completed this book

Robert Nozick, the American philosopher, welcomed me to Harvard

John Rawls, a political philosopher with firm egalitarian beliefs

Harrison White, a sociologist of striking originality

Daniel Bell, author of *The Coming of Post-Industrial Society*

Pangloss, a second-hand bookstore in Cambridge Mass, no longer exists

Into-camera piece: John McCormack BBC television documentary, 1984

recall most from that occasion is the manner in which she was pursued by an open-shirted young man, whom I gather hung around the theatre bar every night. He was certainly much in evidence on the night I was there. She seemed to have considerable power over young men and clearly relished it.

Ghiaurov, McKenna and Barrault are dead. Miller is still going strong, and long may he continue. After his Boris Godunov performance, I sought an interview with Ghiaurov. A member of the management simply told me with a near-triumphalist air: '*Er hat gesagt nein*'. That was a disappointment because of the admiration I had for the possessor of such an extraordinary voice. I heard him sing once more in a concert performance of Boris at Tanglewood, outside Boston, some time in the 1980s. He was married to the singer Mirella Freni. Nicolai Ghiaurov died in 2004. He, Kurt Moll, and Robert Lloyd in his prime were among the leading basses of the late twentieth century.

When the great classical scholar E. R. Dodds published his memoir *Missing Persons* (1977), I suggested to Robin Wylie that we should record a television programme with him. Dodds was from Banbridge, County Down, which meant that whatever populist reservations Robin's programme controller in Belfast might have had about giving a half hour's air time to an aging classical scholar, would be overcome by the force of the regional argument that he was a local boy. In March 1978, we went to Oxford to talk to the Emeritus Professor of Greek. Dodds's appointment to the chair by the prime minister Stanley Baldwin had been controversial: Maurice Bowra was expected to get the job. Dodds' predecessor, Gilbert Murray, had recommended Dodds to Baldwin.

In an edition of The *Times Literary Supplement* in early 1978, I read a review of *Missing Persons* by the historian F. S. L. Lyons, then Provost of Trinity College Dublin. What caught my attention in that review was a seemingly gratuitous remark to the effect that Dodds would scarcely go down as one of the towering classical scholars of the century. The reason the remark jarred was that I wondered how an expert in Irish history could pronounce in so oracular a manner on a scholar of classical Greek. My suspicion that it was a second-hand opinion was confirmed when I raised the matter with Dodds himself. He told me that Lyons had since apologized to him. What happened was this: Lyons sought the opinion of the Professor of Greek at Trinity College, W. B. Stanford, who happened to be an old academic foe of Dodds. There is an odd postscript to this. One day I had lunch with Stanford at Trinity at a time when my curiosity about the interplay between the Graeco-Roman and Judaeo-Christian worlds was growing. 'There's someone you should talk to,' he said. 'Who's that?' I asked. 'Eric Dodds in Oxford.'

What struck me about Dodds's library in his rooms at University College, Oxford was how rigorously specialized it was even for an academic's library: there was nothing at all in it that did not bear on his own *specific* scholarly concerns. The only book I can recall asking him about was a piece of secondary literature by the French classicist, the Dominican friar André-Jean Festugiere, a specialist in Neoplatonism, and a good friend of Dodds. In the matter of friends, Dodds could count quite a number of poets among them, from Eliot to Yeats to MacNeice and Auden. In fact, he was responsible for MacNeice getting a job at the University of Birmingham in 1930.

I have always been impressed by the clarity of Dodds's writing, which I first noticed in *Pagan and Christian in an Age of Anxiety* (1970). In the early stages of that book he says that scholarly progress is made either by means of new questions or new data, or both. That about sums it up, doesn't it? I wasn't surprised to learn that the novelist John McGahern was such an admirer of Dodds's perceptiveness. In *Missing Persons* Dodds is eloquent on the difference between the occultist and the explorer of psychic phenomena. He says the last thing the occultist wants is an explanation. His book *The Greeks and the Irrational*

(1951) owes a lot to Nietzsche in focusing on the darker side of the Greeks: they weren't all reason and light.

There was one terrifying moment for me in the interview which I just about recovered from with a modicum of dignity. In his memoir, Dodds claims that most academics stop thinking at forty. I raised the matter with him because it *is* quite a claim. He didn't withdraw it. I then followed up with: '*You* haven't stopped thinking, though?' Then came the clincher. 'How do *you* know?' he said. At moments like that, you see your whole life flashing before you. It was as if this man was saying: how dare you presume to know such a private matter. Here in front of me was one of the greatest classical scholars of the age, in a direct line with forebears in the previous century as illustrious as Nietzsche. The man Gilbert Murray anointed. The best I could do was to say: 'I've read your book'. Not the most brilliant of comebacks, but it saved the day.

The first journeys abroad for the RTÉ radio series *Inside Europe* were two visits to Rome. The first in September 1978 coincided with the death of Pope Paul VI. The second was a stop-over there on the way to Athens. On that first visit to Rome, we stood in the Via Della Conciliazione, close to St Peter's and witnessed the arrival of Paul VI's Milanese family in a black limousine. It was a reminder that the death of a pontiff is a family affair as well.

Because both the producer Pat McInerney and myself were interested in Vatican affairs, the timing of our visit was perfect. So, apart from recording pieces about Italian life with the likes of Peter Nicholls of *The Times* and the writer Luigi Barzini, we found time to attend a press conference given in the Hotel Columbus by the late American sociologist Father Andrew Greeley, outlining the ideal qualities the new pope should have. The unkind said the job specification bore a close resemblance to Father Greeley's own skills-set.

Eurocommunism was all the rage in 1978, a new de-Stalinized variant of the Soviet version. It surfaced in almost every discussion, though not I recall with that superstar Luigi Barzini. The author of *The Italians* (1964) lived then on the outskirts of the city in what looked like a modern palazzo. On the desk of his library were new publications in French, English, German and Italian. Barzini was an old hand at 'state of Italy' or 'state of Europe' interviews. 'We have it all here in Europe', he said, 'from Mozart to camembert.' That opening line determined the tone of a set piece that he must have delivered a thousand times. The bronzed visage, the slightly greying locks, the high-ceilinged library. This was surely not his study, but a movie set on the outskirts of an ancient city.

On a second visit to Rome in October 1978, on my way to Athens, I spoke to Gore Vidal about American attitudes to Europe. As well as a house in Ravello, he had a flat in the capital, located beside a Jesuit church. We called to see him on a Sunday morning. The late Pat McInerney, my producer and a Dominican priest-theologian to boot, had a highly discriminating take on matters like the cultural significance of whether one was offered coffee or not by a host in various continental countries. Vidal did not offer us coffee.

This was treated by Pat as a cue to hold forth afterwards on the comparative cultural anthropology of it all. It was a convoluted analysis, the only part of which I remember is its opening proposition, namely that Vidal would have known we expected coffee, and therefore *deliberately* didn't offer it. Pat then offered an elaborate exposition of how different cultures approached this matter, but in truth that was no more than an expression of his annoyance at not getting something he expected and wanted. But then I'm not a coffee drinker.

The first thing Vidal asked me was if I knew Charlie Haughey, then a minister in the Irish government, who would become Taoiseach the following year. In 1969, as minister for finance,

Haughey had introduced tax-free status for overseas writers and artists living in Ireland. Vidal lived briefly in County Donegal in the early 1970s to avail of the new dispensation, but as with other writers who came to Ireland for the same reason, found that tax privileges alone didn't encourage him to stay.

In the warm-up chat, I raised the matter of his infamous confrontation with William F. (Bill) Buckley Jr., who had called Vidal a faggot in those 1968 election debates the two men had on ABC. In turn, Vidal called Buckley a crypto-Nazi. The only change I got out of Vidal on Buckley was, "Oh, is *he* still alive?' That Vidal could have done better than that is evidenced in a memoir by John Kenneth Galbraith. 'Where is Buckley, these days?' Vidal is asked. 'Over sewing hoods with George Wallace, I believe.' Having just seen a documentary film, made in 2015, covering all ten television debates in 1968 between Vidal and Buckley, I regret not having pressed Vidal on the matter. On the other hand, the new documentary attests to such an intense level of mutual loathing between the two men that I was probably lucky to have got the response I did. It is worth noting that Vidal was the one who prepared for those 1968 debates. Buckley did so eventually, when he recognized that it was paying off for his sparring partner.

The main focus of that morning's conversation with Vidal in his flat in Rome was American attitudes to Europe. 'Americans don't think about Europe', he boomed in his highly distinctive stage-baritone. He told me that the only art form America had invented was the talk show, but if you wanted to air the kind of conversation that he and I were having, it could be done happily any time after three o'clock in the morning.

Denis Donoghue told me he once heard Vidal address a room with, 'I've nothing to say, but I *do* have something to add.' Speaking of academics, while Vidal tended mostly to refer to them disparagingly as schoolteachers, I noticed that when referencing a member of the academy who had highly praised his own work, he described him as 'that distinguished Professor of English literature, Dr. so-and so.' It may have been Jay Parini, his eventual biographer.

Vidal was a formidable figure. I felt a bit nervous meeting him in his flat that Sunday morning in Rome. Oddly enough, he said on that occasion that he had never met anyone as nervous as Dick Cavett, one of the most gifted American television hosts of the era. Vidal added that what surprised him about this was that Cavett was the intellectual equal of the people he was talking to, including Vidal himself presumably. At any rate, you can imagine my surprise when I later read a piece by S. J. Perelman, who made the very same point about Cavett that Vidal had made.

One thing that really impressed me about Vidal was that when I asked him about the New York art world, he refused to pursue the matter, on the grounds that it was not a subject with which he was familiar. More than likely, the topic came up in our warm-up conversation, given that our arranged subject that morning was American attitudes to Europe. But even after a gap of close on forty years, Vidal's refusal to bluff has stayed with me. Vidal had a sufficiently broad knowledge-base and command of language to have waffled on about that particular topic, but he chose not to.

The significance of such behaviour is that it reassures us that when the individual concerned *does* contribute, he really knows what he is talking about, and that what he is saying matters to him. It is of a piece with what Simon Heffer tells us in *Like the Roman: The Life of Enoch Powell* (1998) about the great lesson Powell learned from his tutor A. E. Housman at Cambridge: never pretend to understand anything you don't. I firmly believe that Powell's adopting of that maxim accounted for his remarkable self-confidence. Because all his life he had abided by that maxim; he knew that he could vouch for whatever claims he made in conversation. I have a sneaking suspicion that that is equally true of Gore Vidal.

Although travelling to various European capitals with McInerney in 1978/79 to record material for the RTÉ radio series *Inside Europe* was both stimulating and thoroughly enjoyable, it came at a bad moment as far as my research work at Trinity College was concerned. At the very time I had moved to the writing stage, this very attractive distraction came my way: it lasted a full year. Then, after a final trip to Helsinki in August 1979, I became a home bird for long enough to concentrate on finishing my academic research project.

Chapter 17

A Rejuvenating Year at Harvard with Robert Nozick

BY THE TIME I HAD FINISHED MY research in psychology at Trinity College, my interests were shifting in a rather inchoate manner towards social theory, historical sociology, political economy and international relations. It is not that I had lost interest in psychology, philosophy and religion, but that I wanted to widen the frame to include a greater acknowledgement of societal issues. In the light of that, a sabbatical year at Harvard in 1982/83 couldn't have come at a better time.

My first visit to Cambridge, Massachusetts in 1980 was a life-changing one because I met a woman there who had a significant influence on my subsequent life. To begin with, it is due to her that I have spent up to a third of each year in the United States for the past thirty years. Moreover, it was thanks to her persistent prompting that I eventually undertook this account of my life and times. Irene Goodman was then a doctoral student at Harvard, having arrived the year before from the University of Wisconsin at Madison, where she had been teaching child psychology. A native of Los Angeles, Irene had had to adjust to the inhospitable mid-west winters and likewise was bracing herself for the rigours of New England winters. We met at Harvard Hillel, a Jewish Centre where I had gone to hear a couple of talks about Judaism and early Christianity. Irene was not the first person I befriended there. The week before at Hillel I had met Professor Benjamin Schwartz, who taught Chinese history at Harvard, and who invited me to his home for dinner. Benjamin and Bernice Schwartz lived on Kirkwood Avenue, not far from William James House, home to the psychology and sociology faculties. Professor Schwartz told me that he was particularly interested in the role of ideas in Chinese political history. Even in those pre-internet days, I had little trouble finding out that his first book was *Chinese Communism and the Rise of Mao* (1951). He was yet to write *The World of Thought in Ancient China* (1985).

The following week I met Irene. After the lecture and discussion, we walked along Mass. Ave. towards Central Square. There was a local march about something or other that day, with Tip O'Neill at its head. O'Neill represented North Cambridge in Congress, where he was Speaker of the House. For Irene and me it was a leisurely pre-lunch Sunday walk. Little did I realize that we would traverse the same ground so regularly for the next thirty years and more. The journey between Harvard Square and Central Square was to become more familiar to me than any short to medium walk I had ever known. That particular urban landscape hasn't changed all that much in the intervening period, though the Orson Welles cinema, Bel Canto pizzeria and Barsamians market store (a later addition) are all sadly missed. Irene and I had dinner later that week at Autre Chose, also now gone.

Because my doctoral research in psychology had raised further questions that were located at the intersection of psychology and moral philosophy, the philosophy department at Harvard seemed a more appropriate home for the year than other departments. Robert Nozick, chairman of the philosophy department, took the same view: he confirmed in the summer of 1982 that I would be attached to his department as a visiting fellow for the upcoming academic year. Nozick himself in the spring of 1983 conducted a seminar on 'The Philosophy of Psychiatry'. I also attended a full term of seminars on psychoanalysis at the Boston Psychoanalytic Society and Institute, but in many ways those choices weren't typical, because what I really wanted to do was find out what was going on in social theory and international political economy. I eventually succeeded in redressing my previous over-emphasis on psychological and philosophical topics by arranging to attend seminars on social theory, economics and politics. At Harvard, Harrison White conducted a seminar on social theory and Edwin Winckler on world-systems theory; at MIT, Nazli Choucri gave a class on international political economy; and at Boston College Bernard Lonergan held forth on his approach to macro-economic analysis.

It was thanks to the then director-general of RTÉ, George Waters, that I was able to avail of this sabbatical at Harvard. Not merely did I get a year off, I was paid a salary for the duration of the sabbatical. All that was expected of me before I left was that I pre-record as many programmes as I could. Such a deal would be unthinkable today. I am greatly indebted to George. What I learned from that experience is that if you want a favour from an organization, you should always go to the top. It may not work, of course, but if it does, you will have no problems down the line. I went to Cambridge, Massachusetts in September 1982 with an open mind as to what I wanted to do afterwards. In other words, I felt that for me to really benefit from the year, I should not decide in advance whether I would go back to Dublin or not. I decided towards the end of September that I would keep a daily journal. My original intention was that it was for the sabbatical year only, but I have continued with it until now.

Since it was Nozick who sanctioned my sojourn at the philosophy department, I felt I should visit him soon after my arrival. But first I wanted to get a flavour of the man at work. So I went to hear him talk to an undergraduate class on the subject of happiness. He looked and dressed like a successful showbiz performer: expensive blue jeans, stylish belt, dark blue jacket and tall white polo neck. He had film star good looks, with immaculately coiffed greying hair, brushed forward and stopping short of his eyes. He lifted a can of Tab from the rostrum every so often in what seemed like a carefully choreographed set of movements. Could a man so obviously concerned with his appearance be taken seriously. Why not?

That afternoon I called to see Nozick in his office at Emerson Hall in Harvard Yard, close to both the Houghton and Widener libraries. Down the corridor were the logician W. V. O. Quine and the philosopher Hilary Putnam, both of whom were well known for having collaborated in the philosophy of mathematics. Whereas Nozick was famed at that time for his differences with John Rawls in the matter of political philosophy (Rawls was an egalitarian, Nozick a libertarian), both Quine and Putnam took the same side in one of the great debates in the philosophy of mathematics: they believed that mathematical objects exist independently of human awareness. On reflection, that was quite an impressive faculty line-up in 1982/83: Quine, Putnam, Rawls and Nozick. As I write in early 2016, Hilary Putnam, the last survivor of that quartet, has just died.

I was surprised that Nozick's office was so dark, so starved of light, but then this was the home of philosophy not design. Nozick and Rawls had both at that stage achieved international fame as political philosophers. Rawls was the first to come to international attention with *A Theory of Justice* (1971). Nozick's *Anarchy, State, and Utopia* (1974) was a response to Rawls: it was essentially a libertarian tract. An article in *Esquire* in the spring of 1983 made much of the fact that each man's current political orientation ran counter to his social origins: it was Rawls, the Baltimore WASP who espoused equality; and Nozick, from a less opulent Brooklyn background, who was making noises congenial to the privileged.

I soon gathered from Nozick that he had little interest in being pegged as a *political* philosopher, let alone tagged as a champion of the right. His book *Anarchy, State, and Utopia,* certainly did take a libertarian line, but the impression he gave me was that in a few years time he could just as easily argue an opposing view. His was a restless, questing intelligence. It was clear that, despite the international success of his book, he had no interest in furthering his reputation mainly as a political philosopher. Besides, not everyone on the right found Nozick's ideas congenial. John O'Sullivan, former RTÉ London correspondent, one-time Thatcher speech-writer and later editor of Bill Buckley's *National Review,* was at the Kennedy School in Harvard that year. He told me he doubted if Nozick and he would see eye to eye, because of the obvious negative implications of Nozick's libertarianism for defence spending. O'Sullivan, like many others on the right, was perfectly happy that the state should have a minimal role in the ordering of a nation's affairs, but drew the line at it not having a role in providing for defence spending.

I was far less interested in the Nozick of *Anarchy, State, and Utopia* than I was in the man who wrote *Philosophical Explanations* (1981). This book revealed him as a thinker who clearly revelled in philosophical inquiry and playful argument. In *Philosophical Explanations* he was critical of Anglo-Saxon philosophy for being wedded to a legal model of reasoning which privileged proof over inquiry. His readiness to write about Heidegger indicated a willingness to think outside the traditional Anglo-Saxon box. I sensed that for Nozick it was the *process* of thinking that really mattered. As with Heidegger, the process of thinking was for him as important as *what* was thought. You can see that emphasis on *process* in Nozick's last book *Invariances* (2001) where he says that two and a half thousand years on, it is not for his results that we find Plato exciting but for his method of thinking. In addition to his delight in the process of reasoning, Nozick was constantly exploring new horizons: that last book on approaches to truth displays an easy familiarity with the most recent work in physics and mathematics.

When I called to introduce myself, he said, 'Oh, you're the journalist,' in a manner that indicated that I stood out from the other post-doctoral students who tended to come from within the academy, and who also would have been much younger than me. Beyond that, he expressed no surprise that I was swapping the radio and television studios for a year of Harvard seminars. I found that I was a bit nervous on first meeting him, which was surprising given that I knew I had no tasks to complete under his direction. The truth is I was probably a bit in awe of his star status. He was courteous, welcoming and eager to help. I met him many times in later years, in Harvard Yard, Cambridge bookstores, or the local public television station.

Because I visited Cambridge, Mass. a few times a year for many years after my sabbatical, we tended to meet. On those occasions, Nozick was always friendly but in a brisk kind of way. Generally, he didn't dawdle unless the topic engaged him, on which occasions he always found time to ask questions. In the course of one of the last conversations circa 1993, we discussed death. He asked me if there was any particular reason I was mulling over the topic at that point. The reason was personal: my sister Charlotte had died earlier that year in Germany. Had I read anything on death recently, he wondered, which had stopped me in my tracks. Yes, a book by the Jesuit theologian Ladislaus Boros called *The Mystery of Death* (1965). Boros talks about the moment of death as a kind of peak experience in which we are more fully alive to the world than ever. It's as if the little epiphanies we have in life are a dress rehearsal for that moment, not just of expiry but of embrace. Nozick himself would get a fatal stomach cancer soon after.

Our very last conversation in the Harvard Bookstore about 1995 involved a reference to the British philosopher John Gray, then at Oxford and later at the London School of Economics.

Gray, whom I had interviewed at Oxford not too long before, had expressed criticism of the kind of political philosophy taught at Harvard, in particular the writings of Nozick and Rawls. 'I don't think Gray cares for America in general,' I said. Nozick's face looked drawn. I may well have been seeing the first signs of the illness that would prove fatal. He was indifferent at that point to what anybody thought of North America in general, let alone to what they thought of that continent's professional philosophers. 'Ah fuck *him*,' he said, as he moved to the counter to pay his bill. A sudden flash of humanity from a man I tended to think of as all intellect. What Nozick was really saying to me was that he now suspected that his time was short: it was not to be wasted on trivia. The face was still handsome but weary; his mouth seemed tighter. I watched him pay his bill and walk out into the Mass. Ave. sunshine. It was the last I saw of this brilliant Brooklynite, who would be remembered as one of the leading American philosophers of the twentieth century.

That Nozick asked questions of others was a good sign. I had noticed that from the beginning. The first day we met in 1982, he asked me about my research at Trinity College, and then spoke about his own interest in material on psychological growth for his courses on ethics. It so happened that he had scheduled a seminar session on the topic I had researched at Trinity. He asked me what I thought of Erik Erikson's work. I made the point that although Erikson's theory dominated the literature as an analytic tool, it had received surprisingly scant empirical research attention. Nozick immediately went to his office blackboard to sketch out the stages of Erikson's theory, about which he had his own conceptual reservations and which he expressed with a kind of agitated rapidity. Oddly enough, it was his jerky body movements that were unsettling, rather than his actual vocal delivery. He returned quickly to his desk and switched to more personal matters, such as what I planned to do after my sabbatical.

I could see what people meant when they said Nozick was clever. If intelligence is the capacity to grasp connections (or indeed the absence of connections), cleverness has to do with the *speed* with which that occurs. I'm not sure if there's necessarily a direct relationship between speed of thought and rapidity of delivery: Nozick's delivery, though fast, was not exceptionally so, unlike say that of Isaiah Berlin, of whom it is said that he could manage the word 'epistemological' in one syllable. Nonetheless, you had no doubt about Nozick's speed of thought. As to how wise or penetrating he was, you might not be sure, but you had no doubt as to how clever he was. Gilbert Ryle is reported to have said of the philosopher Bernard Williams that 'he understands what you're going to say better than you understand it yourself, and sees all the possible objections to it, and all the possible answers to all possible objections, before you get to the end of your sentence.' Ryle might have been speaking of Nozick.

Raymond Geuss, who teaches political philosophy at Cambridge, knew both men. When I floated Williams's name to him some years ago as someone who reminded me of Nozick, his immediate response was: 'Oh, Bernard was well able for Nozick,' thereby underlining the fact that both philosophers were comparably nimble. Geuss himself and Nozick were both taught by the quick-thinking Sidney Morgenbesser at Columbia University. As indeed were Jerry Fodor and Derek Parfit, all distinguished philosophers. Those of us envious of quick-as-lightning thinkers can point to the absence in them of other cognitive skills, that usually amount to variants of the gift of judgement, but everybody recognizes that flash of lightning when they see it.

Cleverness, of course, isn't everything, even in philosophy. Far from it. There's a school of thought, spearheaded by Wittgenstein, that cautions *against* cleverness in philosophy. Wittgenstein, far from endorsing the value of speed of thought, said that in philosophy what is difficult is *slowness* of thought. A classic exemplar of the Wittgensteinian approach is the late

Philippa Foot, who taught at Oxford and at UCLA for years. She herself often referred to the slowness of her philosophical journey. Foot continued working until she was ninety, which may amount to some kind of indirect endorsement of the more painstaking approach to philosophy. It so happens that I have always warmed to her critique of the received mid-twentieth century view that facts and values belong to different logical orders, but the issue in hand is that of the usefulness or not of speed of thought in philosophical argument. I suppose both speed and slowness have their place: the former in dialogue, the latter in private rumination. The first may well dazzle, but it's the second that is more likely to deliver.

Because I mentioned to Nozick that I was developing a growing interest in the history of ideas, he suggested that I see his friend Daniel Bell, the sociologist. He said Bell was especial-ly interested in the interplay between culture, technology and religion. I was well aware of Bell by reputation. Two of his books were regarded as widely influential not just in the academy but elsewhere in society: *The End of Ideology* (1960) and *The Com-ing of Post-Industrial Society* (1973). I went to see him at his office in the William James building. I found him courteous but not particularly warm, with just the slightest undercurrent of self-importance. Such a posture was indeed more than justi-fied by his published work. After all, terms he had coined like 'the end of ideology' and 'post-industrial society' had by then become commonplace in public discourse. There was, though, an uneasy rhythm to our conversation, perhaps because he was a better talker than a listener. Bell switched rather rapidly from talking about his interest in whether cultural universals existed or not to discussing economics, technology and religion. How-ever, he offered no overarching framework linking these vari-ables. At best, he simply compared the components with one another in regard to their respective trajectories. So, he pointed out that in the domain of technology, something more efficient replaces what has been there. But in the cultural field there is no replacing activity; Boulez does not replace Bach. So, the news isn't all bad. As to religion, certain core aspects of it survive, as, for example, the injunction to love one another, an unchanging feature of Christianity.

As to Bell's failure to offer an overarching analytic framework, I should add that that is the kind of judgement I could not have made at the time. It was only after a year reflecting on these matters that I became aware of the usefulness of a framework that tried to understand social change in terms of the interplay between economics, politics and culture. Later, I learned from one of Bell's books that he was happy to describe himself as a socialist in economics, a liberal in politics and a conservative in culture. So, in fairness to Bell, the fault was mine for not asking that he specify the kind of framework he could easily have provided. I would learn that Bell took the view that (a) each of the framework's three domains was governed by a different logic, and (b) the domains were often in severe conflict with one another. To that extent, he sounds more indebted to Weber than to Marx. Almost twenty years later, Anthony Giddens, the director of the LSE and a prominent sociologist, told me that little empirical research had been done on the interrelationships of the three components of economics, politics and culture.

I was surprised to hear Daniel Bell speak on that occasion against the value of periodization in history and also against the usefulness of concepts like Karl Jaspers' s idea of axial turning points in history. He said he himself was deeply influenced by R.G. Collingwood, who considered knowledge to be a matter of question and answer, rather than of abstract logical propositions. I knew that in *The Idea of History* Collingwood had quoted with approval Lord Acton's famous injunction. 'Study problems not periods.' Perhaps that is what informed Bell's distrust of periodization, but he didn't elaborate on the matter. I was perplexed by his attitude because I did not see a necessary contradiction between simultaneously subscribing to the concept of periodization and to an understanding of historical knowledge (à la Collingwood) as essentially a matter of questions and answers. I believe that, provided it is understood as a provisional concept, periodization has to be a most valuable tool. In fact, by definition, periodization appears to be a construct under constant review. As, for example, in the case of something like 'the end of the ancient world', a term particularly prone to revision in the matter of both what the term means and how long it lasted. If by 'periodization' Bell understood something fixed and not subject to revision, then no one could object to his reservation. Finally, it seems to me that Collingwood and Jaspers are far more reconcilable than Bell implies: the fact that you assign primacy to problems over periods, doesn't necessarily mean you want to dispense with the use of periods.

What I didn't realise at that point in 1982 was that the Harvard sociology department was informally divided between Daniel Bell and his ilk, who approached sociology mainly through the lens of the history of ideas, and Harrison White, who was equally attentive to historical data, mathematical modelling and social theory. Broadly speaking, the first group stressed process; the second, structure. This was the faculty once graced by Talcott Parsons, a close friend of and collaborator with the economist Joseph Schumpeter. Parsons was with the department for over forty years from its beginnings in 1931. It was a department of high intellectual standing, but also steeped in controversy following the rejection for tenure in 1980 of the distinguished sociologist Theda Skocpol. It was subsequently established that her claim that she had been discriminated against because she was a woman was true. Skocpol *was* offered tenure in 1985 and accepted.

Before meeting Daniel Bell, I was unaware of the department's history and internal politics, but I had already decided to attend Harrison White's doctoral seminar on 'Complex Organizations in Historical Perspective'. The objective of this seminar was to look at different organizations across time from ancient China to the BBC, to discover if and how they broke down into recognizably different types. I noticed that although he continued to talk about a classification of four or so categories of organization, he didn't say what these categories were. I discovered there were two reasons for this pedagogical foxiness: first, he was in the process of changing his mind on the matter; secondly, he seemed fearful that if he presented a neat theoretical package at the outset, his seminar participants would just file his classification away without any real sense of the process involved in arriving at the classification of organizations in the first place. In the jargon of the time, the danger was that his listeners would 'reify' the concepts. White seemed to want to alert us to two things: the need to have respect for hard data and the provisional nature of whatever categories one devises. I noticed that over the weeks, the number of participants at these weekly doctoral seminars dropped from ten to five, consisting of three Asian-Americans, one Japanese woman and myself.

At that stage, I was drawn intuitively towards the role of organizational structures in determining outcomes; before that, I felt I had been unduly influenced by psychological factors. White really caught my attention when he said that the difference between Stalin and Trotsky was that, whereas Stalin focused on organizational structure, Trotsky concentrated on policy. Stalin, who was written off as second rate by Trotsky admirers, studied the structural features of life around him, and emerged on top; Trotsky, the policy man, fell by the wayside. If that's not provocative, I don't know what is.

The fact that Harrison White had equal time for data and theory was impressive. On balance, though, he was fearful that those social theorists adept at constructing conceptual edifices might lose sight of the relevant empirical data. At least that is how I interpreted his comments about Jeffrey Alexander, who visited Harvard from UCLA that year to talk about the first volume of his *Theoretical Logic in Sociology* series (1983). At any rate, White impressed me perhaps mainly because he was not trying to impress. I liked the idea of enlarging my view of the world to include a rigorous sociological perspective; up to then my approach had been primarily psychological. White made the point that his own brand of sociology was weighted towards economics. But even economics, he insisted, had been too concerned with questions of motivation and intention, and not enough with the impersonal logic that governs the social architecture of systems themselves.

In early October 1982, Irene and I attended an engagement party near Harvard Square for Eric Wanner and Carla Seal. It was hosted by Carol Dweck, now professor of psychology at Stanford, and author of a highly influential book, *Mindset* (2006). Eric Wanner ran Harvard University Press in those days and subsequently became president of the Russell Sage Foundation; Carla was a fellow doctoral student of Irene's. I spent much of the evening in conversation with two distinguished psychologists and educational theorists, Jerome Bruner and Howard Gardner. Bruner was particularly interested in the fact that I had recently recorded a radio programme with Oxford philosopher Michael Dummett. Bruner thought that Dummett's idea that philosophy consists of a pyramid with the philosophy of language at the base was old-fashioned atomism. In that context I quoted Dummett's invocation of Wittgenstein to the effect that no philosophical problem would be solved until *all* philosophical problems had been solved. That's what led to Dummett claiming that when the philosophy of language at the base of the pyramid had been sorted out, then something like the philosophy of religion at the apex would be got right. Bruner said Dummett was the prime example of 'pure' philosophy at Oxford; there were none purer, he said.

I had expected Howard Gardner to be a much older man. He was then in his late thirties, with a nice line in self-deprecation ('I'm a man of breadth not depth'). I was surprised that he deferred so much to Bruner but then he had once been a student of the much older man. Gardner had won a MacArthur Fellowship, alternatively referred to sometimes as the 'Genius Grant'. Recipients are currently paid in excess of half a million dollars over a five-year period by the MacArthur Foundation. Gardner's interests were in both the gifted and the brain-damaged. The following year, 1983, would see the publication of his book *Frames of Mind*, in which he would outline his theory of multiple intelligences. This led to his international reputation as an educational theorist. That was all to come. In October 1982, Gardner was still in Jerome Bruner's shadow. When Bruner died in June 2016 at the age of one hundred, Howard Gardner, in a *New York Times* obituary, described him as the most important contributor to educational thinking since John Dewey.

In the context of a chat about academic bitchiness that evening in Cambridge, Massachusetts all those years ago, Gardner made the point that he found it refreshing to encounter writers who were very much aware of the work of *other* writers. I had made the point earlier that it was now an *idée reçu* that Oxford philosophers not merely maintained not to have read the work of other philosophers, but in some cases, not to have heard of them. Switching fields, Gardner cited John Updike and Robert Lowell as examples of the opposite: they admitted to knowing the work of every other living writer one could think of. Bruner told us that he had recently read Popper's *Objective Knowledge* (1979) on a flight from Europe. He had also been reading J.O. Urmson on philosophical analysis between the two world wars. What else would one read on a transatlantic flight, I thought, ever mindful of Wodehouse's hero 'curling up with the latest Spinoza.'

About a week later, I met Howard Gardner at Reading International, a bookstore at the corner of Church Street and Brattle. That books outlet is, alas, no more; nor is the Crate & Barrel household goods store that was opposite it. Reading International was particularly well stocked with journals in international relations and literary criticism. I asked Gardner about his simultaneous interest in both the gifted and the cerebrally damaged. He said for him it was the appeal of two contrasting populations; each group provided a respite for him from the other. In his book *Quest for Mind* (1976), Gardner had discussed the work of structuralists like Piaget and Levi-Strauss. I argued that sociologists like Harrison White belonged in the same camp. Gardner replied that he thought Piaget would respect White, but not vice versa: Piaget would not be mathematical enough for White. Gardner asked me why I was taking Harrison White's seminar. I replied that I wanted to complement my existing psychological and philosophical perspectives with one grounded in social theory. He then asked me if White was contributing anything other than expressing what was already known in more precise mathematical terms. For Gardner, the question was: what new knowledge resulted? I said it was clear to me that White was more interested in generating new knowledge than in converting what was already known to mathematical notation. I pointed out that White's reputation as a sociologist interested in mathematical modelling had occluded the fact that his primary interest was in generating testable theory. What I personally was interested in was the precise perspective he brought to the study of social realities; this I was still trying to figure out. I spoke in praise of White's integrity in constantly navigating his way with equal regard for theory, mathematical modelling and complex empirical realities. Gardner then added that he recalled that as an undergraduate he had found White impressive, acknowledging his integrity.

The theologian Harvey Cox had been something of a star at Harvard ever since the publication of *The Secular City* (1965). I decided to attend his seminar devoted to the construction of a postmodern theology. Cox's basic argument was that both fundamentalism and liberation theology shared two things: an interest in the Bible and an interest in politics. He hoped to recover enough sustenance from these two sources to articulate a postmodern theology. His attempt to do this wasn't all that convincing, but he did stimulate a good deal of thought about the missing partner in that mix, namely liberalism. As for myself, the main value of the seminar was that I was learning something about fundamentalism.

I volunteered to present a review to the seminar of George Marsden's *Fundamentalism and American Culture* (1980). For Marsden, two things define fundamentalism: the fact that it is a coalition of representatives of other movements; and is militantly opposed to modernism. He concluded that fundamentalists experienced profound ambivalence towards American culture. For example, despite the anti-intellectualism they displayed in the 1920s, they stood in an intellectual tradition that had the highest regard for scientific method. Moreover, their emotional revivalism stood in stark contrast to the more positive attitude to the intellect that characterized Calvinism. This struck me as a fair and balanced account of Christian fundamentalism.

A woman from Brazil at the seminar asked me for an example of the kind of objection that fundamentalists had to modernism. I pointed out that fundamentalists objected to attempts by Christians to express their religion in terms of the categories of the prevailing secular culture. I then suggested that, for me, theological modernism meant two things: the attempt to relate one's faith to one's experience; and in moral theology, the primacy of conscience.

Harvey Cox then added that one of his colleagues at Harvard, W. R. Hutchinson, had argued that there were *three* factors involved in the modernist impulse in Protestantism: the expression of Christianity in terms of contemporary culture; immanentism (the belief that God was immanent in the world) and the notion of progress in history. I suggested that since the first of those factors involved integrating two components, perhaps what characterized the modernist impulse was a need for integration, and that what defined fundamentalism was the need to keep these orders apart. The dominant psychological impulse at work in modernist thought appeared to be the desire to integrate things; the corresponding impulse in fundamentalism bespoke a need for security. James Barr, the renowned scripture scholar who had written a book on fundamentalism, once told me that at first he resisted approaching the subject in terms of psychological categories, but eventually he changed his mind.

The fact that the Boston Psychoanalytic Society and Institute was offering weekly seminars on psychoanalysis was an ideal opportunity for me to familiarise myself with this particular therapy, its theory and methods. By way of preparation for the first session, we were asked to read Janet Malcolm's articles, which appeared in book form as *Psychoanalysis: The Impossible Profession* (1981). Malcolm was provocative in describing psychoanalysis as an unhealthy profession, in that analysts were continually taking the scab off a wound. At the first seminar there were seven people, three of whom looked as if they would be good contributors: a teacher/therapist who had written a dissertation on the American psychoanalyst Harry Stack Sullivan, a woman lawyer who wanted to work in therapy, and a first year doctoral student in history at Brandeis University. Jonathan Kolb and Elliot Schildkrout were the two presiding psychoanalysts. Schildkrout seemed the more open and indeed the more relaxed of the two; Kolb was the more conventionally authoritarian. The Institute, as indeed was the case with its New York counterpart, had the reputation of being quite authoritarian. Nothing new here for someone like myself with a conservative

Catholic background. Still, these were early days for me at the Institute. Both analysts were just out of training. I thought Kolb was the more defensive of the two in fielding Janet Malcolm's criticism, but he did have interesting things to say. For example, he said that while psychoanalysts are not appraising people all the time, they do tend to listen in a certain way to the latent as well as to the manifest content; the analyst develops a feeling not so much for what is said but for what is not said.

Further sessions confirmed the accuracy of my first impressions of the two analysts. I noticed that my questions at the second session pertained mainly to the role of the analyst himself. To what extent does the analyst impose himself; to what extent is the autonomy of the patient respected? This was of a piece with my concern about respecting personal autonomy in all processes of transformation, whether therapy, education or religion. There is a sublime irony in the fact that institutions, which are in the business of transformation, and whose guiding purpose is human liberation, can so easily inhibit that very process of liberation. The reason is that relationships in psychoanalysis and education or whatever are fraught with power/control implications. There is always a danger that the enablers will be lured into a power trip.

Despite my championing of autonomy, I noticed residues of infantilism in myself, traces of still wanting an infallible omnipotent enabler. At one point during a discussion of slips of the tongue, I mentioned that when discussing Janet Malcolm's articles, I had said the opposite to what I wanted to say. What did that mean? Schildkrout jokingly replied: 'Lie down there and I'll psychoanalyse you'. The point was that I was lapsing into the frame of mind that invites and reinforces authoritarian attitudes.

Schildkrout's central point about matters like slips of the tongue, jokes, forgetting names, dreams was that by themselves they tell us nothing. They have to be seen in the context of everything else that is ascertainable about the patient. I suggested that the forgetting of names appeared to be the most context-free of all these aberrations, and here Jonathan Kolb referred me to the first ten pages of *The Psychopathology of Everyday Life*, where Freud gives an elaborate explanation as to why we do not remember names. Kolb added that the explanation was not a common sense one. I had a final question for both analysts. Was Freud's use of a leading question in the Lucy R case – where he said to her, 'You're in love with your employer, aren't you?' – typical of contemporary analytic behaviour? Answer: although it depended on the individual analyst, generally such a response was avoided. They both roundly condemned the received view of the analyst as someone with pat solutions.

Later that week, I went to the basement of the William James House to hear the great B. F. Skinner, one of the most famous psychologists since Freud. Skinner was tall, thin, frail, grey-suited. He was something of a hero to a sizeable section of the psychology department at Trinity College Dublin, when I did research there in the 1970s. The Skinner term 'operant conditioning' was one of the buzz notions of the time. The term was a reference to the experimental finding that any behaviour that had pleasant consequences tended to be repeated. Skinner was a remarkably lucid speaker. His line was straightforward enough: behaviour doesn't need anything from within the organism to explain it; it is simply the outcome of environmental factors. Behaviour is shaped by the *consequences* of our actions. It seems reasonable enough to say that *some* behaviour is determined by consequences, but all? When asked how he explained differences in behaviour among people who are shaped by the same environmental forces, he spoke of differences in genetic endowment and personal style. And if that's not a case of slipping in internal factors by the back door, I don't know what is. What a wonderfully clear speaker, though. Many teachers could learn from Skinner.

A dictum that I am fond of repeating is that there are two kinds of research: the more immediate kind where one mugs up on the relevant brief; and a more ultimate kind which consists of the questions that one is addressing in one's life. These are questions that we keep returning to, questions, say, about what it means to live a good life, to be psychologically healthy, to be creative, to be open to others or whatever. Perhaps our questions explore the other end of the continuum, about the meaning of destructiveness, of evil. Clearly the second, more ultimate kind of questioning is irrelevant to many kinds of programme-making. I recall asking myself how much time I would have for the deeper kind of questioning now that I had decided to get more involved in broadcasting than I had been for the past decade.

I figured there might be some difficulty making time for reflection, once I had opted for a busier life of the kind that I had, say, in the 1960s and early 1970s. However, the intellectual capital I had built up in the last decade would allow me a good deal of leeway. I presumed it would be a cyclical affair from now on, alternating the two approaches. That is to say that, for a given period, I would concentrate on career and then switch back again to a life of study and reflection. In fact, it didn't work out quite like that, but nonetheless my life did fall into a satisfactory pattern that managed to combine work satisfaction with the delights of learning and reflection.

In the last session of his first semester, Harrison White spoke in an interesting and lucid fashion about elites. He began with a general outline. There is no such thing as an organization, only a *population* of organizations. Within any chosen organizational field there will be a first order structure (any one of four or five organizational types or a combination of each), and a second order structure which consists of an elite. This second order, the elite, may well be a by-product of the first order. It is governed by a different logic than the first order structure. Thirdly, there are interlocking mechanisms between these two structures with their own logic of interfacing. The main feature of the elite structure is that it will be confusing. It will not usually be a clear structure; it is constantly changing and fluid. Yet across different structures this kind of organization tends to be the same. What I found extraordinary was that it took so long for Harrison White to present his thoughts in such a clear fashion. As I have said, in all likelihood he feared that if he had done so earlier, his listeners would just file away the map and not look at the terrain. Besides, he was also in the process of changing his own mind.

As to individual members of this elite, they will tend not to have a time frame; they choose not to be so constrained, and they will have no definite goals either corporate or personal (other than general goals, such as survival). The interlocking mechanisms linking the first order and the elite structure are of two kinds: from below there will be a stochastic movement –patronage systems going all the way up to the top; from above, there may be a hieratic system or a committee system but the primary interconnecting mechanism is *congestion*. Congestion is a controlling mechanism which people in the elite structure can take advantage of to manipulate people at the bottom by making access a problematic affair; the elite group can keep people waiting. One of the most important features of an elite is that its members don't do anything: it is more a case of people coming to the elite. It is not so much a proactive group as one that takes advantage of the existing structure and its mechanisms. An elite controls access to itself by means of congestion.

I remember a lively discussion about how one identifies elites. The two indicators cited, (a) people without a time frame (i.e. those not committed to carrying out anything within a particular timespan), (b) people without goals either personal or social, don't take us very far. I raised a number of questions to help clarify the matter for myself. I spoke about Antony Jay's book *Machiavelli and Management*, in which he argued that the really effective divisional head in an organization (let us suppose the BBC) does the following. He rids himself as much as possible of obligations pertaining to his own division by delegating everything, and leaves himself free to engage in the wider politics of the organization. What did Harrison White think of Jay's line of thought: how did it fit in with his structural perspective? It made sense to him, but he added that it may not necessarily be the divisional head who was a member of an elite structure. Yet if he wasn't, someone usually did emerge who hooked into the upper elite. Being a member of an elite, White suggested, had nothing to do with one's formal position within an organization. The conventional upper echelon of an organization may or may not be members of the elite structure. I pointed out that in my own experience what characterized the successful 'operator' in organizational life was the fact that he or she appeared to be tied in to no value system; it was as if commitment to values of any kind would be a hindrance to that person's activities. White fastened on that with enthusiasm as characterizing all members of an elite.

When I raised the question of power, White got quite agitated. I suggested that one could look at power in two ways: as a means of exercising control over others, or as a desire to be independent of one's immediate environment. This touched some nerve because he said rather sharply that if one were after control of people, one became a military general. In other words, that was not what elites were about. White apologized that he had no proof for his theory of elites. It was just a hypothesis. Very little work had been done on elites. He mentioned Pareto's work in this context. For all his championing of the primacy of structure, White could not avoid turning to the psychological domain. So we spent a lot of time discussing particular personalities as likely or unlikely members of elites.

Two related preoccupations surfaced from time to time during my sabbatical: the role that Ireland's history played in shaping my identity and how best to integrate the remembered experience of having been conquered by a neighbouring power. As a result of reading an essay by the historian Margaret MacCurtain in *The Celtic Consciousness* (1983), edited by Robert O'Driscoll, I was stimulated to further reflection. In 'The Roots of Irish Nationalism', MacCurtain traces the roots of Irish nationalism to the Elizabethan conquest in the sixteenth century. At the end of the sixteenth century we find a cluster of writings shaped by that conquest, which offer clues to the nature of Irish nationalism. The Irish writings of Edmund Spenser ('The Faerie Queene' and 'A View of the Present State of Ireland'), Fynes Moryson's *Itinerary,* and William Camden's section on Ireland in his great book *Britannia* are attempts to show the Irish what they *are* and what they must *become* in order to be accepted within a 'superior' British culture.

The general context of interpretation in which MacCurtain situated her essay was that of the previous twenty years (the 1960s and 1970s), during which time historians had increasingly interpreted the Elizabethan wars as a conflict between two civilizations. The one was a centralized Renaissance state, superior in its technology and culture; the other fragmented and backward. European countries in the sixteenth century began to regard countries on the outer edges of civilized Europe as being in the same category as the primitive environments being discovered in the New World. Both needed to be civilized. In Ireland, the conquering administrators set out to destroy the existing cultural institutions. The irony was that the Elizabethan conquerors eventually came to have regard for what had been destroyed. In the 1620s, Anglo-Irish antiquarianism was an expression of regret for what had been allowed to happen. An example is Sir James Ware, who collected writings that represented the older, displaced culture.

MacCurtain's key argument is that antiquarianism (the search for a golden past) in the seventeenth century became the great reconciler of the two conflicting outlooks. A classic example of such reconciliation was the cooperation between Ware and an Irish scholar, Dudley Firbisse, who was Ware's amanuensis. What appears to distinguish Ware's Anglo-Irish contribution from Firbisse's recovery of an old Gaelic order is that Ware was in a position to discover parallels between early Irish civilization and what he had studied in classical antiquity.

A number of questions arise here. Does antiquarianism occur only in the context of conquest? MacCurtain says at the outset that her perspective is that of someone 'divining the perplexities of a society that never had to question its identity, until it was confronted with the challenge of having to articulate its raison d'être, not only of its cultural and religious traditions, but of its system of law, and way of life.' This implies that the society would have continued on its robust way, were it not for the Elizabethan conquest. But would it have needed an injection from the golden age of 700-1200 anyway, regardless of whether or not there was a conquest?

Given the fact of conquest, one can ask what are the prime differences between Anglo-Irish and Gaelic antiquarianism. I suppose the difference will be a matter of differing reasons why people explore their past. It is more likely that the Gael is motivated by a desire to bolster a sagging self-esteem in the matter of conquest; the Anglo-Irish more likely to be motivated by a search for meaning. This, though, is a crude oversimplification: one is likely to have a combination of both in any one explorer. Another difference will pertain to perspective: is the pursuit of the past being set in a comparative context or not? For example, it looks as if Ware's framework in the seventeenth century was to set the Elizabethan conquest in a wider European context. About Firbisse's frame I am not too sure.

Arising out of all that, I began to ask myself how endemic the master-slave relationship is to the human condition. Patterns of dominance and submission around the globe provide a key to patterns of battered identity feelings. One tends to assume that the master-slave relationship is not totally eradicable, though the first big wave of decolonization in the middle of the twentieth century augured well for the future. Nonetheless, even where *political* freedom occurs, there may still be vestiges of economic or cultural slavery. In the case of Ireland, which secured political freedom in 1922, you still encounter a residual form of slavery that is cultural in character.

This expresses itself whenever we Irish refuse to define ourselves other than in terms of the oppressive behaviour of our former colonial occupiers. We should acknowledge conquest and the nature of its injustices as a fact, but then move on by salvaging whatever of value the alien invader brought. That is what freedom is, the capacity to let go and move on. Effective subjugation occurs when the put-upon person becomes incapable of defining himself except in relation to the conqueror. The ultimate in subjugation is when the victim is rendered incapable of forgiveness. It is a theme brilliantly explored in Lina Wertmuller's 1974 film *Swept Away*. Though the film's context is that of interpersonal relations, the wider political resonance is unmistakeable. In this particular situation it is not simply that the exploited person is unable to define himself except in relation to the exploiter, the only response he is capable of is revenge. To deprive someone of the capacity for forgiveness is the ultimate in subjugation. The ultimate in freedom is when a once subjugated people can look dispassionately at the culture and history of the conqueror in their own right and not simply as they intersect with the history of the people(s) they once made subservient.

That 1982 Christmas in Cambridge, Massachusetts was inordinately mild: no need for central heating. So there is a tendency to say, 'it's not a bit like Christmas.' Of course, what we're really talking about there is our lost youth, that loss of innocent wonder, of the capacity for a certain kind of exhilaration. I think of the intensity of the manner in which I anticipated Christmas presents in childhood. What used to animate me to the point of ecstasy on Christmas Eve was the realization that gifts would miraculously appear in the sitting-room the following morning. The core of the delight was the feeling of *certainty* that the gifts would materialize.

I presume the conjunction of intense anticipation and certainty of fulfilment can lead inevitably to a great sense of trust in one's environment. What would the outcome be if, say, one particular year, my expectations were not fulfilled. When we are told later in life that it was our parents who provided the gifts and not Santa Claus or some other mysterious agent, the puncturing of the illusion at that point did not matter: our deep sense of trust has already been engendered. But if in early childhood the gifts did not arrive, that would have more serious consequences: the let down could be acute enough to disrupt in a fundamental way our basic trust in the world around us.

When I tried to analyze the intensity of the pleasure of gift-anticipation that I used to experience in childhood at Christmas, it seems that what occasioned that intensity was (a) the sense of *certainty* that some gifts would be there the following morning, and (b) the sense of *curiosity* as to how change occurred without an apparent cause. This was one of the most intense pleasures I have ever experienced. What an innocent life, the knowing reader is thinking; and he or she is probably right. The more I reflect on it, I feel that what makes the experience unique is the fact that it ministered both to our need for security and our need for understanding, two of the most powerful drives we have. I would not want to exaggerate the curiosity component, though, because the intensity of the emotion resided primarily in the certainty that the miracle would occur, whatever the explanation for it.

I was reminded of a passage in Dostoevsky's *The Brothers Karamazov* (translated by David Magarshack in a

Penguin edition, 1982) where he alerts us to the crucial role of a happy memory from childhood. Young Aloysha, in his address to a group of young boys, says: 'My dear children, perhaps you will not understand what I'm going to say to you now, for I often speak very incomprehensibly, but, I'm sure, you will remember that there's nothing higher, stronger, more wholesome and more useful in life than some good memory, especially when it goes back to the days of your life at home. You are told a lot about your education, but some beautiful, sacred memory, preserved since childhood, is perhaps the best education of all. If a man carries many such memories into life with him, he is saved for the rest of his days. And even if only one good memory is left in our hearts, it may even be the instrument of our salvation one day.'

I began my sabbatical trying to resolve a conflict in myself between a desire to get more involved in broadcasting again and a desire to focus on personal enrichment through study. By January 1983, that is to say after four months' reflection, I made up my mind that I wanted to concentrate more for the foreseeable future on my career in broadcasting. I felt a great sense of liberation after coming to that conclusion. I was amazed at how long it took me to arrive at that point. From my early days in broadcasting I had dealt with this on the whole 'creative' conflict, by which I mean I can think of personal conflicts of a more destructive kind.

Between 1962 and 1972, although I did not neglect private studies, on balance my career as a television newsreader and presenter came first. Then in 1972 it was the turn of studies: I gave up a newsreading career and thereby cut my workload in half. I returned to do graduate research at Trinity College. That was the position right through to my sabbatical in the United States. Now in January 1983, I had decided to change gear again and concentrate more on my broadcasting career. At that point I had no idea how long my return to a more intensive phase of broadcasting would last. The point was: I now felt that I had harvested enough intellectual capital to keep me going for a while. That decision to focus more on broadcasting than had been the case was adhered to strongly for the 1980s and most of the 1990s; then it began to wane.

During my sabbatical year, I began to interpret my interest in international economics, organization theory, international politics, the nuclear issue and in British history, as indications of a desire to get away from a too exclusive concern with religion, psychology, the arts and philosophy. Not that I ever wanted to abandon those interests, but I found I was becoming a bit bored with my own thinking on certain topics. I suspected that all these interests were likely to integrate themselves as I went along. It is hard to exaggerate how important the nuclear issue loomed in the early 1980s: the world seemed anything but a safe place. By 1984 President Reagan had switched from his 'evil empire' rhetoric to a kind of emollience in dealing with the Russians which eventually got results. Up to that point he and his henchmen created a climate of aggression and fear.

It was in Cambridge, Massachusetts that year that I first took an interest in one of the most complicated and sometimes reviled figures in contemporary international relations: Henry Kissinger. For anyone even casually interested in the intricacies of power machinations *within* an administration, let alone outside it, Kissinger is something of a goldmine. My introduction to the complexity of the man was Stephen R. Graubard's *Kissinger: Portrait of a Mind* (1974). In early 1983, Seymour Hersh's *The Price of Power* had not been published, let alone Anthony Summers's *The Arrogance of Power: The Secret World of Richard Nixon* (2000) or Christopher Hitchens's *The Trial of Henry Kissinger* (2001), which draws on the two earlier books.

Hitchens moves his analysis of Kissinger to a more prosecutorial register than the others do: he accuses the former

Secretary of State of being a war criminal, whose crimes include the deliberate mass killing of civilian populations in Indochina, and collusion in mass murder and the assassination of Sheikh Mujibur Rahman, Prime Minister of Bangladesh in 1975. My own position on Kissinger's alleged war crimes is that even if the accusations are true, it does not undermine the validity of his geo-strategic thinking. Just as the value of a writer's work is itself unaffected by whatever misbehaviour that writer is guilty of, the same applies to a geopolitical thinker.

I haven't yet read the first volume (2015) of Niall Ferguson's study of Kissinger, but according to Andrew Roberts's review in the *New York Times*, Ferguson gives the impression that by the time he gets around to the second volume, he will have acquitted Kissinger of the war crimes of which he has been accused. Intuitively, I am slow to give Kissinger the benefit of the doubt in these matters, but in the end, evidence is everything. Greg Grandin's *Kissinger's Shadow* (2015) is a book I haven't yet read either, but reviews todate indicate that he takes a view closer to Christopher Hitchens's. What is certain is that Henry Kissinger is endlessly fascinating.

Graubard, writing in 1974, argued in his book that to get a handle on Kissinger's thinking did not require access to secret documents: his ideas were to be found in many books and articles. Kissinger had written revealing critiques of Truman's, Eisenhower's and Kennedy's foreign policies. Graubard claims that journalists who are aware of Kissinger's study of the Napoleonic era, have not read his book about Metternich and Castlereagh, *A World Restored* (1957); nonetheless the tendency was to treat Kissinger in a simplistic fashion as someone who identifies with a scheming Metternich.

What was unusual about Kissinger, Graubard reminds us, is that he was one of the few academics who managed to create the opportunity for himself to apply his ideas in the world of international politics. His originality consisted in developing his hunch that a study of nineteenth-century Napoleonic politics would give him a fruitful perspective on current politics. Not that he felt one could study Metternich and Castlereagh with a view to finding out what one ought to do in the present situation, but rather that a study of these men, who had succeeded in establishing an international framework that brought about a hundred years of peace, would yield some insight into the kind of order that might be most conducive to peace.

When Kissinger wrote his dissertation at Harvard (completed in 1954), the expected course for him would have been to have chosen a topic in postwar international relations. Not merely did he choose a nineteenth-century topic, but also in his interpretation of it, he departed from received opinion which tended to assign most of the credit for the emergent international order in the 1820s to Talleyrand. Central to Kissinger's thinking is the interrelatedness of diplomacy, military strategy and domestic politics. Peace, in his view, was achieved not by a calculated search for it, but was the by-product of a stable international order. So, if there was to be a search, it should be for a stable order. Stability depended on there being 'a generally accepted legitimacy'; an international agreement about the nature of workable arrangements and about the permissible aims and methods of foreign policy.

I also took note of Kissinger's thinking about Charles de Gaulle. Kissinger claims that the United States and France have very different ideas as to what makes for a stable international order. The former believed that peace and stability were part of the natural order of things; that crises were caused by personal ill-will and not by objective conditions, and that twentieth-century tensions were produced by unreasonable Communist leaders. If a favourable political climate could be created, there would be an atmosphere of trust; excellent personal relations could then be expected to produce the change of heart that might lead to agreement between the parties concerned. The

Americans tended to believe that the cause of conflict had to do essentially with differences between individual leaders. General de Gaulle saw matters very differently: he took a historical view of the problem. Peace, in his view, was not what gave a final settlement, 'but a new, perhaps more stable, balance of forces.' Tension was caused not by individual leaders but by the dynamics of the system. In other words, de Gaulle was a structuralist in his geo-strategic thinking. So, too, was Kissinger.

There is an irony here: de Gaulle is usually seen as validating the 'great man' type of explanation in international affairs. Perhaps the great men are themselves effective precisely because they are alert to the structural/systemic components, as opposed to personality factors in understanding international relations. And what of significant leaders who do not have such a grasp? Maybe there are no really effective leaders who do not view the world in that way. Perhaps this is what defines a great leader and international strategist.

I unexpectedly got an opportunity to pursue the Kissinger theme when I sat beside Carl Kaysen at a lunch break during an MIT seminar on arms control in early 1983. Kaysen was then Professor of Political Economy at MIT. He had been deputy to George McBundy, National Security Adviser in the Kennedy and Johnson administrations. At the same table was Spurgeon M. Keeny Jnr., who also worked in the Kennedy administration and in subsequent ones, specializing in nuclear defence matters. I raised the topic of Stephen Graubard's study of Kissinger. Kaysen thought it a bad book. He had some ideas as to why the book was written, but he was not forthcoming about them. My own impression was that Graubard, who taught at Brown University and was editor of *Daedalus*, was flattered to be a friend of Kissinger. *Daedalus* is a quarterly that is published by MIT Press on behalf of the American Academy of Arts and Sciences; it devotes issues to single topics in the sciences and humanities. Kaysen had been a fellow graduate student at Harvard with both Kissinger and Graubard. He thought Graubard's thesis 'that Henry was a great conceptual thinker' absurd. Kissinger was a bright man, he said, but no better than the average professor. This is a view that tallies with one of Kissinger's biographers, Jonathan Aitken, to whom I spoke a decade later, when he was Minister of State at the Department of Defence in Mrs. Thatcher's government. For Aitken, it was Nixon who was the important conceptual thinker; Kissinger he considered no better than Nixon's 'intellectual valet'.

Carl Kaysen, when I met him, was on the board of *Foreign Affairs*, a leading magazine on American foreign policy and global affairs; he was also on the Foreign Affairs Council in New York. Spurgeon Keeny joined in our conversation. Both he and Kaysen agreed that Kissinger's main strength was a formidable set of interpersonal skills and a good way with the press. His approach consisted of telling everybody what they wanted to hear, but eventually, this caught up with him and now he had lost all credibility and influence. Kaysen used the word 'liar' about him, which tallied with the impression of him formed by Tony Crosland, a foreign minister in a former Labour government under Harold Wilson. This was reported by Crosland's wife, Susan Barnes, in a biography of her husband.

Keeny had served with Kissinger in the Nixon administration. Apparently, Kissinger made a point of always being late for meetings. He once said it was fatal to be on time for anything. Arriving late is a great expression of power. Kaysen then told a story about Kissinger's secretary (when he was a professor at Harvard) ringing up the Russian political expert, Adam Ulam, and saying, 'Professor Kissinger would like to speak to Professor Ulam'. And then having waited for what seemed like three minutes but was in effect thirty seconds, Kissinger would come on the line and say: 'Adam, I would like to talk with you. I have seventeen and a half minutes to spare'.

Kaysen said Kissinger's *Nuclear Weapons and Foreign Policy* (1957) was a load of rubbish, a book that even Kissinger himself subsequently disowned. But Kaysen admitted to me that he hadn't read *A World Restored: Metternich, Castlereagh and the Problems of Peace 1812-22* (1957). Both Keeny and Kaysen made the point that Eisenhower and Nixon were much more liberal and flexible in their foreign policy than other recent U.S. Presidents. President Kennedy was actually elected on the ticket of increasing the arms supply. Kaysen told us that Kennedy called only one meeting with the generals and air force experts about the likely scenario in the event of a nuclear war. When it had concluded, he waited behind and said to George McBundy, 'And we call ourselves the human race?' Kennedy never called another meeting of this kind.

When holidaying abroad, I have never been one to make a point of contacting fellow Irish men and women living abroad unless I already know them from a prior existence or have been introduced to them by close friends. My thinking on this matter is that the reason you go abroad is to meet people from backgrounds different to your own. Besides, I tend to be more interested in what someone does, what views they hold and their interests than in their nationality, let alone if I share their nationality.

Where I tend not to follow those general rules is on *working* trips abroad where I have often relied for professional assistance on Irish contacts in embassies, religious orders and government agencies. Even though Boston is a celebrated Irish stronghold, it did not prove an exception to my general rule. However, thanks to a contact in the Boston police, I had the rare privilege of a most interesting evening in south Boston in early 1983. Phil Doherty, a former Boston policeman turned lawyer, whom I had met in Dublin some months before, invited me one evening to South Boston. When we met, he took me to Amrheins. This had been a German restaurant before the

early 1960s, but at this stage was Irish. It featured in the movie
The Verdict, a story about the recovery of an alcoholic Irish-
American lawyer, played by Paul Newman. I wasn't quite sure
what kind of evening lay in store. Would it be a case of familiar
stereotypes of immigrant offspring waxing sentimental about
'the auld sod'?

What I encountered was quite different. The first two people
I met at the long bar were a detective-sergeant, whose parents
came from Cork and Leitrim, and a man named Bulger, a magistrate's clerk, whose parents came from Wexford. Bulger was a
brother of William (Billy), then President of the Massachusetts
Senate. Both Bulgers were brothers of the notorious 'Whitey',
the Boston crime boss and eventually a convicted murderer.
Phil introduced me jokingly as someone who had come to Harvard to learn Irish history. A non-drinker at the time, I opted for
a ginger ale. The detective-sergeant said quite curtly: 'I thought
you said he was Irish.' This made me feel a little uncomfortable,
but the attitude of the magistrate's clerk was compensatingly
warmer.

The detective-sergeant asked me where I lived. Cambridge,
I replied. 'Cambridge is a very cosmopolitan place,' he said, with
a slight hint of sarcasm, as if he were saying, 'You're a long way
from Cambridge here.' He continued with this general theme.
'South Boston is a very cosmopolitan place; we have Irish, Germans, Poles and Lithuanians.' At that point I was trying to figure
out Phil's allegiance to this community. Phil and I had just come
from Charlie's on Newbury Street, a smart pub/restaurant that
catered to some of Boston's young professionals. Where, I wondered, did South Boston fit into Phil's social world. Did it represent a form of exotic ethnic slumming, or were these people his
real friends and the Newbury Street crowd mere frothy social
shadows, one-night stands in a world of more lasting allegiances? Phil the detective-sergeant and I sat in a capacious booth
to eat. I expressed admiration for the quality of the woodwork

that ran along the top of the wall behind the bar counter. 'You couldn't reproduce that,' the sergeant responded. 'Couldn't be done today.' I ordered the corned beef, cabbage, beetroot and potatoes, which turned out to be the kind of portion that I had doubts about being able to do justice to.

We were then joined by a man named Sullivan. He told me that he was a federal funds co-ordinator for the County of Middlesex in Massachusetts. He had fought in France in the Second World War, had been an air pilot and was a retired marine colonel. He had a degree in government from the Jesuit university of Georgetown.

The turning point in the evening came when I raised the question of local politics. I began to sense the remarkable political shrewdness of these men, particularly Sullivan. What about Governor Dukakis's reputation for honesty? I asked. I made the point that I had heard that it wasn't that corruption had not gone on during his period in office, but that he and his aides distanced themselves more from it than his predecessor Governor King had done. Sullivan replied that he and his cronies never consulted Dukakis. Dukakis was a media creation who didn't know what was going on in government. As the conversation developed, I was reminded of Harrison White's discussion of formal and informal structures and his discussion of elites. These men I was talking to, particularly Sullivan, had a real feeling for where power lay.

I began to sense their contempt for media, and by the same token to be become aware of the hollowness of any view of politics that depends too much on media and academic sources. Sullivan had been a fund-raiser for both John McCormack and Tip O'Neill, both Speakers of the House. He told a story about McCormack's patience and discipline in waiting for thirty years as a virtual errand-boy for the Democratic party bigwigs before eventually being made speaker. The only reason he survived even as a gofer was that his brother donated millions of dollars to the party. Then, out of the blue, Sullivan said to me, 'the important thing is to have friends'. He told me he regarded the restaurant where we were as his real office; he was more likely to treat problems sympathetically there than in his 'official' office. As to the larger arc of local power, it was clear that as far as the group around me was concerned, Billy Bulger, the president of the Senate, was their man. The detective-sergeant remarked that Governor Dukakis could get nothing through without Bulger's okay. Phil said he would take me to meet Bulger: we would have coffee together. That night I had three coffees as the boys wolfed down about a dozen Irish coffees each.

Phil began to ask the detective-sergeant about the ratio between black and white people in various parts of Boston: it was information he needed to guide him in the choice of location for a new club. I noticed from the outset Phil's obsession with blacks. One of the first things he told me when we arrived at the restaurant was that I would see no blacks in South Boston. He referred to this issue several times. In fact, all three men seemed obsessed with other ethnic groups, as if their own sense of identity was negatively derived. In other words, being Irish was essentially about not being black, Jewish or WASP (or 'Yankee' as the detective-sergeant tended to say). Italians, Poles, Germans, Lithuanians did not seem to enter the picture, at least not in the sense of causing these men any problems.

Sullivan felt that the WASPs were determined to wipe out, indeed had succeeded in wiping out, any contribution by the Irish to the American Revolution. Interestingly enough, neither Sullivan nor the detective-sergeant seemed to have much interest in Ireland; Phil alone had the kind of sentimental yearning that would take an Irish-American to Dublin for St Patrick's Day. Sullivan was particularly concerned with the WASPs. He told me that Martin Kelsen at Harvard had produced data showing that since the 1970s, although the Irish made up only 9.8 per cent of the population and the Jews 1.2 per cent, these two groups had taken power from the WASPs in the country as a whole. He added: 'The WASPs don't know how to behave, having lost power; the Irish and the Jews don't know how to behave as the groups who have taken power.'

That night in South Boston was a welcome change from the regular round of seminars, and in its own way every bit as instructive. One of the men there said to me: 'Forget the *New York Times* and Harvard seminars; we'll tell you what's really going on.' Quite. Later that week I was impressed by a Harvard doctoral student who told me that the question he asked about all speakers, local and visiting, was, 'What does this person want?' His point reminded me of my own threefold approach to evaluating writers and artists. We spend much of our lives trying to identify the good in its many manifestations, not least in the matter of creative output. The first question I tend to ask in that context has to do with authenticity. It asks: what does the question or preoccupation a particular person is pursuing *mean* to them? How important is it to them? Next, one can ask how *significant* is that preoccupation itself? The criteria by which significance is judged will vary from the philosophical to the religious to unspecified criteria, but the process should result in an evaluation of the comparative importance of the particular theme being pursued. Finally, one can ask how well made is the artefact that results from this particular preoccupation? So there are three levels of assessment involved: those of authenticity, significance and craftsmanship. I have found this a useful schema in assessing creative output of all kinds.

I went to see a fine Australian movie, *Don's Party*. The sheer honesty of the dialogue led to my reflecting on the tinselly, artificial nature of a lot of academic discourse. How meaningful is it to distinguish between different kinds of discourse anyway? Aren't we all trying to move closer to one another or move farther away. Isn't that the size of it? The chit-chat at various seminars is different from but not necessarily superior to that of the pub. I keep forgetting the importance of just looking at people, as distinct from monitoring what they are saying. Very often the chit-chat is secondary to other things that are going on and being worked out. We're back to that distinction between manifest and latent conversational content. Are those of us who get involved in these intense abstract discussions avoiding something else? There is something about getting absorbed in abstract argument that renders us insensitive to much of what is going on around us. It is easy to fall into the trap of thinking that one kind of discourse is inherently superior to others. How much of intellectual discourse is grounded in the disinterested pursuit of truth? How much is it grounded in other needs? In so far as it is grounded in the pure desire to know, I suppose it does justify itself as a separate kind of discourse, but in so far as other needs are at play (security, self-aggrandisement), it is no better and no worse than any other kind of discourse.

World-systems theory, as a Harvard seminar topic, appealed to me straightaway as an interesting subject. It slotted perfectly into my wish to amplify a view of the world that in my case had been, up to that point, largely a compound of psychology, philosophy and religion. The first seminar I attended, conducted by Ed Winckler, looked promising. About fourteen people turned up, most of them Asian-Americans. He told us he was going to look at two basic approaches to world-systems theory: a neo-Marxist one and a neo-Weberian one. The essential difference between the two is that the neo-Marxists see economics, politics and culture (or ideology) as all of a piece; the neo-Weberians see them as autonomous domains. Winckler declared himself to be a neo-Weberian. The only theorist in this field with whose work I had any degree of familiarity is Immanuel Wallerstein. Winckler said he regarded him as a good analytic historian rather than as a theoretician. I think that's fair enough, but only up to a point: Wallerstein has emerged more and more as a theoretician than as a historian. As to Wallerstein's prediction that socialism will replace the capitalist system we've had since the middle of the fifteenth century, I wasn't so sure in 1982. Even in 2016, it doesn't look like it, despite the crisis in 2008.

I went to hear John O'Sullivan talk at the Kennedy School of Government on JFK Street in Cambridge. He was one of six Institute of Politics Fellows that year. A former colleague of mine, John was RTÉ's news correspondent in London. I hadn't seen him since 1971 when we were both involved in a minor scare in the RTÉ newsroom that involved a leaking fire extinguisher. It was soon brought under control by Maurice O'Doherty, the newsreader on duty. John and I threw ourselves to the ground, a natural enough response during the early 'Troubles' in Northern Ireland. John had forgotten the incident.

On the other hand, I had forgotten that he had interviewed both Joan Sutherland and Ingrid Bergman for a radio arts programme I was doing in the early 1970s. In his talk at the Kennedy School in early 1983, John made no attempt to give a philosophical justification for his conservative Tory politics; that was how he grew up in Liverpool viewing the world. Perhaps, that is not altogether true: his father voted Labour. However, by the age of fourteen, his Conservative leanings were quite clear to him; he was very much in favour of the Suez invasion in 1956.

After the talk, we adjourned for dinner with three other Kennedy School Fellows: Andy Maguire, from New Jersey, a former Democratic member of the U.S. House of Representatives; Madeleine Kunin, who at that stage had been Lieutenant Governor of Vermont from 1978 to 1982; and Kenneth O. Hartnett, managing editor of the *Boston Herald*. Andy Maguire's father had been a conservative clergyman who changed into something of a radical under the influence of socialist Christian thinkers like Walter Rauschenbusch, a Baptist pastor. Andy in turn had imbibed something of his father's socialist leanings.

Given that O'Sullivan and Maguire had different starting points, I raised a question at dinner that had been preoccupying me for some time: namely, what happens when intelligent, well-intentioned people disagree. I argued that the way people are politically oriented is usually not a function of intelligence or of a rational process. Given their initial orientation to the world, which may either be inherited or the result of an emotional attraction of some kind, the best they can hope to do is to operate intelligently within that particular orientation. In other words, the best we can do is submit our initial orientation to critical scrutiny.

We inevitably got around to Ireland. I challenged the wisdom of the Thatcher government's decision to criminalize the IRA. Prescinding from the rights or wrongs of their case, it was a mistake, I argued, to redefine that body. The intelligent course would be to realize that men who are willing to die cannot easily be defined as criminals. The next step would be to try to understand what they're about. This would not necessarily mean going soft on the IRA. If you were in charge of a society and found that a particular group within it was wrecking it (or part of it) through violence, the intelligent thing would be to try to find out first of all why they were doing it. If we assume that the Thatcher government did in fact do this but decided nonetheless to criminalize those involved, then that is another issue. Even at the level of practical policy, though, it would be subject to questioning. By refusing to recognize a group's definition of itself, you are denying that it even exists. Isn't such a strategy likely to provoke even greater violence in return? The foregoing led to my sounding off about the best strategy for the future a once conquered people like the Irish should adopt. Our best hope was to begin with an informed awareness of what the British had done in Ireland, and then get over it. Otherwise, we would never achieve real freedom. The so-called songs of freedom are ultimately songs of slavery because it means we are still defining ourselves in terms of the conqueror.

The way forward is to work out an identity for ourselves that involves an exploration of our Gaelic, Christian, Graeco-Roman and British past. To my mind it was not enough simply to acknowledge whatever benefits the British had brought us, we eventually needed to move to a point where we could assess the British experience as a phenomenon in itself, regardless of how the British interacted with us. Therein would lie true freedom. This would involve, say, looking at the rise of the British empire and its decline in more global terms than those relating to the manner in which that empire interacted with our own Irish experience. One is then asking the question: who are these people with whom our history is interconnected? If we are to understand ourselves, we must understand our neighbour since they are part of what we are. Does the corollary hold, namely, that the British should try to understand the Irish? Of course they should, but my impression of London dinner tables over the years is that the British have very little interest in Ireland, let alone in exploring it as a component in their make-up.

The conflict in Northern Ireland that erupted in the late 1960s understandably had a narrowing effect on British attitudes to Ireland. For example, Robert Kee's BBC television series about the history of Ireland was really propelled by the following question: who are these Irish who are still fighting with one another and with the British in Northern Ireland? On both the Irish and British sides, the attempt at understanding should be as open and generous as possible. The aim should be to see the other as a society with which we have been involved, not as one simply that has conquered us (on the Irish side) or whom we have conquered (from the British side). That is not an easy task, but it's the way freedom lies. If the other is to be part of your self-definition, it is better that you choose him to be so in a way that doesn't exhaust your energies through bitterness or hatred, but rather in a way that actually energizes you. So what I'm proposing is a strategy for dealing with the past that is most congruent with our psychic welfare. Whether the British in turn ever undertake such an enterprise is entirely up to them. We can at least take responsibility for ourselves.

In February 1983 I began to list the themes that had been preoccupying me since my arrival in Harvard: the weakness of the 'great man' hypothesis in approaching socio-political questions; a corollary of that – the importance of group or structural factors in politics; the problem of what can be done when intelligent people disagree about fundamental questions; the desirability of exploring the meaning of being British as part of understanding oneself as Irish; an interest in advancing my understanding of the kind of comprehensive analytic framework that might shed light on what drives social change. All those concerns fed into my broadcasting work in a subterranean way, in that most of my work from now on, if not all of it, was informed by a perspective that transcended psychology, philosophy and religion to include social, economic and political realities. More precisely, that perspective would consist of an analytic framework that had a three-pronged character, consisting of economics, politics and culture. The last-mentioned category of culture should be wide enough to include the humanities (philosophy, history, literature), the sciences and religion.

Chapter 18

Does a Good Row Make for the Best Radio?

My return to Dublin and RTÉ in the early summer of 1983, after my year's sabbatical, occasioned mixed feelings. I was refreshed and invigorated but also anxious about what lay in store for me in radio and television programme-making. Most of my encounters soon after returning were 'unremarkable' (to use a term beloved of physicians when they wish to indicate the absence of pathology). One meeting stays with me not because of anything that was said but because of its tone. I had gone to a preview of *The Gigli Concert* at the Abbey Theatre in late autumn of that year. About half an hour before the curtain went up, the play's author, Tom Murphy, was standing in the long bar of the Abbey. We hadn't met for a year. What registered with me that night was the penetrating look he gave me just as we first shook hands. He was prospecting for the most minute changes in my facial expression. Despite the pressures of a preview night, he seemed unusually alert to monitoring whatever a year abroad had wrought in me. That was quite flattering and part of what makes Murphy a great writer.

That the playwright was under pressure was an understatement. That night, after watching towering performances by Tom Hickey and Godfrey Quigley, I stayed around for a brief post-mortem in the bar. 'The text needs to be cut,' said Jim Fitzgerald, a much-respected theatre director of the day. Murphy stared at the ground: 'What would you cut, Jim?' was Murphy's rejoinder. At a subsequent press conference there were complaints that the play's length prevented people from catching the last bus home. Just think about it: you write a masterpiece and all people want to talk about are bus timetables.

The following day, in a phone conversation with the playwright, I discussed the play and its production, including the idea that the two protagonists, the building contractor and the therapist, could be viewed as two different aspects of the same individual. Patrick Mason's direction was successful not merely in integrating the play's overt musical interludes, but in his alertness to the inherently musical character of the text. Tom was as eager as the next to hear praise but has often drawn my attention to the fact that on these occasions 'we all lie to one another'. He is one of the few people I know with the kind of honesty that is both a precondition of and a consequence of self-knowledge.

In those years I was not merely a regular theatre-goer but was actively involved in chairing the panel of critics who chose the annual Harvey's Irish Theatre Awards. The highlights of the preliminary meetings with the theatre critics were the mildly anarchic solo runs of Des Rushe in the *Irish Independent.* Des invariably waited until the panel had laboriously worked out a consensus before he raised a myriad objections. In 1987, at the last theatre critics lunch I attended at the Grey Door restaurant, writers Fintan O'Toole, Colm Tóibín and I talked about theatre and books as if there was no tomorrow. Both of them on that occasion kept me abreast of the delights of working with the highly gifted, if unpredictable, Vincent Browne.

A radio producer with whom I worked closely on my return from America was Donal Flanagan, formerly a professor of theology at Maynooth and an expert on Marian theology. Erudite and witty, he was an excellent companion on journeys to London and to different parts of Ireland. It was Donal who said that the Irish Catholic Church must be the only persecuted *majority* in the world. We worked on a variety of book-based programmes. In one such series, *Once a Book,* we examined Walter McDonald's *Reminiscences of a Maynooth Professor* (1925). A man of droll wit, McDonald said of a fellow professor of theology at Maynooth, a Dr. Healy, that 'he had not sufficient sympathy with error to be a profound theologian'. The overriding impression I formed of McDonald was that he loved to question everything he heard and read. And rightly so.

My favourite Donal Flanagan story was one he told about a vigorously contested hurling match in the west of Ireland. It was not unusual in the 1940s to find a Catholic priest playing on one or other of the competing teams. One such cleric who had had to endure the unwanted physical attentions of an opposing forward, was approached after the game by the offending player: 'I'm terribly sorry, Father, but I thought you were a Christian Brother.'

One particular radio guest of mine who generated an unusual level of interest in the year 1985 was John Moriarty, the Kerry-born mystic and thinker, who had been introduced to me by the theologian and spiritual writer the late Father John O'Donohue. A philosopher by training, Moriarty had abandoned academic life in Canada in his early forties to become a gardener in Connemara. Disillusioned with Renaissance and Enlightenment culture, he sought to undo the effects of that culture on his thinking by getting in touch with the natural world. He found, however, that a return to nature was not enough either: he still needed culture. But the culture that at that stage met his needs was that of the medieval Rhineland mystics, of people like Meister Eckhart. That discovery led to a reawakening of his childhood religious impulses; he became alert to what he called 'the divine ground of being'. Moriarty reaffirmed his inherited Christianity, but now wanted to integrate it with other traditions of a religious, mythical and scientific kind.

Conversations with John Moriarty were always exhilarating, not least because you felt everything he said had been tested on the anvil of his own interior life. As a result of that kind of rigorous, personal filtering, he tended to speak of Plato, Jesus, Darwin and Nietzsche as if they were his daily companions. On the other hand, some complained that John was not a great listener. My own experience of him in a one-on-one context was otherwise, but as a panellist on *The Sunday Show* in the mid-1990s, he was less inclined to engage in debate when challenged. In other words, my impression was not so much that he wasn't a good listener as that he had lived the life of a hermit for so long that he had grown unaccustomed to having his ideas challenged.

After the earlier 1985 radio interviews with him, I had querulous phone calls from two members of the Cistercian order who queried his closeness to God. One of the callers accused John of fundamentalism. The provenance of the calls was a source of amusement to me: the only people who had complained about the Connemara-based mystic were themselves living in a monastery. Perhaps they felt threatened by a freelance. On the other hand, writers like Paul Durcan and Aidan Mathews recognized him for the seer that he was. John Moriarty died in 2007. I introduced the John Moriarty programmes in 1985 by describing him as one of the most remarkable people I had ever met. He remains so.

A radio producer with whom I had a particularly fruitful relationship between 1985 and 1988 was Pat Leahy, a native of County Limerick who was much given to lateral thinking, and who sported a graduate degree in English from UCD. We worked together on *Books and Company*, a programme that transformed my broadcasting life. It did so because it unleashed fresh aspects of myself on air. I began to really savour the activity of chairing panels and to nurture the more mischievous side of my nature. Nothing particularly subversive, but different all the same. I stole the programme title from a bookstore of the same name, alas no longer there, that used to lurk in the shadows of the old Whitney Gallery in New York.

Books and Company was primarily a talk show. Before I got around to discussing the books, I would talk to guests about what they had been up to recently and create the kind of convivial atmosphere that audiences responded to. One contributor, who should have known better, thought it was a ruse to cover up my not having read the books. Au contraire, it was a carefully thought out strategy. In fact, both producer and I firmly believed that a well-prepared host means an extra contributor, but by also focusing on the contributors, in addition to the topics, one added to the general entertainment value of the proceedings. Pat also rightly believed that this strategy was applicable to all kinds of broadcasting, from agriculture to sport. Working with him was one of the high points of my broadcasting career, because of what new energies it released in me.

Occasionally Pat and I had a drink afterwards with some of the contributors. I recall a particularly enjoyable session we had with Denis Donoghue in February 1987, on the eve of a working trip to London to collect material for the programme. That edition featured Denis talking about his collection of essays *We Irish*; Ruth Dudley Edwards had written a biography of the publisher Victor Gollancz; Terence de Vere White discussed his novel *Chat Show*; and Patrick Mason reviewed a book about the Royal Court Theatre. At supper after the programme in a pub in Booterstown, Denis revealed an interest in the way that the setting of a discussion can influence the participants. The context he had in mind was Anglo-Irish relations in the 1980s. More specifically he was referring to the manner in which the setting for talks between Irish and British civil servants at Murrayfield in Scotland favoured a British agenda. This led to my suggesting that at international conferences, form is content: the fact that the participants interact at all is itself more important than whatever resolutions are declared at the end. In turn, this led to our discussing the manner in which each of us is influenced in particular social situations by the prevailing consensus. My own view was that 100 per cent integrity is impossible in all social situations: there are times when the wiser course may be not to speak your mind. I was thinking of a dinner party in Dublin circa 1975 when I was surprised to discover that all the guests bar none took a much less liberal line on Catholic schooling than I did. I didn't think there was anything to be gained in those particular circumstances by going out on a limb.

Denis told two stories that illustrated a more uncompromising approach. At the centre of the stories was Diana Trilling, widow of the illustrious Lionel. At a recent party in New York, given by a senior figure from Columbia University Press, the guests were all ridiculing Ronald Reagan's handling of the Iran/Contra crisis. The Reagan Administration had facilitated the sale of arms to Iran to fund the Contras, an anti-Communist rebel group in Nicaragua. It was unclear whether or not Reagan himself had authorized the diversion of the money from the arms sales to the Contras. Either way, he came in for sharp criticism at this New York party. It gradually dawned on those present that Diana Trilling was remaing silent. At a certain point she said she wanted to dissociate herself from the views expressed; she told them she backed Reagan all the way. She believed it was right to employ the Contras to oust the Sandinista government in Nicaragua. She left the party within five minutes.

At another dinner party, this time in Diana's own house, one of the guests was the American composer Ned Rorem. On that occasion, Rorem's boyfriend criticised a recent New York recital given by an Israeli soprano. His main target was the programme, which he said lacked an American component. Diana Trilling challenged him. Rorem took his friend's side. As the discussion continued, Rorem said, 'I think you will agree, Diana, that I have some expertise in this matter.' To which she replied, 'I am not without qualification in the matter myself.' When Rorem and his friend departed, she said to Denis, 'It's dreadful the way we let them get away with it; we don't stand up to them.' Denis replied that she had stood up to them. She continued, 'Once it was blacks, now it's gays.' In other words, the issue for her was not the concert, but that of dealing with minorities. Part of me admires Trilling's uncompromising stand, not so much the substance of it in this particular case, but the fact that she was willing to take an unpopular stand. However, that part of me indebted to what Catholic theologians call a tradition of 'prudential judgement' realizes that taking such a stand isn't always the wise course of action.

In her memoir about Lionel and herself, Diana Trilling says her husband taught her how to think and she taught him how to write. A friend who taught writing classes used to say, 'If they can think, they can write.' There are those who insist it is the other way around. Also in that memoir, I was quite surprised to learn that Diana had taken singing lessons and had a deep understanding of voice production. That explains her remark to Ned Rorem.

I travelled to London the following day with Denis Donoghue's stories about Diana Trilling still ringing pleasantly in my ears. I was on my way to collect material for both *Books and Company* and *Dialogue*. The first programme guest on that trip was Owen Chadwick, author of a newly published book about *Britain and the Vatican during the Second World War* (1986). A Herbert von Karajan lookalike, Chadwick taught at Cambridge all his life. I asked him about his classic book on *The Secularization of the European Mind in the Nineteenth Century* (1975). He had planned to write a different book but on a trip to Austria someone drew his attention to a host of baroque church steeples. That set him off in a different direction.

He remarked to me that nobody today devoted much time to religion and science. When I pointed to A. R. Peacocke at Cambridge and T. F. Torrance in Edinburgh, he agreed there were exceptions. Chadwick then said he didn't understand most of what Torrance wrote. In some cases, he said, it was difficult to know whether a person had nothing to say and was hiding behind jargon or whether they had had to invent a new language to express what they had to say. In response, I argued that some authors who had mastered a large amount of material sometimes achieved a clarity that was deceptive: it amounted to the distillation of much thought. Whereas it appeared simple, the reader had still much work to do. 'Someone like Martin Buber', he said. The person I had in mind was Bernard Lonergan. Also Eric Dodds.

The following day, I went to hear a lecture at London University on 'The History of Ideas in Theory and Practice', given by John Burrow, Professor of Intellectual History at the University of Sussex. In a stimulating talk, he suggested *eavesdropping* on a conversation, and *translation* as appropriate ways to think about what intellectual historians do. These suggestions followed his rejection of attempts to construct a theoretical language to deal with the discipline. In a delicate balancing act, he stressed the need to be simultaneously sensitive to whatever unities and patterns existed in the intellectual context of a given period, and also to those unique features not amenable to such treatment.

Browsing and buying that week in Foyles, Waterstones, and the Oxford University Press outlet on Charing Cross Road, I bought two books by E. H. Gombrich, who was on my interview list. One of them, *Tributes* (1984), is devoted to some of the great interpreters of the western cultural tradition. I was beginning to notice that the history of scholarship itself was becoming a big interest of mine. That is to say an interest in scholars who interpret and transmit their cultural traditions: people like Harry Wolfson, Ernst Gombrich, E. R Dodds, Arnaldo Momigliano, Jacob Neusner, and E. R. Curtius. Steve Katz, the Jewish scholar, told me once that he had sat beside Momigliano at dinner in Cincinnati. The only exchange between them was Momigliano asking him if he knew of a German translation of Vico that would have influenced Hegel. More coffee, anyone?

On the Monday following, I called to the Warburg Institute to meet Ernst Gombrich. Not something that happens every day, as they say. I knew I was talking to one of the great interpreters of the western tradition, someone with a place in a distinguished line that included Lessing, Hegel, Burckhardt, Wolfflin, Panofsky and Warburg. Gombrich agreed that the Warburg project, which is devoted to exploring the classical heritage (i.e. the way we have interacted with the legacy of the ancients) presupposes the continuing study of the classics. However, he said they had not foreseen that interest in the classics would wane to the extent it had done.

A few things struck me about this globally renowned scholar. First, I suspect I unwittingly touched a nerve in raising the point about the dependence of the classical heritage on continuing interest in the Greek and Latin originals. In doing so, I was drawing attention to the fact that Gombrich himself, on his own admission, had read Plato in translation or at best in a Loeb edition. Perhaps I shouldn't have been surprised at this, but I was. Secondly, Gombrich struck me as quite self-conscious about his indebtedness to Karl Popper. Thirdly, given the kind of work he did, he seemed surprisingly indifferent to developments in the field of theory of interpretation. But, that could be a misreading on my part. Finally, his own general analytic framework (insofar as I could decode it) was narrower than I expected: it was heavily weighted towards the psychological and cultural, when I expected it to include a nod as well towards the socio-economic, the technological and the political. In 1987, Gombrich was

seventy-eight and not the sprightly self I might have encountered in early years. This great scholar lived until 2001.

The following day I went to South Kensington to talk to
Susan Crosland (nee Barnes) about her collected journalism,
mainly assorted profiles. Her late husband Tony Crosland had
been Foreign Secretary in Harold Wilson's Labour government
in the 1960s and 1970s. She was a tall, long-legged blonde from
Baltimore who had been to Vassar. Black trouser suit with white
scarf tied at the neck. As I reread my notes, it strikes me that I
didn't remark what Ernst Gombrich was wearing, but then why
should I give free publicity to Burton tailoring?

An underground train ran under Susan's apartment block.
Some of her late husband's books were on either side of the
sitting room fireplace. These were mainly novels such as early
editions of Graham Greene. She was welcoming but also made
it clear that she didn't want to dally too long before completing
the recording. I concentrated on the first essay in her book, an
account of her life five and a half years after her husband's death
in 1977. She had come to enjoy the freedom of being single, but
found that many of her friends wanted to fix her up with a partner. She spoke about meeting Henry Kissinger at a dinner party
not long after her book on her husband came out. Kissinger
ignored her. At first, she thought he didn't recognize her. The
reason for his behaviour was that he was very hurt by what she
had written, namely that at first Henry and Tony got on quite
well, but eventually it dawned on Tony that Henry had lied to
him. She did not elaborate further on the matter.

Susan had got an advance from Weidenfeld & Nicolson to
do a book on Anthony Blunt, but she couldn't make it work. She
abandoned the project because no one she interviewed could
bring the man alive for her. I said Blunt sounded to me like
perfect espionage material, pure silhouette. John Banville tells
a story about being inspired to write *The Untouchable* (1997),
having watched Blunt at a television press conference. I wonder

did Susan speak to Brian Sewell about Blunt. Maybe if she had done, she would have wanted to write about Sewell instead.

On Friday night of that week, I went to dinner at Roy and Aisling Foster's house in Kentish Town. Roy was then teaching at London University. The other guests were Tom Dunne, an Irish historian then at University College Cork, his friend Clare O'Halloran, who was researching a PhD at Cambridge, and novelist Terence de Vere White and his partner, the biographer Victoria Glendinning. There was also another woman guest, a photographic artist. The most remarkable feature of the evening was that no one mentioned the recently held Irish general election. In fact, Irish politics didn't surface in any guise.

I found Victoria Glendinning immensely charming. However, she took me aback somewhat when she said that what she and I were doing then (1987) in the realm of cultural journalism would not last for us for ever, that we should enjoy it while we could. I agreed, but deep down saw myself at fifty-two, going on for quite a bit. In fact, I continued working regularly for another twenty-six years. The irony is that a year after that conversation, my workload increased again when I returned to more mainstream broadcasting as host of *The Sunday Show*. However, I always kept a hand in minority-based fare. This meant that when one particular mainstream phase ended, I still had more rarified pastures to rely on. The Sunday morning assignment came about because of Ed Mulhall's regard for the work Pat Leahy and I had been doing on *Books an Company*. Ed was then assistant to the legendary Michael Littleton, shrewdest of radio administrators and long-time crafter of programme schedules.

Being assigned to *The Sunday Show* meant that what one could, at a stretch, call my broadcasting career had now come full circle. Having begun in the mainstream in the 1960s as a radio and television newsreader and thereafter in the 1970s as a presenter of a popular radio magazine show, *Lookaround*, I was now returning from the shadows of niche broadcasting to a more mainstream outlet. Fortunately, I held on to my niche slot of books programming as well. I was happy with a working life of intense reading.

I noticed when I returned from my sabbatical in 1983 that I had a new taste for conflict in my programmes. I felt much more aggressive when in studio. This first expressed itself in television programmes I made for the religion department. How do you mean *three* Persons in the Trinity; where did you get that? Just kidding. First of all, I found that a year of doctoral seminars at Harvard had sharpened my reflexes considerably. Secondly, I was becoming more alert to the entertainment value of a modicum of conflict on a programme. Looking back on it now, I confess to a mild uneasiness about the manner in which for a period, at least, I was in hock to the idea of 'the row' as the *summum bonum* of broadcasting. Paddy Glackin, producer of *The Sunday Show*, was the one who first nudged me down that road. In case of any misunderstandings here, let me add that I was a willing accomplice. If truth be told, my heart lies in the more dispassionate exploratory kind of broadcasting, but I must confess that when it comes to entertaining a listening or viewing audience, you can't beat a good row. The point about a row is that the subject-matter is irrelevant. We will stop in the street just to see what is going on.

During the period of *The Sunday Show* from 1988 to 2000, the primacy of conflict gradually tended to became an article of faith for me in other programmes as well: eventually wherever possible a show had to be transposed to that particular register. For example, while presenting a season of *The Arts Show*, a series which Mike Murphy had usually conducted with commendable decorum, I managed to steer a straightforward programme about the teaching of singing in the direction of a fisticuffs-type confrontation. The late Bernadette Greevey, a leading contralto, and Veronica Dunne, a one-time Covent Garden soprano and distinguished singing teacher, were to be found at each other's throats over the relative importance of practising scales in the development of the human voice. Bernadette Comerford, who produced that particular programme, told me that it took her weeks to recover from the shock. Tapes of that particular confrontation changed hands for ages in musical circles both at home and abroad, particularly in various conservatories.

I must confess that I was beginning to allow the notion of conflict as a production value to run away with me. As a device, it has to be used judiciously. Too many confrontations on air, and the currency becomes debased. Anyway, they're time-consuming: they require more planning than usual. Life would have been much easier for us on *The Sunday Show* if we had chosen either a magazine format with discrete items one after the other, or a discussion format based solely on the newspapers of the day. Among the earliest producers of *The Sunday Show* were Julian Vignoles, Liz Sweeney, Phil Crotty, Peter Mooney and Doireann Ní Bhriain. In later years, Micheál Holmes, Kate Shanahan, Carol Louthe, Michael Campion and Michael Kealy produced the show. One inexplicable management decision at the time was a refusal to assign any one producer to the role of producer-in-charge. That meant that for most of the show's existence no single producer had overall responsibility; I, the host, was the only constant from week to week. As a result, it was difficult for any of the revolving producers to develop a sense of programme ownership. The producer who came closest to that was Paddy Glackin, who is also a well-known traditional musician. On the other hand, the show really worked despite its unstable production structure.

Paddy was the most brilliantly innovative of us all; he was also by far the most mischievous producer ever to work on the show. He saw lively programme potential a mile off. One of his most daring ideas for what was usually a current affairs show was a live Sunday morning hook-up with Nora Hayden, a sex therapist in Frankfurt. Nowadays that is probably commonplace. Well, maybe not. The switchboard operators on duty that morning had never seen anything like the response. The RTÉ Authority denounced the programme uncompromisingly at its regular meeting. The entire team was summoned by John P. Kelly, head of feature programming, to his office to account for itself. You want ratings, we said under our breath, we'll get you ratings. That particular programme was quite an unusual outing for someone like myself who was mostly associated with more sober material. After all, I had also worked in religious programmes, and in Ireland people are convinced that religion, at its core, is all about sexual abstinence.

An item I was associated with that caused even more furore had taken place a few years before that in 1989, not on *The Sunday Show* but on a television programme, *The Late Late Show*. Its regular host, Gay Byrne, asked me to chair a segment of his own show devoted to a discussion of his newly published autobiography. The senior management of the day was none too keen on the host himself handling that. So Gay asked me to interview his co-author, Deirdre Purcell. Because the interview got off to a dull start, I attempted to liven things up by asking *personal* questions of Deirdre about her relationship with Gay. I also later asked Gay *personal* questions about his own marriage and his earnings. My main concern was to ensure a lively item. This was in a way presumptuous of me: it wasn't my show. But on these occasions our professional instincts take over. That instinct was to make the interview as watchable as possible.

The upshot, whether in the matter of media reaction, correspondence or corridor gossip, was that I was seen to have overstepped the mark. The episode gave me an insight into how sheltered a life I had been living. For me, it was a matter of a few weeks of intense public dissection, but Gay Byrne, as host of *The Late Late Show*, had to put up with that kind of hassle for thirty-seven years. I got a brief insight into what he had to deal with. As to the 'controversial' interview itself, I watched it recently after an interval of twenty-six years. Yes, it did have a mischievous 'where is this interview heading?' quality but I wondered why it had created such a storm. My main regret about the piece is that I failed to do full justice to Deirdre Purcell's exhaustive knowledge of her subject. After all, at that point, she was regarded as the most insightful profile writer in the country. But I was so concerned with 'livening things up' that I didn't explore as fully as I might what Deirdre had to tell us.

Most of my television work for RTÉ in the 1980s was with the network's religion department. In the early part of the decade, Marian Finucane and I alternately presented *Wednesday Plus*, with Agnes Cogan in charge of production and Ann McBride as researcher. Agnes pursued an admirably provocative editorial policy, mainly through a current affairs lens. Later in the decade, I made quite a number of television documentaries that, among other things, reflected the kind of authoritarian regime ushered in by Pope John Paul II in 1978. Some of these programmes, made for Radharc Productions under the direction of Fr. Joe Dunne, analysed Dutch Catholicism; the rest were made in Rome for RTÉ and dealt with global Catholicism. The purpose of the 1985 synod in Rome was to celebrate the Second Vatican Council; the 1987 synod examined the role of the laity in the Catholic Church. Both gatherings laid bare a conflict at the heart of the church between the centralizers and the non-centralizers, between those who thought authority and power should reside with the pope and his civil service, the curia, and those who believed it should be tilted more in favour of the bishops worldwide. It is a source of embarrassment to me from this distance that my into camera piece summing up the 1985 synod was so mealy-mouthed about a conflict that would consume the church in the coming decades. Two years later, it had become clear to me that the strategy the 'centralizers' had deployed in this conflict was the following. They made it clear that they unequivocally backed Vatican II, but then interpreted it to suit their viewpoint, namely, one that favoured continuity at the expense of change. Whatever rhetoric they deployed about embracing change, they wanted power to continue to remain in the hands of the pope and the curia.

Apart from the two television documentaries in Rome in 1985 and 1987, I recorded two television half-hour interviews there in 1987. The first was with John Magee, former secretary to two popes and on that occasion newly appointed Bishop of Cloyne. Of greater interest to me was an interview with Leonard Boyle, a Dominican priest who was prefect of the Vatican Library. He gave me a tour of the library after lunch at San Clemente, the renowned Dominican monastery. Leonard was a delightful man and an outstanding medievalist. He told me that when he went to Oxford in the early 1950s to do a doctorate in medieval history, he just wanted a degree. However, in due course he became hooked by the subject of education in the medieval period. When his supervisor asked him if he wanted to edit a medieval priestly manual, he replied that he didn't think it would be sufficiently rewarding. But then he began to explore the subject and discovered that a local parish priest had done a doctorate at Oxford in his spare time. How did this come about, he asked? And on he went from there.

Topics that emerged at lunch as possible interview material included why he found Canadian academic life at the Pontifical Institute of Medieval Studies at Toronto (1961-84) more rewarding than academic life in Europe. The renowned Etienne Gilson set up the Toronto Institute in 1929 because he felt that Europe was finished. I gather he failed at the time to interest Harvard in such an institute. Leonard Boyle later sent me a copy of his critique of Le Roy Ladurie's *Montaillou* (1975). This was a study of a medieval village in southern France that was renowned as a locus of the Albigensian heresy. The book was indeed a publishing sensation. Leonard's main criticism of it was that Ladurie never checked the work of his graduate students, who had compiled index cards based on a reading of the various texts. I asked him what kind of reaction he had got to his critique. Nothing from Ladurie himself, but critics of Ladurie, like Georges Duby, a medievalist at the Sorbonne, were not displeased.

The television interview itself was reasonably good despite Leonard's opening nerves. I was aware of his distinguished lineage at the library: Pope Pius XI (Cardinal Ratti) was a predecessor. Leonard said that Cardinal Tisserant in his papers points out that although Ratti was very close to his staff in the library, when Ratti became pope he scarcely acknowledged them. My own view is that that may tell us more about Tisserant than about Pius XI. What put that idea into my head was hearing the producer of the programme, Romuald Dodd, say, 'That's how Tisserant would have treated his staff'. Leonard Boyle, over a decade later, told me that if he had his life all over again, he would become a New Testament scholar rather than a medievalist.

One year later to the day, I was in completely different terrain: I had arranged to record a programme with the Irish actor Donal McCann about his life and times. We had known each other for twenty years, but I never found Donal easy to relate to. Lots of hesitations and pauses, and that was just me. He spoke first about a marked difference between English and Irish actors. To the English it's a job; for Irish actors like himself it was an obsession. I commented on the fact that he had praised fellow actor Tony Doyle on a recent television programme. Clearly there was something about the character of this tribute that caught my attention. In reply, Donal simply said Tony was one of the few actors who didn't hate other actors. Perhaps the most memorable thing Donal said in the interview was his description of a career as that which someone leaves behind, like a snail glistening.

After the programme he said to me, 'are you living with anyone at the moment? Forgive me, I'm not curious about your sex life'. And then, as often happens when people ask questions of that kind, you realize it is merely a prelude to their wanting to talk about themselves. He went on: 'Can you imagine what it's like to live with someone who doesn't know what you're talking about half the time. At times, it can be refreshing, but at other times deeply depressing.' As an indication of how wrapped up he became in a part, he said that during the run of *Juno and the Paycock* at the Gate he slept alone. He added that he really shouldn't be playing Captain Boyle for another fifteen years, 'but I'll be dead by then', which indeed he was. He died thirteen years later at the relatively young age of fifty-five.

Donal was due to leave early the following year for Los Angeles to play opposite Angelica Huston in her father's film of Joyce's short story 'The Dead'. He seemed to enjoy getting regular phone calls from certain people, among them the poet Paul Durcan and the actor Anthony Hopkins. And then before leaving he said: 'Ring me. I have few friends that I can talk to. Maybe it's the same with you.' I was in Cambridge, Massachusetts in July 1999 on the day Donal's death was announced. It was gratifying to see that the *New York Times* obituary caught the measure of his greatness.

Between 1978 and 2013, I travelled to London, Oxford and Cambridge a few times a year to record on each visit six one-on-one radio interviews for a series called *Dialogue.* These conversations were usually book-based, which meant that I was provided with substantial learning opportunities in speaking to scholarly authors across a range of disciplines from history, literature, religion, philosophy to politics. The producer who organized most of these trips (for 24 years) was Michael Campion, a qualified lawyer who had been a teacher and actor. Bernadette Comerford, a history graduate of Trinity College Dublin with a deep interest in music and a radio presenter herself, produced the programme for ten years. Aoife Nic Cormaic, a music graduate, composer and Irish language scholar, was in charge of the programme for its final year. I was spoiled in having such outstanding colleagues.

These regular trips became a highlight of my life because, in addition to meeting rewarding guests, I had an opportunity to see theatre, opera, art shows, and visit bookstores in one of the world's great capitals. Trips to Oxford and Cambridge had the added bonus of Blackwells and Heffers. Rather than pick on individual interviews at random, I have decided to select one week and for that particular week give details of some of the people I recorded material with. That week beginning 28 March 1994 will give the reader a flavour of an experience I thoroughly enjoyed over a period of thirty-five years.

The first *Dialogue* was with Anthony King, professor of government at Essex University, who lived in a low-ceilinged seventeenth-century house not far from Colchester station. This Canadian academic was well known to us from his election night BBC broadcasts. As we arrived, he said he was expecting an 'important' phone call. I noted the qualifying adjective with some amusement. The Beeb eventually called to hire him for the upcoming local elections. Apart from university teaching and BBC work, King wrote for the *Daily Telegraph* and was consultant to Lloyds on voting systems. The topic I had lined up for discussion was why world leaders en masse seemed so unpopular in the early 1990s.

Frances Partridge, the last surviving member of the Bloomsbury group, lived off Sloane Street, near the King's Road in Chelsea. She was incredibly lively for a ninety-four-year-old. Roy Foster had already told me how clever she was. He had met her a number of times, occasionally with the historian and broadcaster Robert Kee, a close friend of hers. Partridge mentioned that Kee was off to Ireland that week to stay with the Duke of Devonshire. She showed radio producer Michael Campion and me three volumes of essays by Montaigne, which had once belonged to Napoleon. She had a full set of Virginia

Woolf and of Freud, but said she had given many of her books to charity. Among recent publications, I spotted Ray Monk's biography of Wittgenstein. She recommended it highly, though, as she spoke, I recalled a negative review of it by Michael Dummett. I couldn't get over Partridge's energy. She said she had got a new lease of life in her seventies, but now at ninety-four she didn't want to go on much longer. She showed us a recent portrait that Derek Hill had done of her, but though she looked very young in it, she didn't care for it. She had a number of paintings by Duncan Grant (now out of fashion) and a portrait of her friend Julia Strachey by Augustus John. Frances Partridge spoke forcefully about a belief of hers that one should not live alone, which she herself had done since her husband Ralph died in 1960. Her son died of a heart attack at twenty-eight in 1963. It struck me that it is possible that without the loss of her husband and young son she would not have had as active a social life as she clearly still had at ninety-four.

She told me she really didn't care much for Noel Annan's much-lauded book *Our Age* (1990) because the people he wrote about, namely those at university between the two world wars, did not constitute a real group. Agreed, it wasn't as socially and culturally cohesive a group as the Bloomsbury lot, but nonetheless it was ample testimony to the emergence of a post-war liberal intellectual consensus that was characterized by an economically interventionist approach to the world. Besides, the founding father of that view was one of Frances Partridge's Bloomsbury favourites, John Maynard Keynes.

Meeting her reminded me that the only other women in her nineties I had previously spoken with was the Irish painter Mary Swanzy. In 1977, thanks to my friend Pat Murphy, a major art collector and champion of Swanzy, I recorded a conversation with her in Buswells Hotel in Dublin. The occasion was an exhibition of her work at the Dawson Gallery in Dublin. Both Partridge and Swanzy in their mid-nineties displayed the energy and mind-set of much younger people. When I asked Mary Swanzy about her longevity, she said she was not a person who had enjoyed the best of health. If anything, she had been quite delicate in her younger days. The best advice she ever got was never to give any action more energy than it required: she learned to conserve her energy early on in life. It sounds perfectly in accord with what I have learned of the Alexander Technique from Frank Kennedy, an outstanding teacher of it in Dublin. If Swanzy was recommending careful treading, Frances Partridge argued against living too carefully. Perhaps Partridge had a more robust constitution. In any event, both women impressed me no end.

Later, in 1994, I made some more *Dialogue* programmes in London and also one in Oxford. Over the years both Oxford and Cambridge were regular locations for recordings because so many of my scholarly guests lived and taught in those cities. In early December 1994, I spoke to the philosopher John Gray, then at Jesus College Oxford. He sat in a corner of his college lair and held forth for a good twenty-five minutes before we recorded his thoughts on a pamphlet he had written critiquing the manner in which conservative thought had been hijacked by free market fundamentalism.

We spoke first about a mutual friend, John O'Sullivan, a former RTÉ London correspondent about whom I have written in the Harvard chapter. Gray's assessment of O'Sullivan set out the terms by which he evaluates everybody, namely, how open or closed they are, how sceptical or how dogmatic. It is an evaluation model dear to my own heart. He said he was convinced that O'Sullivan is full of nostalgia for some kind of *ancien régime* which had prevented him from seeing things as they are. Gray saw the Tory intellectual Roger Scruton in similar terms.

Gray spent a year at Harvard as a visiting professor of philosophy in 1986. He regarded Bob Nozick as very clever but superficial. When I pointed out Nozick's imaginative gifts as well as his brilliance, Gray conceded, 'Ah yes', he said, 'good at thought experiments.' He said that in all probability Nozick intended his book *The Examined Life* (1989) to be an airport bestseller, but that it contained too many technical terms. In addition, Nozick was a bad writer, he said. Gray quoted what Santayana said of someone else as being appropriate to Nozick: he devises deep solutions for superficial problems. Again, I felt the need to make a case for Nozick as someone who in *Philosophical Explanations* (1981) tried to subvert the legal mode of reasoning that pervades American philosophy, a mode that privileges proof over understanding and explanation. Gray agreed to some extent, but said that in that book Nozick was trying to subvert reason itself. My own impression is that Nozick was attacking the coercive use of reason: that he was making a case for *understanding* as opposed to *proof.*

Gray went on to lambaste American academic culture in general. He used to spend three months a year there (Harvard, Yale, New York, the midwest). Now he had decided to give that up, partly because of his new marital arrangements, but partly because he was finding too big a gap between European cultural values (the emphasis on tradition, the sense of different particular cultures within Europe, the lack of a monolithic capitalism) and American values (which insist on the appropriateness of the US economic model for universal use, the lack of a sense of history and so on).

In the interview itself, Gray, in the manner of Edmund Burke, came across essentially as an anti-universalist, a champion of the irreducibility of the local. He did agree that there were certain transcultural moral values of a minimum kind, but beyond that he was not prepared to go. In other words, he would agree that certain kinds of behaviour are not on, if we are to describe ourselves as fully human, but that leaves a residue that doesn't fit into a neat set of transculturally valid prescriptions.

In addition to my regular radio programmes *The Sunday Show, Off the Shelf* and *Dialogue,* I occasionally did the odd special. Among them was an hour long interview with Edward Said, the distinguished cultural critic. Michael Kealy produced the programme. The most recent reference I have seen to Said was in a memoir (2012) by Bernard Lewis, a leading authority on Islamic history. The names of both men will forever be linked. Said considered Lewis to be the leader of a group of western scholars of Islam he called 'Orientalists', by which he meant that in outlook they represented the intellectual wing of western imperialism. In turn, Lewis claimed that Said and his acolytes had continued to exercise unhealthy control over the direction of Middle Eastern studies in western universities. In a word, each accused the other of bias.

At the end of June 1999, I was all set to travel to Galway to meet the scourge of Bernard Lewis's life, when I got a phone call from Said at close to midnight. He said his wife had had a brilliant idea, namely, that since he was travelling to Dublin on the following day, he should do the interview in Dublin. That was a relief to me, since much as I love Galway, it suited me that particular weekend to remain at base. Meeting Edward Said turned out to be a real pleasure. I was naturally impressed by his intelligence, warmth and his easy chat about the glitterati of the music world (music for him is as much a passion as literature), but what really struck me was the impression he radiated of being a good man. He exuded a sense of generosity. Instead of bitching about people, he tended to follow up any criticism of them that I introduced with an enumeration of their good points. The only exception was the pianist Alfred Brendel. Edward said that Brendel wrote to him regularly insisting that Glenn Gould was not a great pianist, ever since Said had told Brendel how much he admired Gould. Said spoke also of being a good friend of Daniel Barenboim and Yo Yo Ma. He spoke very highly of the musicologist and pianist Charles Rosen, whom he knew well.

He claimed Rosen was the greatest musicologist he had ever met, a man of incomparable learning. I recall it being said of Rosen that he was incapable of asking someone to pass the salt without quoting Schlegel.

Among the interesting points he made was that the heart of the modern dilemma facing westerners confronted with the Palestinian situation is that the Palestinians are victims of the victims. It is one of the ideas Said was most associated with, namely, that what undermines Palestinian appeals for sympathy in the face of Israeli aggression is that the Jews were themselves the victims of unspeakable treatment. On personal matters, he said that when he discovered that he had leukemia he began to research the topic intensely, but then he met an Indian doctor who advised him to desist, and let him (the physician) do the worrying. The problem here is that in order to be willing to let someone else do the worrying, he has to be the kind of physician in whom you have complete trust. Said had overcome the fear of death by learning to live every day. He did not believe in an afterlife.

Some bookish addenda to our conversation: at first he was dismissive of a recent book by Rüdiger Safranski on Heidegger (1995), but then accepted my point that the author had shown how crucial the phenomenon of mood was to understanding Heidegger's philosophy. Perhaps 'accepting my point' isn't the most accurate way of putting it: he said that I had got more out of the book than he had. I can't remember, but I suspect I had initiated the topic because I was very much taken with the book. Said told told me a story about the literary critic Frank Kermode losing all his books. As he sat outside his home in Cambridge, Kermode mistook the garbage truck for a removal truck. As he sat watching the truck move away, he suddenly realized that his books were being devoured by the garbage machine.

Said recommended I get in touch with a brilliant Irish academic, Joe Cleary, whose PhD on colonialism and literature he had supervised at Columbia. Said was insistent I call to see him in New York, which alas I never did. I am surprised I never did: what impressed me even more than the man's erudition and charm was the sense of goodness he radiated.

In the following year, 2000, I ended a twelve-year run with *The Sunday Show* but continued with *Off the Shelf* and *Dialogue.* I have already dealt with *Dialogue,* many of whose editions, if not most, were recorded in London because of author availability. *Off the Shelf,* in contrast, was a discussion programme which tended to favour nonfiction because of our interest in exploring the ideas that girded economics, politics, the sciences, religion and biography. Not that we neglected fiction, not least because we could call on the services of two outstanding reviewers: Niall McMonagle and Julia Carlson.

At the request of Helen Shaw, director of radio, I recorded a series in 2001 about all the Taoisigh (Prime Ministers) of the country since the foundation of the Irish State in 1922. Also at Helen's request, I recorded a series in 2002 celebrating the country's thirty years in the European Union. The most controversial of all recent Irish political leaders, Charlie Haughey, agreed to talk to me off the record about himself for the series about Irish leaders: he refused to agree to a recorded interview. Michael Campion, the producer, and I arrived at his landed estate in Kinsealy in County Dublin on a Friday morning at the end of February 2001. Haughey began by telling me that he always associated me with David Timlin, with whom I had shared television news anchoring duties in the early days of Irish television. David's sister had been married to Charlie Haughey's election agent, Pat O'Connor. The former Taoiseach's opening gambit suggested to me that he had probably researched me as part of his preparation for the interview. After all, he was now a man of leisure. Besides, research would mean no more than asking a trusted source: 'Fill me in on so and so.' At any rate, I felt flattered by the attention.

He offered us tea and biscuits in a study replete with framed degrees and diplomas. There were two copies of *Le Monde* on his desk. When tea arrived, Haughey insisted on doing the pouring. He was in an amiable if wary mood. He began by talking to us about his general mistrust of RTÉ. Even a recent series produced by Seán Ó Mórdha, which had treated him well, upset him because an old political foe, Des O'Malley, was given air time in the last programme to counter some of what Haughey had had to say.

My impression of Haughey was of a very bright, observant individual, a man of action more than a thinker; a person of menace as well as an undoubted charmer. I was disappointed to discover that he was such a closed, tribal type who could see no good at all in people he disliked. For example, when I asked him if he regretted the loss of Des O'Malley, whom he had expelled from the Fianna Fáil party, he replied that O'Malley was something of a fraud. There was no acknowledgement by him of O'Malley's undoubted ability. Haughey said O'Malley wanted to build a power station at Carna, but 'we stopped him'. I asked Haughey if he had ever considered not expelling O'Malley, but instead 'using' him as the 'liberal' voice of Fianna Fáil should the occasion arise. But it was clear from his reply that his personal dislike of O'Malley got in the way of any such *realpolitik* manoeuvring.

When I asked Haughey for an assessment of his predecessor, Jack Lynch, he replied: 'Pass'. What role did he see for the Progressive Democrats in Irish politics: 'All they do is try to destroy people.' He was surprisingly dismissive of the Taoiseach of the day, Bertie Ahern, whom he said was 'getting away with murder'. I have always linked Irish Taoisigh Bertie Ahern, Eamon de Valera and Jack Lynch because in my view they have a high measure of inscrutability in common. Haughey, by comparison, was an open book: he signalled what he thought and what he wanted. In football parlance, Haughey was the sort that, for all his intelligence, responded predictably and swiftly in kind to a foul committed against him. The ones to watch are the unpredictable ones who are difficult to read, the ones who retaliate when we are least expecting it.

A decade before that encounter, I had lunch with Haughey's mistress of many years, Terry Keane, whom I had already known for thirty years. She was then a columnist with the *Sunday Independent* and was on that occasion interviewing me for a brief series with people about their regrets in life. The only part of our conversation I recall is the part where I sounded off innocently about senior political figures of the day, including Charlie Haughey. I must have been the only journalist in Dublin at the time who did not know of their affair. She must have derived immense satisfaction from hearing an innocent like myself hold forth.

Haughey died a disgraced man because of the eventual disclosures of his corrupt behaviour in politics. That outcome obscured two things: whatever good he did as a politician, and his outstanding ministerial ability. In the brief hour-long meeting I had with him, I could see both the menace and the charm. It must have been exhilarating to work with him, but also at times scary. He had a disconcerting way of looking at you through hooded eyes. He asked me several times where our chat was leading, as if he was convinced it was merely preparatory to hitting him with questions about the charges of corruption against him, how he had funded himself and so on. But, in fact, my concern that day was with other matters, given the kind of programme I had in mind. Besides, I had been supplied with enough intelligence about other recent encounters with C. J. Haughey to realize that he could just suddenly close down and end proceedings. I did ask him towards the end why he thought Mrs. Thatcher preferred *him* to Garret FitzGerald. Though a decidedly soft-ball question, I thought it might be productive. All it yielded was: 'Isn't it obvious?'

Chapter 19

LORD REITH WAS RIGHT:
INFORM, ENTERTAIN, EDUCATE

W HEN MEDIA HISTORIANS LOOK BACK on this past half-century of television, the talk show is likely to assume a prominent and, possibly, a defining role. When I began broadcasting in 1960, the genre did not exist, even in the United States, apart from the Jack Paar Show, which ran from 1957 to 1962. Then Johnny Carson's *Tonight Show* took to the airwaves from 1962 to 1992, defining a whole era in American television. Gay Byrne did likewise in Ireland with *The Late Late Show*, which enjoyed an even longer innings from 1962 to 1999, and then continued with Pat Kenny and Ryan Tubridy.

What defines the talk show in the second decade of the twenty-first century (and for some time past) is that *all* the guests are now selling a product of some kind. There was always an element of product-selling, but of late it has become the defining feature. One welcome corollary of that is a greater availability once again of big-name performers. That represents a return to a period of almost forty years ago when top showbiz names were equally available. The difference, as broadcaster Michael Parkinson keeps reminding us, is that in earlier times the public relations cohort kept a looser rein on their stable of stars in the matter of what would be discussed. The result was more spontaneous freewheeling exchanges with the likes of James Stewart, Bing Crosby, Orson Welles and Bob Hope. In those days, *The Late Late Show* had similar exchanges with stars like Danny Kaye and Fred Astaire. Bette Davis was a guest on BBC's *Wogan.* Today, the Graham Norton show, though attracting major stars, is obliged, according to Norton himself, to work within the narrow confines of what the public relations people ordain.

Another defining feature of today's talk show is the absence of writers, artists and thinkers. Thirty and more years ago, this was a regular feature of such programmes from Johnny Carson to Michael Parkinson to Gay Byrne. Now, the material discussed on these shows has become more restricted: there has been a narrowing of horizons. This may be the way that national conversations are heading for the next century. It seems to me not unreasonable to invoke a rudimentary economic explanation for this to the effect that this is what current markets decree. That seems to me a more rational explanation than simply saying it is a matter of changing tastes.

As talk shows go, Vincent Browne's show on Ireland's TV3 is a unique phenomenon. It is an example of how the format can evolve, mainly as an expression of a particular host's personality. Vincent was a latecomer to broadcasting, although in the early stages of his career in the late 1960s he was a researcher on *The Late Late Show.* He was a print journalist for most of his life, having been editor of *Nusight* and *Magill* magazines, and eventually editor of *The Sunday Tribune.* Not until the mid-1990s did he become a broadcaster, when he joined a Dublin commercial radio station at the age of fifty. Shortly afterwards he moved to RTÉ Radio 1, where for a decade he presented a nightly radio show. Thereafter, he took over a late-night television news show for TV3. Browne has none of the obvious skills required for smooth radio and television presentation, but he is one of the most listenable to and watchable broadcasters working today.

He doesn't have a particularly good voice, and his on-air skills are patchy. His introductions are marked by fumbling and mistiming, but this doesn't matter, such is the power of his personality, the keenness of his intelligence and the infectiousness of his humour. Above all, there is the unwavering moral passion. He is one of the few who are completely themselves on air. Terry Wogan, Graham Norton and Chris Evans also spring to mind, though these broadcasters adorn light entertainment rather than broadcast journalism. I was a slow convert to Browne's style of broadcasting because of what I thought at first was an excess of moral outrage. Often that was accompanied by a lack of preparation. It could grow tiresome when he would repeatedly say to whomever his guest was, 'that is absolutely outrageous.' Even to this day, I get irritated with an excess of outrage on his part, mainly because once you have condemned something you have to move on; repeated condemnation of something or other for the duration of a show may have some moral justification but is not intellectually interesting.

Vincent can be a bully; he can continue badgering somebody long past the point of it being productive. But, on balance, he has decent instincts; he's a fair man. Which leads me to his egalitarianism and his consistent flying of the flag for social justice on his programmes and in his columns. In that regard, he has remained true to those young members of the Fine Gael party, who in the 1960s gathered around lawyer Declan Costello in an attempt to move that party to the left. The sixties, for all its faults, had its heart in the right place. Young people know that, in the end, politics is not that complicated, at least at the level of moral choice: you are either in favour of protecting the interests of the less well off or you're not. Vincent Browne has never wavered on that one. It is easy with all this talk of moral passion to forget what a brilliant entertainer he is, not in the song and dance sense, but in the manner in which his complete lack of reverence for the electronic media allows him to behave as if in his own kitchen. There is also, of course, a lack of reverence for politicians and public officials, which just about stops short of outright disrespect.

The informality of his shows is unparalleled because of his supreme self-confidence. One night in the middle of a very harrowing discussion about an earthquake, Vincent suddenly turned to a guest and said: 'Our former ambassador to the United States, Seán Donlon, has some great stories about being trapped in an earthquake in Iran; we must invite him in some night to talk about it.' What struck me about that remark was that it's the kind of thing someone says at a programme conference, but not on air. For Vincent, the studio has no special, sacred status: it is just another venue.

Eamon Dunphy is also a print journalist who came to radio broadcasting relatively late in life, though he had considerable experience as a soccer pundit on Irish television. Like Browne, he is not what you would call a natural broadcaster. He too doesn't have a particularly attractive voice, nor is he the skilful reader of a script, but such is the power of his personality that none of the foregoing matters. Above all with Eamon, what impresses me is his intelligence and his desire to understand the world. His political compass is less consistent than Browne's. At best, he is the champion of the little guy, a posture that, unfortunately, can be made congruent with the most reprehensible of political positions. There is an element of the sentimentalist in Dunphy: easily brought to tears but still capable of condoning the kind of policies that led to those tears. The banking crisis of 2008 onwards was perfect fodder for him, with its big guy/little guy framework. I prefer Dunphy when he's trying to understand the world than when he's trying to change it, because I don't think he has a coherent sense of the kind of change he wants.

Dunphy's best work was on a show called *The Last Word*, which ran on Today FM from 1997 to 2003. Here he displayed a masterly command of international as well as national affairs. What I liked about this show was that he was not afraid to discuss ideas, the besetting sin of contemporary current affairs programmes. In fact, Eamon tended to give one-off events a wide berth, knowing that on such occasions a programme team can do no more than offer an on-the-spot report. He always opted for the discussion of ideas and tended to conduct conversations rather than interviews.

RTÉ's Ryan Tubridy is a better television broadcaster than a radio one, and that's saying something because of the high quality of his radio work. It is on television, though, that we see Tubridy at his best. He listens carefully and can respond with lightning speed. Reaction shots of him listening to a guest are always revealing: they have an 'across the kitchen table' quality of naturalness. He radiates little sense of being brief-dependent, the besetting sin of many. His laughter is unforced and infectious and he moves like Fred Astaire. His early interviews with politicians were less than successful, mainly because he seemed uncharacteristically more governed by the research brief than by the personal encounter. His more recent interviews with politicians have been excellent. In fact, one can truly say now that his interviews with politicians exhibit the best of Tubridy. He is sharper than many broadcasters who work exclusively in current affairs. The one flaw I see in his approach to broadcasting is that he doesn't seem to be sufficiently involved editorially in his programmes: he gives the impression of being happy to be just a front of house man. These days, that is a perilous route for a broadcaster, who should insist, at the very least, on being a co-producer of his or her own show.

As to British broadcasters whose work stimulates me, there is, first of all, Melvyn Bragg. It is his radio work that I find really interesting, though I know that he's been a stalwart of television arts programming since the early days of BBC's *Monitor.* That dimension of his career culminated in a lengthy run of

The South Bank Show for ITV, which he subsequently switched to Sky Arts. Television is a medium that tends to reduce personality. Bragg on television is but a shadow of the Bragg we encounter on radio. That has to do with the structuring of an arts show as much as anything else. Were he to present a *Start the Week*-type discussion on television, it is possible the two Melvyns would come closer. His heyday on radio was with *Start the Week* on BBC Radio 4 on Monday mornings throughout the 1990s.

Bragg could sometimes make listeners uncomfortable when he began to needle guests, presumably to get the show going. There may have been an element of bad temper as well, very occasionally evident in his stewardship of the excellent *In Our Time* series on Radio 4 on Thursday mornings. However, I do recall meeting a therapist in the 1990s who told me that the producer of *Start the Week* asked him before the show if he would mind if Melvyn attacked him. That suggests that whatever about occasional bad temper, there was a deliberate strategy afoot to make the show hum. But it's slender enough evidence. The main point is that whatever Bragg was up to, it worked. The main feature of his broadcasting work is that it demonstrates how passionate he is about ideas. That, more than anything else, appears to account for his consistent success in animating a panel of talkers. Those who succeeded him as chairman, apart from Andrew Marr, were less successful at knitting together different topics on the show. Lord Bragg in his cultural programming over the years has 'done the state some service.' He shares Lord Reith's conviction that working people require more than bread and circuses.

The television interrogator Jeremy Paxman of BBC 2's *Newsnight* was the first to succeed Bragg in *Start the Week*. Jeremy seemed less than comfortable in that new role because, while highly intelligent, he didn't seem to have the passionate interest in ideas that the programme requires. After him came

Andrew Marr, who has made the show his own. Three things strike you about Andrew Marr: the beauty of his voice, his nimble command of language, and his high intelligence. For my money, he is the brightest broadcaster in Britain today. And what a voice. Clive James is one of the few who has pointed to the significance of vocal quality in Terry Wogan's success. It was too easy to be distracted by Wogan's banter from the sheer quality of the vocal instrument that made it all possible. In Marr's case, we're more aware of that presiding instrument, because of the very nature of the work he does. As with Vincent Browne, Marr was a newspaper editor, which experience has sharpened his command of language and his conceptual skills. Marr suffered a stroke in early 2013 when he was in his early fifties. Fortunately, he has been able to return to the BBC, which network I hope he continues to adorn for many years to come.

Among American broadcasters, I have a particularly high regard for Charlie Rose, Fareed Zakaria, Rachel Maddow and Christopher Lydon. I saw the very first edition of the syndicated *Charlie Rose Show* on PBS in the early 1990s. The fact that his first guest was Bill Cosby gave a misleading impression of where the show was heading. After more than twenty years, it has struck an adroit balance between economics, politics, culture, technology and entertainment. I am often amused by the way Europeans patronize American television. Because what most Europeans see are American telly-fodder exports, they have no idea of the existence of intellectually stimulating material such as the *Charlie Rose Show*. To some degree, that is changing now, because the Bloomberg channel has begun to transmit the show worldwide.

Charlie Rose trained as a lawyer and began his career in local television before working in an editorial capacity for Bill Moyers, one of PBS's leading current affairs presenters. There-after he moved to CBS and then in the early 1990s to public television, where he was given his own show. If he has a bias in the selection of guests, it is towards chief executives of start-up high-tech companies. A typical guest of that kind is someone like Sebastian Thrun, a former professor of computer science at Stanford, who founded UNACITY, an online educational company offering computer science classes. Thrun's major interests are robotics and artificial intelligence. On the occasion of that particular interview with Thrun in December 2015, Charlie Rose displayed not just a deep curiosity about artificial intelligence, but expressed an interest in assembling, on a monthly basis, a panel of like-minded creative types working at the frontiers of communications technology.

Probably the most accurate way to describe Rose's political colouring is as the unofficial media voice of American corporate philanthropy. We're talking about that slice of corporate America closely identified with figures like Bill Gates and Warren Buffet. The unofficial *political* voice of that grouping is that of Bill Clinton, who has his own philanthropic foundation. The rock musician Bono is their most visible link with the world of entertainment. American corporate philanthropy is a terrain perched somewhere between government and corporations which sees itself as augmenting the work of government. These privately funded foundations certainly do good but if we assume that there are donor strings attached, it is not altogether clear at what cost. Some ventures are best left to government. Moreover, it is particularly a source of concern whenever we find philanthropic activities substituting for full compliance with tax demands.

Charlie Rose's erstwhile mentor, Bill Moyers, former press secretary to Lyndon Johnson, is notably more socially radical than his protégé. Rose is perilously perched on the precipice of private sponsorship. That imposes its own constraints, but if there is a likely conflict of interest, he tends to be open about it. If you want to get a really good sense of what is going on not just in America but in the world at large, this is a show you need to watch: this is the *Financial Times* of the airwaves. Originating in New York on PBS, the *Charlie Rose Show* is viewable in many countries on the Bloomberg cable channel. Charlie Rose has a particular interest in U.S. foreign policy, international affairs, economic issues and developments in technology. He also caters for film and theatre lovers and does special miniseries within the framework of his show on scientific topics like current developments in neuroscience. Rose gives generous coverage to major art shows, important new buildings and to lengthy interviews with the leading architects of our day. And to cap it all, he's a dedicated sports fan, with a special interest in golf. With scientists, one of his perennial questions is: what do you yourself most want to know, but he asks it not in a ritualistic, memo-pad way but as something rooted in deep curiosity. Susie Orbach, author of *Fat is a Feminist Issue* (1978), and one-time therapist to Diana, Princess of Wales, said to me once, with commendable accuracy, 'most interviewers don't give a shit.' American television produces more than its quota of dross but the *Charlie Rose Show* demonstrates that it is also capable of consistently delivering the best conversation to be heard anywhere.

I was never a regular CNN watcher, but from the moment I discovered Fareed Zakaria, I wanted to see more of his work. In his Sunday programme, *The Global Public Square,* he discusses current issues with newsmakers and panels of commentators. More than most presenters on mainstream channels, he editorializes, but not in the in-your-face, obnoxious manner of the other cable news channels. His opinions are obviously grounded in hours of reading and reflection. There's a compelling clarity about his introductions. He has a worked-out position on geopolitics, as you would expect from a one-time managing editor of *Foreign Affairs.*

Zakaria is an Indian-American journalist, a self-confessed non-practising Muslim, who works for both print and broadcast outlets. He studied at Yale before completing a doctorate in political science at Harvard. Apart from his work for CNN, he writes a weekly column for *The Washington Post*. More than any other presenter I know, he brings his knowledge to bear on current issues with a devastating clarity. Also, having analysed a situation, he then offers his own opinion in a way that enhances the debate rather than shuts it down. The opinions are more acceptable than they otherwise would be because they are the product of knowledge and rigorous thought. Whatever flaws contaminate cable news networks, the presence of Fareed Zakaria is proof that they can accommodate intelligent programmes as well. Full marks to CNN for making such effective use of him.

Rachel Maddow was a relative newcomer to Cable News when I first saw her in 2011: she still fronts a nightly news show for MSNBC. She was a Rhodes scholar who did graduate work at Oxford. I indicate elsewhere that I am not too happy with the stridently partisan nature of either Fox News or its mirror image, MSNBC. However, if we're to have partisanship, let it be Maddow-style. Clearly liberal/left in her political sympathies, she doesn't distort her material, as far as one can judge, and her gift for exposition is peerless. This woman is so intelligent, she's a joy to behold and listen to.

The career of the Boston broadcaster Christopher Lydon raises questions in my mind about the direction of National Public Radio in America, simply because that network did not seem able to accommodate someone of such outstanding journalistic ability. In fairness to the public radio station in Boston for which he worked, I know there was a contractual dispute between the parties about fifteen years ago. But without traversing the ins and outs of that particular dispute, it does seem sad, on the face of it, that the public radio audience lost such a rare talent. Lydon is equally comfortable with both politics and culture at a very high level of discussion. I first encountered him when he did a nightly television newscast for WGBH public television station in Boston in the 1980s. Next, he presented a radio show called *The Connection* on public radio in Boston, which enjoyed national syndication. Currently, he presides over *Open Source*, which originates from the Watson Institute at Brown University; it has a strong web-based character.

The editorial content of *Open Source* is of such high quality that it once again gives the lie to European preconceptions about American broadcasting. There is certainly a lot of dross in American broadcasting output, but on the other hand the kind of material heard in the old days on WGBH's *The Connection* and more recently on *Open Source* would put elite European channels like BBC's Radio 3 and France Cultur to shame. Lydon's 2008 conversation with the British conductor Colin Davis which explored, among other things, the conductor's interest in Hermann Broch's *The Death of Virgil* was of a kind still found in some of the broadsheets, but which is becoming rarer even in public radio. The only broadcaster this side of the pond who swims regularly in those waters is BBC's Tom Service who adorns Radio 3; he is the best informed music presenter I have ever heard.

Let me turn now to the kind of broadcasting that gets under my skin. The main culprit is American cable network news. It began with the founding of Fox News in 1997. This represented a major fissure in the news broadcasting landscape, because where Fox went, its competitors, MSNBC, and to a much lesser extent CNN, were bound to follow. The undeniable fact is that Fox met a gap in the market; it was phenomenally successful as a news channel. Up to that point, the traditional post-war news ethos had prevailed. CBS, NBC and ABC had aimed at impartiality in their news coverage. Probably, on balance, its anchors and reporters were more liberal than conservative, but they did aim at impartiality of coverage, at overall fairness.

That concern with impartiality was what defined being a professional journalist. Both the news itself and editorial shows subscribed to that ethos. With the arrival of Fox News, all that changed. To be fair to Fox, its news reporters still subscribe to the traditional news ethos, but its news show anchors and commentators do not. Not merely that, the entire character of the network is determined by the expressed views of the individuals who are anchoring the programmes. In turn, MSNBC developed a mirror network that responded in kind. For every Bill O'Reilly on Fox, you had a Chris Mathews on MSNBC. The difference is that MSNBC hosts like Mathews are capable of occasionally torpedoing positions beloved of the liberal left; Fox allows no comparable doctrinal deviations, though Megyn Kelly, the latest Fox star, appears to be 'her own woman'. Overall, the MSNBC posture is an inherently smarter one, in that it immediately captures whatever 'swing' viewers happen to be watching.

While my sympathies lie with the more liberal network, I am no happier seeing a liberal channel than I am a conservative one. I believe the move towards agenda-driven channels is a bad one. So, let's have neither Fox nor MSNBC in their present form. The old system wasn't perfect, but at least journalists *tried* to be impartial. The problem with the departure initiated by Fox News is that it is a slippery slope. The most subtle of the liberal commentators was the former comedy host Jon Stewart, who ran the risk that all ironists do, of being taken literally. The same applies to Rachel Maddow on MSNBC. We liberals like to think liberals are intellectually smarter than conservatives, but then we remember the late Bill Buckley. The best line I've heard from Jon Stewart was one about Glenn Beck, the American conservative political commentator. Stewart said, 'Glenn Beck tells us what people who are *not* thinking are thinking.'

The really pernicious aspect of agenda-driven news broadcasting is that, in time, large sections of the community may come to believe that the only option for news presentation is an environment that consists solely of partisan channels. So I was surprised to hear a former director-general of the BBC, Mark Thompson, say, circa 2010, that he would welcome a news landscape in Britain which featured partisan news channels in the manner of Fox and MSNBC. It is quite significant that Sky News which, like Fox News, is also owned by Rupert Murdoch, has not gone down that route. It is clear that Sky's proprietors recognize that the British public would not welcome such a development. Hence my surprise at Thompson's remark. I was taken aback by an hour-long interview he gave to Charlie Rose on Bloomberg in the last decade. Not alone did he not mention flagship radio or television programmes, but he gave broadcast content as a whole a wide berth.

Managing a broadcasting network involves controlling three broad elements: finance, technology and content. In recent years, I have noticed that chief executives who run vast media organizations, whether Disney, ABC, BBC or RTÉ, tend, in their public utterances, to ignore content beyond perfunctory lip service. In fact, they often begin by asserting that content is primary, but once they have done so, rarely return to it. The language used by these masters of the media universe is one that speaks of monetizable models, integrated digital platforms or whatever, as if they have forgotten these are but part of the picture. There are two obvious possible reasons for this: the 2008 financial crash and unprecedented advances in communications technology. But there is a third factor: programme content is much more difficult to talk about. That is why the ratings system is a godsend for managers who do not want to discuss quality. Technology and finance, heretofore always regarded as merely instruments in the delivery of content, have taken over. Even my use of the term 'delivery' shows how influenced I have been by the new financial techno-babble. If senior executives talk only about finance and technology, then a climate may be created in which those who make the programmes begin to feel that what they are doing day in, day out is ancillary to other considerations such as technology, finance and the making of strategic partnerships. If all that programme-makers hear is talk about integrated digital platforms and adequate monetization models, they will gradually feel alienated from the people running the organization.

In 1999 I went to the Barbican Arts Centre in London to record a *Dialogue* programme with Sir John Tusa, who was then managing director of the Centre. A former BBC executive, he spoke about the fact that interviews were being held that week for the position of director-general of the BBC. Indeed, Tusa himself had been interested in the job at a certain point in his career. Who was likely to get the job, I asked. 'I don't know, but there are three questions the board has to ask of a candidate: What does he know? What does he believe? Can he write?' Greg Dyke got the job on that occasion. What is interesting about those three questions is that they presuppose that content in broadcasting is king, that content is more important than technology or finance. Perhaps that era is over, perhaps nowadays the challenge of controlling content is no longer ultimately the direct concern of the director-general or chief executive but of someone down the line. As far as the BBC is concerned, the appointment in 2013 of ex-Covent Garden supremo Tony Hall as director-general suggests that content may be about to come into its own again.

One doesn't have to be an economic determinist to see the role that the latest incarnation of capitalism, namely financial capitalism, has played in this transformation of the media landscape. In the good old days of social welfare capitalism, underpinned by a Keynesian consensus, public monies were available for cultural and educational purposes, including public broadcasting. That was the position right up to the middle if not to the late 1970s. But for the last thirty years, broadcasting, university education and the arts have been forced to survive in a less bountiful world. As a result, these institutions have had to cut corners, and to narrow their horizons: public broadcasting has become even more obsessed with ratings; universities increasingly see their role in terms of meeting the needs of the economy. The challenge for both institutions is to survive commercially without a total surrender of vision.

Where a network like RTÉ has dual sources of funding, from the public purse and from commercial advertising, it is easy to see how such a network will be under pressure to compromise in the matter of programme content. The demand of advertisers for big audiences inevitably squeezes out programmes of a minority and challenging kind. But why does a network like the BBC, which unlike RTÉ is not even partially dependent on advertising revenue, also have to succumb to pressure to dumb down? The answer is that in order to justify a huge government subsidy, the BBC has to be seen to be competing effectively with commercial television. So it too has to deliver big audiences. This being the case, the character and tone of programme content of all networks, including the BBC, is dictated by the commercial stations. In other words, a government-funded network like the BBC does not operate in a vacuum. In that environment, the BBC has not lost its nerve completely: it still delivers thoughtful programmes of outstanding quality. However, in the past forty years, there has been a discernible pattern at work in the matter of scheduling cultural material, which is a cause for concern.

In the early 1970s, the poet W.H. Auden was a guest on Michael Parkinson's show on BBC1. Such an event would be unthinkable on BBC1 in the second decade of the twenty-first century, and probably unthinkable for some decades past. From the 1970s onwards, BBC1 gradually began fobbing off cultural material to BBC2. Bryan Magee's series of conversations with philosophers is a good example. Then, more recently, BBC2 (with notable exceptions like Simon Schama's series in 2013 on the Jews) has been offloading such material to BBC4. A prime example of that was the transfer in 2013 of *The Review Show* from BBC2 to BBC4. Later, the Beeb saw the error of its ways, and reverted to the earlier arrangement. My prediction, however, is that, eventually, even BBC4 will come under pressure.

One doesn't want to be too pious about the erosion of what admirers refer to as 'quality' programming and detractors as 'worthy', because if current 'lifestyle' genre offerings attract huge audiences that must be recognized as a fact of life, whether champions of minority fare like it or not. Ideally, the matter of scheduled content should never be posed in either/or terms. Why not have both mass market fare and the more intellectually challenging variety. In E. M. Forster's novel *Howards End*, the author presents two families as the embodiment of contrasting values. The Schlegels represent culture and the life of the mind, the Wilcoxes business and commercial endeavour. Forster appears to be saying that we need both. The cultural aspirations of the Schlegels are possible only because of the business achievements of families like the Wilcoxes; the Wilcox approach by itself is so bound up with material considerations, it loses sight of the finer things in life. We know that Forster is making a larger point here about the mutual dependence of German and English cultures, but his binary framework also has direct relevance to recent developments in television programming. Art and commerce need each other. The question is how can commercial television be managed so that it can combine a strand of good quality cultural programming with the kind of mass audience fare that ensures profitability.

I have singled out *commercial* television because it ultimately sets the tone for what happens in broadcasting at large, be that government-funded (BBC) or partly financed by advertising and public funds (RTÉ). The Irish commercial network TV3 is setting a headline for what can be achieved in the influential commercial sector by encouraging the broadcaster Vincent Browne to present regular high-quality discussion programmes in a network otherwise defined by highly populist programming. RTÉ, the Irish network for which I worked for over half a century, is funded partly by public monies and partly by advertising. Over that period, I remain amazed at the degree of editorial freedom I was allowed as a radio broadcaster in the matter of pursuing my own intellectual interests. The network knew that I was engaged in a life-long educational voyage, and was quite happy that I should share the fruits of that journey with our audience, however esoteric the material.

Broadly speaking, I had the freedom to read for programme purposes what I myself wanted to read. The result was book-based discussion programmes that explored whatever ideas were found to be animating economics, politics, religion and culture at different periods. It is because of that very rewarding personal experience that I am surprised at the manner in which in recent years the ethos of the organization has become practically indistinguishable from that of a purely commercial network. My belief is that this does not have to be the case: it ought to be possible to survive commercial pressures *and* remain loyal to some ethos of broadcasting which involves a sense of obligation to *educate* the community to which it is broadcasting.

Commercial pressure is a fact of broadcasting life. But what is having an even more damaging effect, on radio schedules in particular, is the rise of current affairs to the kind of hegemonic position that leads to a narrowing of horizons in the matter of content. In turn, the current affairs perspective has become so heavily weighted towards economic news that it has effectively elbowed *politics* out of the current affairs picture. Admittedly, such a heavy emphasis on economic news and analysis was a consequence of the severity of the financial crisis that Ireland, together with other nations, faced. Nonetheless, that should not be a licence to forget that we humans are driven by considerations other than the economic. Notable among those RTÉ broadcasters who have resisted attempts to reduce current affairs to national economic stories is Richard Crowley, who clearly has a deep interest in international affairs, particularly in developments in the Middle East.

That privileging of current affairs (heavily geared towards economic developments) has in turn squeezed out not only material of a more reflective, enlightening kind but has also eliminated programming devoted to entertainment. I am thinking of comedy shows, music and variety shows and quizzes. So, we're talking about the negative effect on content not just of commercial pressures, but the damaging consequences of a narrow current affairs mind-set. In RTÉ radio, current affairs has become so all-consuming that it has squeezed almost everything else out of the picture. Radio programming is now structured in such a way that what the listener hears from morning until evening is nothing but an extended diet of current affairs. The same stories tend to run right through the day, with current events and issues dominating the schedule. There is scarcely ever a nod in the direction of more reflective material, the kind that would situate what is happening in a richer set of contexts than current personality-led programming allows. Furthermore, as I have pointed out, even entertainment is beginning to get short shrift. In fairness to RTÉ, it should be noted that in putting economic/financial news in the foreground to an unbalanced degree, its producers may simply be reflecting the zeitgeist. In other words, it is an open question as to how much broadcasters are imposing their own view of the world, and how much they are reflecting the priorities of the ruling elite and perhaps of the community at large. Either way, that current affairs perspective on the world (itself only part of the programme content menu) has become too narrow.

One way in which senior executives have successfully distracted attention from their neglect of a duty to educate is by talking about their fidelity to the network's public service obligations. This kind of language has become well nigh vacuous because 'public service' has become a catch-all term that can include anything from state functions to sports broadcasts, but it overlooks the network's obligation to educate its viewers and listeners. There is a case to be made that publicly funded broadcasters should drop the customary guff about a public service remit, and speak instead of a network's obligation to *educate*. In other words, they should retrieve the great three-pronged injunction of the BBC's John Reith to inform, entertain and educate. It is no longer realistic, as Reith did, to put education in first place, but it should be there somewhere. At present, it is rapidly disappearing altogether.

By 'education' in this context I mean the obligation to transmit to the community a sense of the best that has been articulated and achieved by our predecessors and contemporaries, national, European and global. RTÉ, like all networks that depend significantly on the public purse, should have a division that is constantly reflecting systematically on ways to convey to its audience the riches of our human past, its artistic, philosophical, religious, scientific, political, legal and economic achievements. For example, the side of the RTÉ network that soaks up the views and feelings of the community on Joe Duffy's *Liveline* should be complemented by an arm that shares with that same community the literary, philosophical, religious and scientific accomplishments of the past. Such a division would have to fight for its life in the current economic dispensation, but at least its presence would be a constant reminder to those executives inclined to talk exclusively about digital platforms and monetizable models that we live 'not by bread alone'.

One obvious corollary of the unchallenged rise of the concept of ratings is the collapse of the kind of critical language that programme-makers need to analyse programmes. Ratings offer the easy way out. No one any longer is obliged to discuss whether a show was any good or not: all you have to do is quote the figures. About twenty-five years ago John Ranelagh, a highly gifted television executive who was involved among other things in the setting up of Channel 4 in Britain, identified a major malaise in contemporary broadcasting. In the course of a most enjoyable conversation in the centre of London, Ranelagh said to me that the source of the much talked about insecurity that characterizes broadcasting is not the fact that many people do not know where the next job is coming from, but is due rather to the fact that programme-makers no longer know what they mean by the term 'a good programme'. At the time I nodded in agreement, but it was only in the course of the next two decades that I would develop a real grasp of that same point. Ranelagh amplified his claim by saying that at weekly programme meetings everybody waited to get a signal from the top man as to whether something was any good or not. Increasingly, such top executives are in hock to nothing more that the latest audience figures.

The idea that a good show or performance can be reduced to what's measurable has invaded all aspects of broadcasting and showbiz life. For example, some years ago Ryan Tubridy introduced Tom Cruise on *The Late Late Show* as the 'most famous' actor in the world. It struck me that to say of someone that he is the 'most famous' actor in the world is a readily measurable claim in a way that saying he is the best or greatest is not. In effect, this is at best a public relations category, and not one belonging to the language of film criticism. It is a claim that can be established by quantitative means (column inches or digital reach) but it is alarmingly reductive. Maybe that's a portent of what is going to happen to critical languages in everything from film to music to literature. It is already happening in radio and television.

It occurred to me during the run of *The Sunday Show* that programme executives were more concerned with breaches of taste, libel and possible political implications for government than they were with programme content. No one cared all that much whether a programme was any good or not. I am not for a moment claiming that programme executives shouldn't concern themselves with possible legal infringements and breaches of taste, or keep an eye on the likely impact of a programme on those in power, but we can never lose sight of the intrinsic quality of the programme itself.

In more recent times, ratings have tended to eclipse all other considerations for the programme-maker. The mind-set at work here is one seduced by the non-complicated nature of the criterion that determines whether a programme was good or not, namely what ratings did it have. It is bad enough that executives should think only in those terms, but the danger is that programme-makers themselves will follow suit. The problem here is that we are seeing the collapse of a complex language of radio and television programme assessment that was used by practitioners of the trade for aeons. Of course ratings matter; of course broadcasters want audiences to watch and listen, but that should never be the end of the matter. Gay Byrne, who not only presented *The Late Late Show* for almost four decades but also *produced* it, was a classic exemplar of the best of both worlds. He sought the highest ratings possible but also cared deeply as to how *good* a show was when judged by the professional criteria he developed with his team over that long period. It was obvious that good ratings alone were not enough for the greatest television broadcaster Ireland has produced: he was equally concerned with whether or not a show had worked. Once that impulse is lost, all we're left with for assessment are the number of viewers watching and the number of advertisements the programme attracted.

One consequence of taking seriously a network's obligation to educate (as well as inform and entertain) is that greater attention should be paid to the personal culture of senior broadcast executives. We know that the old humanistic mandarin culture of the BBC, PBS and RTÉ had its flaws, not the least of which was insufficient attention to audience needs, but that culture had a lot going for it. Now that it has been more or less swept away, we realize its importance. About twenty years ago, Ian McIntyre, former controller of BBC's Radio 3 and 4, and biographer of Sir John Reith, offered me a snapshot of the personal culture of BBC senior staff. He said if you were to put them up in a hotel for a weekend and invite them to write two thousand words on any subject of their own choosing, most would be hard-pressed to deliver. McIntyre may have been overstating the case. But, even if he was, it is worth remembering he was talking about the BBC twenty years ago. Imagine the result today in a broadcasting world engulfed by talk about digital platforms and monetizable models.

I don't know if the comedian Barry Humphries was referring to an era when the BBC mandarin class consisted almost exclusively of Oxbridge intellectuals, or to a later phase when he told Michael Parkinson that at one point he was such a heavy drinker he could have qualified for a job as a senior executive with the network. Nor do I want to make too much of the difference between the two kinds of mandarin stewardship at the BBC for the following reason. Hedley MacNeice, widow of the poet Louis, told me many years ago that Louis, a distinguished BBC radio producer and writer, couldn't face the 'suits' unless he was well pickled. And that particular period of the 1940s encapsulated the essence of Oxbridge-inflected BBC mandarin culture. The difference in Ian McIntyre's case is that the criticism comes from a member of the tribe: McIntyre ran Radio 3 and Radio 4 at different points.

A classic posture adopted by current broadcast executives who insist that their networks are not outposts of philistinism is to refer to their coverage of the arts. That's the usual get-out reference to indicate they are not completely engulfed by commercial pressures. It is better than nothing I suppose, but not if it's just tokenism and certainly not if such programmes become little more than noticeboards for various cultural events. My unease when I hear senior broadcasting executives speak of their arts programming as an example of their commitment to public service broadcasting is that all too often it indicates an attitude that sees current affairs as the nerve centre of broadcasting output, and culture solely in the particular guise of arts programmes. In turn, such programmes are treated as just icing on the cake of news and current affairs.

The BBC, though equally under financial pressure, has done better than most comparable organizations in maintaining an understanding of culture that is richer than that conveyed by the making of arts programmes. One can sense behind their scheduling across numerous channels a group of people at work who are acutely aware of the role of the organization not just in discussing the latest offerings from the arts world, but in providing its listeners with a broad-based education. Many are interlinked at least informally in an attempt to answer questions that pertain to where their society has come from and where it is heading. RTÉ, which is blessed with some of the finest producers to be found anywhere, both on staff and in the satellite independent sector, has failed in recent years to achieve a comparable coherence in the matter of programme philosophy. That won't be achieved until senior management restores programme content to a primary position in its thinking. Let us hear less about technology and finance, important though they be. And then, when content is restored to a position of centrality, let it mean more than current affairs and sport.

It is not too late for broadcasting management to widen the frame again: first of all to restore 'content' to its rightful place alongside technology and finance; secondly, to enlarge the concept of content beyond a news/current affairs horizon to cater more for culture and entertainment; thirdly, the idea of current affairs itself should be widened beyond its current economic/financial emphasis to pay greater attention to politics; fourthly, our understanding of politics needs to include not just parliamentary and political party nuts and bolts, but to embrace the discussion of political ideas; and finally, we need to broaden our understanding of culture beyond the concept of arts programmes.

I concede that the challenge facing programme schedulers in Ireland is not an easy one in that the Irish appetite for news and current affairs is well above average. Networks have to cater for that hunger and also to minister to those who require more varied fare, whether of a thoughtful or formally entertaining kind. Lest I be misunderstood here, I regard radio and television as primarily information and entertainment media, but I also subscribe to a school of thought that believes that these media should educate us as well. Joe Duffy's phone-in show *Liveline* is one of the jewels in RTÉ's populist crown. Joe is a skilful orchestrator of the concerns of an Irish public that is regularly irate, but never less than articulate. This programme is a superb example of the manner in which the community at large makes its voices heard on the issues of the day. What RTÉ has been less attentive to is transmitting to that same community a deep sense not just of an Irish past but of a more broadly human one, its intellectual, economic, socio-political and cultural achievements. It has also been less attentive than it might be to providing a space wherein we could explore not just the lineaments of our past but debate the choices before us as we face the future. It is not enough to *listen* to the community; a network also has an obligation to *talk* to it through the most gifted people it can find. Its relationship with the community should be a two-way street. Furthermore, that obligation should be met at a decent hour in the schedules, a time when one can truthfully talk of a community and not just of a collection of minority interest groups.

That said, one of the notable achievements of *Liveline* is that in addition to airing the community's concerns in such a powerful way, it is also keeping alive the notion of broadcasting as formal entertainment. Opinions vary as to the quality of the show's Funny Friday editions, but it is good to see *Liveline* flying the flag for light entertainment, which, like education, is in danger of being edged out by current affairs, particularly of a kind weighted towards economic/financial news. Straightforward entertainment shows are a thing of the past on Irish radio, though television is still making a serious effort in that regard. Indeed, David McSavage's television comedy shows on RTÉ 2 are works of remarkable originality. Lord Reith set the template for a comprehensive broadcasting philosophy a century ago. We can argue about the comparative weight that should be assigned to any of Reith's trinity of essential broadcasting functions – those of informing, entertaining and educating – but we should at least try to ensure that none of them is squeezed out. In the second decade of the twenty-first century, the education function in particular is on life support in most broadcasting outlets.

INDEX

Index

Index

Index

Mehta, Ved, 150
Meister Eckhart, 300
Melchin, K. R., 194
Mercier, D-J, 125
Merkel, Angela, 9
Merton, Thomas, 76
Metz, Johann Baptist, 92
Miller, Jonathan, 152, 153-4, 247, 248, 249
Minchin, Scott, 61
Mitchel, Charles, 116, 147, 157
Mitchell, Joan, 222
Mitchelmore, Cliff, 146
Mitterrand, François, 11
Moll, Kurt, 248, 249
Molloy, Pat, 97
Momigliano, Arnaldo, 306
Monroe, Marilyn, 156
Montague, John, 183, 203, 221-2
Montaigne, Michel, 14
Monteith, Charles, 226
Monteverdi, Claudio, 213
Montini, Giovanni, 81
Moody, T. W., 148, 149, 226
Mooney, Peter, 310
Moore, G. E., 129, 137
Morecombe, Eric, 104, 176
Morgenbesser, Sidney, 263
Moriarty, John, 300-1
Moriarty, Michael, 89
Moryson, Fynes, 278
Moyers, Bill, 332
Moynahan, Bon, 67
Moynihan, Pat, 158
Moynes, Adrian, 94
Mozart, W. A., 75, 247-8
Muldoon, Paul, 222, 225
Mulhall, Ed, 308
Mumford, Lewis, 150
Murdoch, Rupert, 337
Murphy, Dan, 212

Murphy, Mike, 87, 105, 309
Murphy, Pat, 101-2, 317
Murphy, Tom, 152, 154-5, 174, 197, 213, 217, 233, 298-9
Murphy, Willy, 70
Murray, Daniel, 45
Murray, Gerry, 143, 148
Murray, Gilbert, 249, 251
Murtagh, Tommy, 220-1

Napoleon, 51
Nash, Heddle, 106, 187
Naughton, Tom, 81, 154, 162-3, 164, 166, 212-3
Neusner, Jacob, 306
Neville, Richard, 166
Newman, Alec, 203
Newman, Jeremiah, 160
Newman, J. H., 43, 61, 81, 83, 142, 190, 194, 203
Newman, Paul, 289
Ní Bhriain, Doireann, 310
Nic Cormaic, Aoife, 315-6
Nicholls, Peter, 251
Ní Dhomhnaill, Máire, 158
Nietzsche, Friedrich, 83, 251, 301
Nixon, Richard, 287, 288, 290
Noble, Dennis, 106
Nolan, Evelyn, 224
Nolan, Mike, 132, 138, 139, 140
Norris, David, 236
Norton, Graham, 120, 326
Norton, Jim, 174
Novak, Barbara, 180, 182
Nozick, Robert, 134-5, 228-9, 257-64, 318-9

Obama, Barack, 20, 21, 36
Ó Briain, Colm, 213-214
O'Brien, Conor Cruise, 170, 206, 211, 219, 221, 228
O'Brien, Flann, see O'Nolan, Brian

359

White, Harrison, 258, 266-8, 270, 275-7, 290
White, James, 33, 75
White, Terence de Vere, 173, 181-2, 302, 308
Whitehead, A. N., 198, 218
Whyte, William, 117
Wilbur, Richard, 58-59
Wilde, Oscar, 41, 80, 85, 101, 153, 218, 234
Wilder, Billy, 72
Williams, Bernard, 263
Williams, Desmond, 152
Williams, John, 162
Williams, Ralph Vaughan, 78
Williams, Raymond, 171
Wilson, Colin, 88-9
Wilson, Harold, 287
Winckler, Edwin, 258, 293
Winnicott, Donald, 6-7
Wittgenstein, Ludwig, 131-2, 135, 191, 192, 240, 263-4, 268, 317

Wodehouse, P. G., 15, 117, 269
Wogan, Terry, 113, 114-16, 119-21, 146, 327, 331
Wolfe, Tom, 41, 165-6, 182
Wolfflin, Heinrich, 306
Wolfit, Donald, 175, 232
Wolfson, Harry, 90, 306
Wood, James, 11
Woolf, Virginia, 316-7
Worth, Katharine, 233
Wright, Frank Lloyd, 181
Wylie, Robin, 224, 225, 226, 232, 237, 249

Yeats, Jack B., 179
Yeats, W. B., 94, 217, 227, 250
Yo Yo Ma, 320
Young, Hugo, 21-2

Xenophon, 70

Zakaria, Fareed, 331, 333-4
Zeldin, Theodore, 10-11
Žižek, Slavoj, 95